FROM BALLOON
TO BOXKITE

FROM BALLOON TO BOXKITE

MALCOLM HALL

AMBERLEY

First published 2010

Amberley Publishing Plc
Cirencester Road, Chalford,
Stroud, Gloucestershire, GL6 8PE

www.amberley-books.com

Copyright © Malcolm Hall 2010

The right of Malcolm Hall to be identified as the Author
of this work has been asserted in accordance with the
Copyrights, Designs and Patents Act 1988.

ISBN 978 1 84868 992 3

British Library Cataloguing in Publication Data.
A catalogue record for this book is available from the
British Library.

Typeset in 10pt on 12pt Sabon.
Typesetting and Origination by FonthillMedia.
Printed in the UK.

Contents

INTRODUCTION 7

I BUOYANCY 9

    1   Hanging in Heaven's Vault 11

    2   Watchers in the Sky 29

    3   South Africa 37

    4   Ballooning Twilight 51

    5   The Dirigibles 65

II KITES – FLYING BUT STILL TETHERED 83

III WINGS 95

    1   Collecting the Breeze 97

    2   Europe Awakes 119

    3   The Pilots Assemble 145

    4   Flying Machines Needed 153

    5   A Gift from France 159

    6   Larkhill 165

    7   A Motley Collection 175

    8   A Matter of Power 181

    9   The Air Battalion and the Aircraft Factory 187

    10   The Looming Clouds 215

    11   They Also Served 227

THE ENDING – AND THE BEGINNING 233

APPENDIX I – Summary of changes to the names of units 241

APPENDIX II – List of balloons operated by the British Army 243

APPENDIX III – Aeroplanes of the Balloon School and the Air Battalion 245

REFERENCE SOURCES 247

ACKNOWLEDGEMENTS (including photographic) 251

INDEX 253

INTRODUCTION

Apart from moving in the same medium, the gentle balloon, sailing slowly and peacefully through the skies, has nothing in common with the modern warplane, ripping its path through the air by the brute thrust of its snarling engines. Nothing, that is, but the family relationship which binds descendant to ancestor.

For, whereas the Royal Air Force was created, some ninety years ago, from the two earlier formations, the Royal Flying Corps and the Royal Naval Air Service, these two had their own direct antecedent, in the form of a small unit of the Royal Engineers called the Air Battalion. To go back a little further still, the Air Battalion had itself been created as the direct replacement of another sapper formation called the Balloon School, whose name reflected the fact that, in those days, it had been the balloon which provided the only means by which military aeronauts were able to ascend into the air. In other words, the RAF can trace an unbroken descent which stretches, not just from the day of its own formation in 1918, but a further forty years into the past, to the high noon of the Victorian age and the foundation of the first unit of the British armed services whose duties were, by means of the balloons which it operated, essentially to be discharged in the air.

It was conceived at a time when the country was enjoying a long period of peace, disturbed only by the minor conflicts and police actions which took place now and again, as the need arose to maintain order amongst the many disparate peoples of her far-flung empire. It was thus not a particularly favourable time for the introduction into the army of a new vehicle such as the balloon, which appeared to many minds as exotic as it was unwieldy, so that the enthusiasts who were advocating its adoption found at first small support in the higher reaches of the army.

The balloonists, convinced of their case, were undeterred by such disdain. From the very early days of warfare (they would have argued), the advantage to be gained by the possession of ground which is higher than that available to his opponent has always been one of the factors taken into consideration by a commander as he manoeuvred to face his enemy. A position on a hill, other things being equal, is more defensible, from both physical and morale considerations, than one which is on the same level as its attackers. In addition – and of more direct relevance to the balloonists' campaign – it gives the occupant a better chance of seeing what the enemy is up to. A suitable vehicle to this end was now available, they pointed out, which could and should now be introduced, greatly to enhance the army's means of reconnaissance in the field. Here was a portable hill – and one which furthermore was likely to be higher than any real hill available. Its elevation could even be varied to suit the occasion. Every general should have one!

The slow and grudging recognition with which their campaign was eventually rewarded meant that Victoria's long reign would be nearing its end before the balloon gained general acceptance and before it found a major war in which it could demonstrate its worth. The consummation was barely in time: by then, ever-advancing science was preparing to produce its more effective successor, the aeroplane, although the slow emergence of the latter was to grant the balloon a few more years of active life before it was pushed definitively to the margins.

Nonetheless, it had served its turn, not least in laying the first foundations of military aeronautics and thereby ensuring a continuity of purpose, which was carried forward as each change in the latter's evolution took place. At each such stage, the existence of the previous formation provided a foundation of professional expertise and, indeed, an embryonic tradition, on which the succeeding one could build, until the ultimate independent flying service was created.

Throughout these formative years, it was the Corps of Royal Engineers (RE) in whose hands the development and operation of the country's aeronautical service had lain, logically so since it was from that source that the impetus for its existence had first sprung. Throughout that period, while balloons - and later on man-lifting kites and airships – comprised the means by which the British Army could raise itself into the air, the sappers retained their ownership of military aeronautics. When the first aeroplanes were acquired, these too were placed in the hands of the Royal Engineers and for a while this monopoly seemed set to continue.

It took a little while longer for the truth to sink in. The balloon, tethered to its launching winch, had been closely confined to the immediate scene of conflict, with a consequent limitation of the range of its effectiveness and the weakening of its claim of superiority over the cavalry as a means of reconnaissance. The aeroplane, once it had demonstrated its ability to range at will over large areas of countryside, was a very different prospect. As its promise to change the face of warfare became clear, its claim to a higher status in the nation's order of battle could not be ignored. For aviation to continue to rub along as an ancillary part of the work of the army's technical corps, rather smaller in scale – and less highly regarded – than, say, bridge-building or signalling, would not do. Aviation deserved to be the business – and the sole business – of a separate and higher military formation. Just as essential was the need for such a formation to be a larger and more powerful establishment than the handful of men, pilots and machines which then constituted the country's aeronautical service.

If the policy-makers had been less than swift to recognise these facts, some of their more forward-looking subordinates, in a spontaneous assertion of the necessity for a change of policy, had not. For, of the handful of pilots which the army then possessed, every one of them had learnt to fly entirely by his own efforts, in his own time and at his own expense, with no official encouragement to do so. Moreover, the status of all but a few of them was that of merely 'on attachment' to the RE, having been found from other regiments across the wider army. Such men, themselves sure of aviation's transcending importance in future warfare, were painfully aware that their efforts and enthusiasm seemed not to be receiving the appropriate recognition from their leaders.

Perceptions in those high places gradually caught up and in 1912 the situation was belatedly rectified. With the formation of His Majesty's Royal Flying Corps (RFC), the stewardship of military aeronautics was finally wrested from the Royal Engineers, whose responsibility it had been for more than three decades. The following pages recount the story of that time – a period of development, expansion and transition, from Balloons to Boxkites and beyond.

I
BUOYANCY

I

Hanging in Heaven's Vault

Although the sunshine which had bathed Aldershot all day had been deposed by the arrival of a large black cloud, its flat base heavy with the promise of rain, the decision was taken to go ahead with the ballooning as planned. It was just before four o'clock therefore, as the official party was arriving, that the order was given to the waiting winch crew to launch *Flo*, the smaller of the two balloons which had been brought out earlier. In accordance with the carefully prepared programme, the intention was that *Flo*, with Lieutenant R. B. D. Blakeney RE occupying its basket, would mark the start of the visit by rising on its cable until it was floating, still tethered to its winch, several hundred feet above the ground. The brake was therefore released and the balloon, urged by the 4,700 cubic feet of low-density but highly inflammable hydrogen inside it, began to ascend, with the Royal Standard attached to its rigging flapping in the gusting wind which had accompanied the cloud. It had got no higher than 200 feet, jerking and swaying at the end of its cable, when the heavens opened, driving the visitors into the shelter of a nearby building. As they peered at the rain lashing down outside, the gloom was suddenly rent by a brilliant flash, as a bolt of lightning, reaching down from the dark mass overhead, consumed the balloon in an envelope of flame and then, content with the destruction it had wrought, travelled eagerly onwards along the cable attached to the winch below. As the accompanying thunder clap boomed out its own alarming contribution, the now-useless cable fell slackly to earth, followed by the limp remains of the balloon and its basket. To complete the cataclysmic scene, the onlookers now realised with concern that three figures were writhing on the ground around the balloon winch, their cries leaving no doubt of the pain they were suffering.

The scene of their discomfort was the home of the Royal Engineers Balloon Section and its sister unit, the School of Ballooning, which occupied a small area known as Balloon Square, a collection of assorted buildings alongside the southern bank of the Basingstoke Canal, within South Camp of the Aldershot Command of the British Army. The date was 5 September 1894 and the occasion was an official visit by the Duke of Connaught, the third son of Queen Victoria as well as being the General Officer Commanding Aldershot District. He was accompanied by his wife, since the purpose of their visit was the ceremonial naming by the Duchess of the second balloon, much larger and brand-new, which still floated nearby, festooned with bunting and quite unharmed. It was to be called – naturally – *The Duchess of Connaught* and, with a capacity of 12,000 cubic feet of hydrogen, was the largest so far produced by the army's tiny aeronautical service. For the men of that unit (they numbered fewer than forty in all), such royal recognition was a welcome event in the long struggle to get ballooning accepted as a significant and useful part of the army's establishment.

The plan had been that, with the subordinate *Flo* already aloft and ceremonially hoisting the Royal Standard in the novel way of which only the aeronauts were capable, the Duchess would be invited to release the rope tethering the larger balloon, allowing it, first to join its small companion aloft, and then, unhindered by any earthly bond, sail off downwind on a celebratory maiden 'free run', carrying in its own basket Lieutenant

B. F. S. Baden-Powell of the Scots Guards – brother of the founder of the Scouting Movement and well-known for his enthusiasm for military aeronautics – assisted by two sappers.

As they spent the earlier part of the day preparing for these events, the army's aeronauts had naturally kept one eye cocked upwards, in the direction of their natural medium. The blue skies of late summer, which they had been enjoying for some days, seemed to suggest that the weather was prepared to cooperate with their plans. However, as the day advanced, a line of clouds, which had begun to assemble along the far horizon, continued to grow and spread, so that by mid-afternoon the sky was well filled with vigorous-looking cumulus with dark, flat bases which sailed slowly downwind, drawing their threatening shadows across the otherwise sunlit land beneath.

As the royal visitors arrived and were received by Sir Arthur Mackworth, Officer Commanding Royal Engineers Aldershot, Colonel Templer, Head of the School of Ballooning, and other officers, Lieutenant Blakeney made to climb into *Flo's* basket. Even as he did so, the wind began to increase, the sun disappeared and strong gusts, accompanied by large drops of rain, began to blow the tethered balloon back and forth. In such weather, ballooning would normally be halted, yet the occasion was an important one and to cancel the show now would hardly help ballooning's cause. Blakeney made his decision – the launch would go ahead: the cable securing *Flo* was paid out and the little balloon began to ascend. As a precaution, however, Blakeney had decided to remain on the ground – as matters turned out, a most fortunate decision.

Although the heavy rain had driven the official party indoors, a number of subordinates were detailed, in defiance of the weather, to remain in attendance on the two balloons. Three of them – the unfortunate Sappers Foster and Mudie and their assistant, young Bugler Bourne – had been sent to wind the *Flo* back to earth and had just begun to do so when the lightning struck. Two of the unlucky trio had laid their hands upon the brass winch handles, while the third was holding the brake. Thus, all three most effectively completed the path available to the lightning's electrical charge as it sought the earth, with the painful results which have been described. The watchers, including the Duke himself, ran to assist the injured men, who were borne off to hospital to recover from the effects of the shock, while all further ballooning was cancelled for the day.

As it happened, the above event took place almost exactly one hundred years after the day which is generally considered to be that which saw the first appearance of a balloon over a field of battle. It was the spring of 1794 and revolutionary France was at war with Austria. At the instigation of the Committee of Public Safety, it had been decided to investigate the possibility of employing the newly-invented balloon for warlike purposes, in particular as an observation platform over a battlefield. A young scientist, Jean-Marie-Joseph Coutelle, was recruited and experiments were carried out under his direction at the chateau of Meudon, near Versailles. These were sufficiently encouraging to result in the establishment of a small balloon unit, *La Compagnie d'Aérostiers*, which was placed under the command of Coutelle, who had by then been gazetted *Capitaine*. With no further delay, it was ordered to proceed to the town of Maubeuge, then under siege by the Austrian army. There the company launched its balloon, *l'Entreprenant*, and in the course of the next three weeks was able to provide the defenders with useful reports of their besiegers' movements. The company's next exploit involved moving the balloon – still fully inflated – some thirty miles across country towards Charleroi – the town where twenty-one years later the campaign was to open which would culminate in a great battle a little further north – the battle which would take its name from the nearby village of Waterloo and bring an end at last to the years of European warfare which were then just beginning.

The fighting which took place on the earlier occasion, 25 June 1794, is known as the battle of Fleurus, which lies a short distance to the north of Charleroi. There, as the double-headed eagle of imperial Austria faced France's tricolour bonnets of revolution, *l'Entreprenant* ascended once more, enabling a General Antoine Morlot, who accompanied Coutelle in its basket, to observe the movements of the opposing Austrian forces. He was said to have communicated his observations to the commanding General by means of flags. Whether or not his efforts influenced the course of the battle, they certainly moved Thomas Carlyle, in his history *The French Revolution*, to lyrical heights:

> Or see, over Fleurus in the Netherlands, [...] hangs there not in Heaven's Vault some Prodigy, seen by Austrian eyes and spy-glasses : in the similitude of an enormous Windbag, with netting and enormous Saucer depending from it? A Jove's Balance, O ye Austrian spy-glasses? [...] By Heaven, answer the spy-glasses, it is a Montgolfier, a Balloon, and they are making signals! Austrian cannon-battery barks at this Montgolfier ; harmless as dog at the Moon : the Montgolfier makes its signals ; detects what Austrian ambuscade there may be, and descends at its ease. – What will not these devils incarnate contrive?

Devils incarnate indeed.

For a while thereafter the balloonists continued to prosper and develop, as *Entreprenant* and its sister balloons, *Céleste*, *Hercule* and *Intrépide*, accompanied the army on its advance towards the Rhine. Even while Coutelle was airborne over the Fleurus battlefield, a second company was being formed, while shortly afterwards *l'Ecole Nationale d'Aérostation* – the National School of Ballooning – was established at Meudon. In 1798, a company was sent with Napoléon's expedition to Egypt, but this was to mark the last flourish of the military balloon for the time being, for by the time that enterprise foundered with the British victory at the battle of Aboukir, the aeronauts had became part of the wreckage of that defeat, all their equipment having been lost when their ship *le Patriote* was sunk by Nelson's guns.

The great Bonaparte, although himself a gunner, would appear to have remained unimpressed by the potentiality of ballooning, or aerostation as it is termed, to observe and report the fall of shot from his guns and thus to enhance the accuracy of his artillery. On 28 January 1799, the *Compagnies d'Aérostiers* found themselves disbanded and no more balloons were to make their appearance during his campaigns, although throughout his time and beyond, proponents of the military use of aeronautics continued to press its claims in all countries.

In Britain in 1803, one of these, Major John Money, published a paper urging the adoption of balloons by the British Army, but the suggestion seems to have fallen on deaf ears. Major Money was followed by others: both the Crimean War and the Indian Mutiny generated campaigners in support of the use of balloons, in those cases particularly as bombers rather than for observation, but it was to be many more years after Fleurus before any nation again sent up a balloon to confront an enemy's eyes.

Once more the French were responsible and once more Austria was the enemy, this occasion being the battle of Solferino in 1859. On that occasion the craft was operated by the civilian brothers Godard, well back from the field of battle, and little or nothing of significance seems to have resulted. It was to be only a couple of years later however – and half a world away – that military aeronauts made their next appearance, and to rather greater effect. In 1861, during the early months of the American Civil War, a balloon contingent, directed by a keen balloonist named Thaddeus Lowe, accompanied General McClellan's Army of the Potomac during its campaign in Virginia. Numerous ascents were made, apparently with useful observations of the enemy's dispositions, as well as some work in assisting the artillery by reporting the results of its firing.

So far, though, the results of such deployments as had come to their attention contained little to excite the interest of British generals, who may well have felt that there were more pressing matters to attend to – and more useful equipment, on the acquisition of which time and treasure might be spent. The re-equipment of the infantry with the

LE COLONEL COUTELLE,

Chef des Aérostiers, en 1794.

Above left: Transporting the balloon *l'Entreprenant* from Maubeuge to Charleroi prior to the Battle of Fleurus. (Paul Chapman)

Above right: Jean-Marie-Joseph Coutelle. (Author's collection)

L'Entreprenant aloft during the Battle of Fleurus. (Paul Chapman)

The portable hydrogen generating system used by the balloonist Thaddeus Lowe during the American Civil War. (Paul Chapman)

breech-loading Martini-Henry rifle, which took place around that time, will undoubtedly have appeared to them as of far greater moment than the incorporation of a few unwieldy and rather ridiculous-looking 'gas-bags'. It was among the more junior officers – perhaps more imaginative, perhaps driven by the promise of new adventures – that a small number could be found who allowed themselves to be convinced of the practical advantages to be gained from the deployment of such aerial vehicles. An observer, raised hundreds of feet above the ground, with the whole battlefield laid out below him, would be in a position, they might have argued, to see far more of the enemy's activities than any cavalry detachment, ranging perforce well forward of the line, in possession of a much more limited field of view and with its movements quite possibly constrained by enemy action. Furthermore, they might have added, the balloonist's report, provided that matters were properly arranged, could be with the force commander well before that of the cavalry messenger, however fast he galloped back.

It was natural that the seat of such new ideas should lie within the army's technical service, the Corps of Royal Engineers. One of its officers, Capt Frederick Beaumont RE, had been an observer with General McClellan's army and had been impressed by the balloons' contributions. On his return to England, he joined forces with another sapper, Lieutenant George Grover RE, and the two of them began to campaign strongly for the introduction of balloons into the British Army. As is so often the case with innovators, they probably suffered from being ahead of their time. In that same year of 1862, the twenty-two-year-old Lieutenant Grover read two papers on the subject of military ballooning at the School of Military Engineering, Chatham, and also submitted a report to the War Office's Ordnance Select Committee – a report which tended to be damned with faint praise, as his seniors on the Committee kindly but firmly put young Grover in his place:

> The Committee have carefully perused Lieut Grover's Report on the adoption of Balloons for military purposes in the British service. This officer recapitulates as has been repeatedly done by others the several instances of their employment in the French Revolutionary War and also strengthens his argument by pointing to two very recent cases, namely their employment by the French before the battle of Solferino in 1859 and by the Americans in 1861, he does not however furnish any authentic information about these latter instances, which is the more to be regretted, inasmuch as the silence of the public papers respecting their use in America for some months

past is calculated to lead to an impression that they have not been found of much utility there, and as their alleged failure in Italy has given rise to a lawsuit in Paris, which attracted attention but very lately.

Nevertheless, his propositions were not treated wholly unsympathetically, Beaumont and Grover being co-opted on to the committee, which then went so far as to sanction the implementation of trials, which were conducted with the aid of a well-known civilian balloonist, Henry Coxwell, who had also been canvassing the claims of ballooning for military purposes. The trials were performed at the army's Aldershot depot, on 14 July 1862, using a balloon hired from Coxwell and filled with coal gas, rather than the more buoyant hydrogen. A number of ascents were made, with different observers, but the exercise was hampered by its subordination to the day's main activity, a 'field-day' for the benefit of the Prince of Wales. With the troops involved being deployed so as to impress his Royal Highness, rather than further off, so as to allow the balloon to demonstrate its true value as an observation platform, the results were of limited assistance to the two officers' campaign.

In any case, in Britain the times were not favourable for such innovatory ideas. While American fought American and, later on, the Prussians crushed the France of Napoléon III, mid-Victorian Britain stayed aloof and peaceful on its island, its politicians more concerned with domestic affairs – in particular parliamentary and electoral reform, not to mention that ever-baffling riddle, the Irish Question. In any case, William Ewart Gladstone was now at the Exchequer, with an ambition to abolish Income Tax. Although he did not succeed, he did manage, between 1860 and 1866, to reduce it from tenpence (4p) to fourpence (1½p) in the pound. With budgets correspondingly restricted and no wars in prospect other than minor colonial ones, any expenditure on the armed services lay well down the list of priorities. From what funds that were allocated there was certainly nothing left over to cover the introduction of new and outlandish equipment, which seemed to be both awkward to deploy and unreliable. There indeed was the rub. Military ballooning's detractors were not without reasons for their scepticism: at that time, balloons still suffered from major practical difficulties which tended to impede their rapid deployment and launching when a tactical need arose – a feature to which we will return later on.

It was perhaps to war-torn Europe that the balloonists might have looked for their best chance of finding examples of the use of balloons to support their aspirations. In 1870, when the Prussian army began its march on France, a balloon company was initially incorporated within its ranks – an enterprise in which Henry Coxwell was also involved. However, by the time the invaders had beaten Napoléon III at Sedan and were pressing on the gates of Paris, the difficulties which had been encountered with the balloon's deployment in service had resulted in the company's disbandment. Aeronautical activities then passed to the other side of the lines, for it is of course a fact that many significant balloon flights took place in that war, although their purpose was the essentially non-military one of enabling important passengers to escape from Paris over the heads of the besieging Prussians, the politician Léon Gambetta being the best-known. Such flights, although highly demonstrative of the balloon's then unique usefulness, had no direct relevance to its employment on the battlefield.

In Britain, military aeronautics did manage to creep forward a little further when a permanent Balloon Sub-Committee of the Royal Engineers' Committee was formed in 1871. Nevertheless, this move was yet to be reflected in the creation of any military unit or appointment, still less any allocation of funds from the official purse. With this limited encouragement, Grover continued to pursue his campaign; in 1873, finding an article on military ballooning in the German military publication *Jahrbücher für die Deutsche Armee und Marine*, he translated it and submitted this to the *Royal Engineer Journal*, accompanying it with some notes of his own. In the course of the latter, he

Right and below: Artists' impressions representing the employment of balloons to enable a chosen few to escape from Paris over the heads of the besieging Prussian army in 1870. (Author's collection)

gazed once more across the Atlantic Ocean, this time to the southern hemisphere, and evoked the occasion, six years earlier, in the War of the Triple Alliance, when the combined forces of Brazil, Argentina and Uruguay, facing those of Paraguay, had made use of a captive balloon, operated by a Mr Allen from the United States. Grover quoted the views of the Argentinian President, General Mitre, who was also commanding the Allied Army, on the balloon's efficacy:

> ... I will inform you that it can be employed to carry out any observations that may be required, and that with the assistance of a glass your view embraces a considerable extent of ground in all its details; but it is absolutely necessary that the observer should have acquired sufficient practice to enable him to balance his body so as to counteract the oscillation of the balloon, otherwise the use of the glass is impossible, and the observations, therefore, of but little importance.

The General's remarks illuminated another unfavourable feature of the balloon – its instability as an observation platform in anything but calm air conditions. This adverse trait not only made focussing on a target difficult, as noted by the General, but could also induce nausea in the observer – an effect not calculated to help in the recruitment of officers willing to fulfil that role.

However, in that same year of 1873, hopes amongst the 'balloonatics' rose when the War Office asked for plans to be prepared for a balloon detachment to accompany the force being sent to West Africa at the outbreak of the Second Ashanti War. A silk balloon was offered by Henry Coxwell, at a cost of £1,200, but a stumbling block lay in the lack of equipment either to make the necessary hydrogen in the field, where it would be needed, or, alternatively, to carry it there.

An experimental furnace for the manufacture of hydrogen had been built at Woolwich, but was clearly far too bulky to be transported to the scene of any action and this project was eventually abandoned. Quite a lot of effort, led by Lieutenant C. M. Watson RE, was then exerted in investigating the possibility of a generating plant being devised which would be made up of components small enough (not heavier than 80 lb) to be portable by native bearers. This project too was found to be not feasible, while transportation of the hydrogen from home was excluded for lack, at that time, of any compact means of carriage. These technical complexities, set alongside what was considered to be the limited contribution likely to be made by the balloon detachment, were enough to tip a balance which was already biased by a prejudice which tended to range from indifference to hostility and the expeditionary force sailed without it.

It was 1878 before the persistence of the balloon enthusiasts at last brought its first practical reward. In that year, a unit called the Balloon Equipment Store was set up at Woolwich, with authority to fabricate and to experiment with hydrogen-filled balloons. Now, for the very first time, some funds were made available, in the shape of a cautiously modest grant of £150, which allowed the army to make a start in producing its own aerial equipment and which resulted in the appearance of the first British military aircraft – the appropriately-named *Pioneer*, at a cost of £71. Its envelope was of varnished cambric and held 10,000 cu. ft of hydrogen. At last, a military formation devoted to an airborne activity was in being. It is this event which may be taken to mark the birth of the British air arm.

Progress was thus being made, even though military aeronautics was still on no more than a semi-amateur, semi-official basis. Amongst the Royal Engineers' various occupations, ballooning languished unhonoured, unsung and very much at the foot of the list. This unpromising situation was made worse by the mobility of the personnel involved, since any who managed to get themselves assigned to ballooning were, following standard practice, always posted after a certain time to other, more traditional sapper duties, taking with them the valuable and specialised aeronautical experience they had acquired. Grover and Beaumont themselves had by that time left the aeronautical scene to pursue other military activities. Happily, though, others took up the torch, since there were always a few RE officers available and keen to continue the campaign – men such as Lieutenant Charles Watson, referred to above, and Captains Henry Lee and Henry Elsdale, who were to figure prominently in the developments of the coming years.

However, the man who was to emerge as the leader of army ballooning, and remain so throughout the rest of the century, was in fact not a sapper, nor even a regular officer, but a member of the Middlesex Militia (later the King's Royal Rifle Corps – the Royal Green Jackets), one Captain James Lethbridge Brooke Templer. Thirty-three years of age when he first came to the Balloon Equipment Store, Templer was an enthusiastic amateur balloonist and to that end the possessor of his own balloon, the coal-gas *Crusader* (25,000 cu. ft), which was to be used 'on official business' on various occasions at a time when so little government cash was forthcoming to fund the making of balloons by the army itself. Being in the militia and at that time as much a civilian as a soldier, he was not subject to the same service exigencies as his regular colleagues and was free to carry on with his task from year to year. Tall and imposing in his appearance and blunt in his ways, he had an uncompromising approach and a disdain for obstructive regulations, which were to prove useful in the long struggle to persuade the army to lift up its eyes to the sky. An anecdote from his later years illuminates the bluffness embodied in his character.

Colonel Templer, as he had become by that time, was walking across the ballooning ground, carrying a large parcel, when he encountered a subaltern coming in the other direction. After the usual exchange of courtesies, Templer explained that the parcel contained a new type of parachute from France, following this up by suggesting that, since the thing needed to be tested, the subaltern might like to volunteer his assistance by being the man to jump out of a balloon with it.

No doubt regretting by that time that he seemed to have contrived to be in the wrong place at the wrong time, the young officer asked what would happen if the parachute failed to open. He was assured that the makers had guaranteed that it would do so.

'But Sir, supposing it doesn't?'

'Well, in that case,' was the unfeeling reply, 'they'll have to supply me with a new one!'

To return to those earlier years: in 1879 Captain Templer, accompanied by Captain Elsdale, managed to get a balloon included in the Easter Volunteer Review at Dover, and again at Brighton the following year. *Pioneer* being not yet available, he used his own *Crusader*, which on the second occasion was inflated with carburetted hydrogen at the Lewes Gasworks and then moved some two and a half miles across country to the scene of action, accompanied by two smaller balloons containing a reserve supply of gas. Unfortunately, the poor visibility caused by misty conditions in the morning, made worse by dense smoke from the firing taking place, prevented Capt Elsdale, in *Crusader*'s basket, from demonstrating the balloon's efficacy by reports of the 'enemy's' positions. Later in the day, however, the haze cleared away and 'a most excellent view of every man and every movement below was obtained'. The balloonists were included in the final march-past and a mental picture is induced, not without an element of the comic as, amid the crunch of marching feet and the jingle of cavalry harness, we perceive Captain Templer jogging along on the balloon wagon, while in his basket 200 feet above, Captain Elsdale stands rigidly at the salute. When the parade was dismissed, Templer seized the chance to end the day's demonstration with a touch of panache, by which he sought to impress the onlookers with the balloon's mobility in the field. With Elsdale and *Crusader* still attached, he whipped up his horses and left the parade ground at the gallop.

Balloons also featured in the manoeuvres at Aldershot in 1880 and 1882, while, in the latter year, the Balloon Equipment Store removed from Woolwich to the Royal Engineers' main depot at Chatham, where it became known as the School of Ballooning and where, for the first time, a few RE officers and men were detailed to attend training courses in ballooning techniques. At the same time, a second, rather smaller balloon, the *Sapper* (5,600 cu. ft), was constructed, this time of silk. Very slowly, balloons were advancing towards acceptance as part of the army's tactical resources, although they were still to be proved on active service. Another chance to do so arose fleetingly in 1882, with a proposal that a balloon should accompany the expeditionary force to Egypt, which had been sent to put down the insurrection led by Arabi Pasha. However, that matter was concluded successfully at Tel-el-Kebir before arrangements could be made, and nothing came of it.

It was also about this time that Henry Elsdale carried out some exploratory experiments aimed at an extension of the balloon's usefulness, namely aerial photography. He installed a camera in a small unmanned balloon and, in an early example of automatic control, added a clockwork mechanism which would not only operate the shutter, but then follow this by removing the exposed plate and replacing it with another, ready for a second photograph to be taken. By this means, it was said, a balloon could be launched and as many as six photographs taken without further human intervention. That there is no record of the device being exploited operationally suggests that it was never taken beyond the experimental stage. There would certainly seem to have been serious drawbacks to be overcome. Its use on a balloon in the tethered mode would scarcely have been likely to yield photographs of great military value, while if the balloon were to have been released so as to over-fly enemy positions, its recovery and that of its exposed plates would have been, at best, uncertain. Even if a solution to that difficulty had been found, the contribution of the ever-capricious wind would have rendered the setting of any timer, so as to start the clockwork mechanism at the desired point above the ground, problematical.

The point has previously been made that, at that time, balloons suffered from being difficult and cumbersome to deploy in the field, making the lack of enthusiasm for their adoption at higher level somewhat understandable. The disadvantages were twofold. The first lay in the undue permeability of the material from which balloons were then made, resulting in excessive loss of hydrogen, while this drawback was compounded by another difficulty – the absence of any compact means for the manufacture of the necessary replacement hydrogen in the field or, failing that, its carriage to the point of use, as was found prior to the Ashanti campaign. Together, they placed a severe limitation on the availability and the mobility of the would-be aeronauts on occasions such as manoeuvres, when the latter might otherwise have demonstrated their usefulness. It is possible to imagine the scorn, even mirth, of ballooning's opponents at such times, as the crestfallen aeronauts found themselves obliged to retire early from the scene of action and to travel back to base, before they were able to recharge their balloon, now (like them) deflated.

But it is in the nature of pioneers to advance in defiance of adversity and disbelief. In 1883, the first problem was greatly diminished when Templer discovered in the East End of London a family of immigrants from the Alsace, called Weinling. These useful people were found to be using for the purpose of balloon-making an organic substance, known as goldbeater's skin, which was obtained from the lower intestine of the ox and was much more impervious to hydrogen than the treated linen or silk previously used. By force of nature, this material could not be obtained in pieces larger than about one and a half square feet, while furthermore, a balloon skin needed to consist of up to seven thicknesses of the stuff, so that very many pieces were needed to make a complete envelope. While this did not represent an insuperable difficulty, the obstacle to their use heretofore had lain in the means by which the separate pieces could be joined together. This was where the Weinlings came in, for it was they who had devised a successful solution to the problem and now guarded its secret jealously. Since the entire family was skilled in the process, they had of necessity all to be taken into government employment. In due course, the 10,000 cu. ft *Heron* became the first fruit of the new construction process.

Soon afterwards, the second problem, that of the ready availability of hydrogen, was overcome by the introduction of steel cylinders with gas-tight valves, in which the hydrogen, having been manufactured at base, could be stored at a pressure of 1,500 psi and then transported in the field on specially adapted army wagons.

The hydrogen itself was manufactured in a plant which had been installed at Chatham and which employed the chemical reaction caused by the combination of zinc and sulphuric acid. In this process, to describe it briefly, a dilute solution of sulphuric acid contained in a barrel was gravity-fed to a second vessel in which had been placed the necessary quantity of zinc particles. The hydrogen thus generated then passed through two further containers, in which it was cooled and washed in turn, before ending in the main storage tank. The plant was completed by pumps which transferred the gas under pressure to the cylinders used for its transportation.

In parallel with these advances, more balloons were constructed, all making use of the new skin material. With the arrival of these improvements, the Balloon Store was, for the first time, in a position to offer a balloon section which could accompany troops on active service and which stood a reasonable chance of deploying its balloon to some effect when needed. Fate then lost little time in ordaining events which would allow this enhanced flexibility to be demonstrated, although, ever perverse, it produced not one, but two campaigns, at almost the same time. While, for both of these, it was decided that balloons should be included in the expeditionary force, this decision inevitably stretched the young ballooning organisation's resources to the limit.

The first opportunity came in 1884, when a new clash of interests arose in Southern Africa between the British colonial authorities at the Cape and the Boer farmers of the Transvaal, this time over attempts by both parties to extend their influence into the tribal territory of Bechuanaland. A British military expedition was dispatched to the area under Colonel Sir Charles Warren, to assert imperial authority. The balloon detachment which accompanied it was commanded by Major Elsdale, assisted by Lieutenant F. C. Trollope, Grenadier Guards, and ten other ranks.

Trollope was no stranger to ballooning and was perhaps the earliest example of

James Templer. (Paul Chapman)

Francis Trollope. (Paul Chapman)

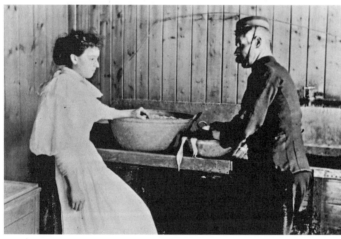

One of the Weinlings preparing goldbeater's skin, helped by a sapper. (Museum of Army Flying)

The hydrogen production installation, as it appeared in 1894. (Museum of Army Flying)

many who were to follow – enthusiastic military aeronauts who were not Royal Engineers, but who hailed from elsewhere in the army. He had been attached to the RE balloonists at Chatham since 1883, but his association with balloons and with Templer began somewhat earlier, although, but for the lateness of a train, his career might have ended before it had properly begun. It was in December 1881 that he had been due to join Templer on an ascent in the coal-gas balloon *Saladin*, for the purpose of making meteorological observations. In the event, Trollope's train ran late, and by the time he arrived, the balloon launch had gone ahead without him, Templer's companions being an army officer, Lieutenant Agg-Gardner, and a certain Walter Powell, the MP for Malmesbury, who was also an experienced balloonist. They started from Bath in a north-easterly wind, which carried them southwards and across the county of Dorset, until deteriorating visibility, a strengthening wind and the approach of nightfall indicated to Templer the advisability of landing. As he emerged from the clouds, his shouted enquiries to the ground revealed that they were near Bridport, with the coastline a perilously short distance beyond. With no time to lose and valving hard, he brought the balloon violently to earth, while the wind continued to drag it towards the cliff-edge which could now be seen a short distance away. In the impact, Templer and Agg-Gardner were thrown clear, the latter suffering a broken leg. Templer clung to the valve line, trying to release more hydrogen, but it was torn from his grasp as the now-lightened balloon swept upwards, out across Lyme Bay and disappeared, bearing the unfortunate Powell with it, to an unknown and watery end, somewhere in the English Channel.

Having been spared from participation in this tragic event, Trollope found himself involved in an enterprise which promised excitement of a different kind, since it was to be the first occasion that a British army was preparing to go into the field with an airborne unit mustered in its ranks. The party's equipment included three balloons: the *Heron* (10,000 cu. ft), the *Spy* (7,000 cu. ft) and the *Feo* (4,500 cu. ft), as well as 27,000 cu. ft of hydrogen, stored under compression in the new steel cylinders.

Operations began at Mafeking on 6 April, with the filling of *Heron*, followed later by the other two. The high altitude in those parts – 5,000 feet above sea level – reduced the balloons' lifting capability, but the party was pleased to find that even the little *Feo* could be persuaded to go up, with a single aeronaut in its basket. However, for those in the expedition who had been looking forward to action – who undoubtedly will have included the balloonists – the outcome was disappointing. The Boers melted away, the British were left in control of what became the colony of Bechuanaland (later Botswana) and the expeditionary force returned home without a shot having been fired.

Meanwhile, some 2,000 miles to the north, trouble of a more serious nature had for some time been brewing in the Sudan, then under the corrupt and inefficient domination of Egypt. The latter country, in its turn, although nominally a part of the crumbling Ottoman Empire, was then, in the complex world order of those days, effectively ruled by British officials, with its army under the command of British officers. It was in 1881, in a remote part of the Sudan, that an obscure religious ascetic, one Muhammad Ahmad ibn Abdallah, had declared himself the *Mahdi*, or divine leader, and had raised the standard of revolt against the Egyptian overlords. The ever-increasing *Mahdist* hordes, known popularly as the Dervishes, went from success to success, culminating, in late 1883, in the defeat of an ill-founded Egyptian army, commanded by a British officer, Colonel William Hicks, which had first been lured deep into the Sudan and then annihilated. By now, the *Mahdiyya* had become the *de facto* ruler of the Sudan, while Great Britain found itself unwillingly but inexorably drawn into the conflict.

The events which followed reflected no credit on the British government of the day, led by William Gladstone. In February 1884, having decided that evacuation of the Sudan by Egypt was the only possible course, it sent the nation's hero General Charles

Gordon to Khartoum with instructions which were open to fatal misinterpretation. Even though Gordon's position, deep in hostile territory and virtually defenceless, was soon seen to be clearly untenable, several months were allowed to pass before the government at last yielded to a popular clamour and dispatched a relief expedition for the purpose of extricating Gordon and the city's many Egyptian inhabitants.

For this campaign also it was decided that the novel airborne reconnaissance vehicle should be tried, even though the earlier departure had taken all the best equipment. Whatever was left over was gathered up and sent out to the Sudan, under the command of James Templer, assisted by Lieutenant R. J. H. L. Mackenzie RE. Even then, it was not considered worthy to be part of the main column advancing up the Nile valley, led by the C-in-C, Lord Wolseley himself, but was added to a subordinate force commanded by Lieutenant General Sir Gerald Graham, based on the port of Suakin, away to the east on the Red Sea coast, which was required to campaign in the desert between the Nile and the sea.

General Graham's orders were firstly to engage and crush the *Mahdi*'s lieutenant in that area, the redoubtable Osman Digna, and then to lay a railway line from Suakin westwards to Berber, on the upper Nile, to provide an additional supply channel to Wolseley, as he made his way slowly upriver. In the event, at the end of a campaign marked by confusion and small military success, neither of these objectives was achieved. In any case, on 26 January, before Graham's force had even set out, the principal purpose of the expedition had lapsed: Khartoum had fallen to the Dervishes and Gordon had been killed. Nevertheless, it was decided that for the time being operations against the insurgents should continue as planned and on 17 February the first troopships sailed for Suakin.

Suakin itself had its basis on two islands in a lagoon which lay at the landward end of a narrow, mile-long creek connecting it with the open sea. One of the islands was occupied by the old Arab town, while the other, which in some earlier time had acquired the name of Quarantine Island, provided the principal moorings for the troopships which now began to arrive in a continual stream, from both Britain and India. In an organised chaos of men, mules, camels and wagons, the troops, with mountains of equipment and stores, were gradually disembarked and transferred to the lines of tents forming the main camp which was taking shape on the mainland. The latter was protected by a defensive line based on a series of redoubts, for beyond lay the arid expanse of the open desert, across which, for the time being, Osman's warriors roamed unmolested.

On 7 March, the undermanned little balloon unit itself arrived. It numbered no more than ten, including the two officers, an insignificant group all but lost amongst an army which when complete would exceed 10,000 men. Its arrival would not, however, have escaped the approving notice of at least one of the officers present, a certain George E. Grover. He was by then a mature forty-four-year-old staff officer bearing a major's rank badges and had long since severed any connection with military ballooning. He must, nevertheless, have felt no small pleasure in seeing his campaigning of twenty years earlier vindicated at last by a tangible result.

Once ashore, the balloonists pitched their own tents amidst the bivouacs already established on the desert sand and near to one of the wells which provided Suakin's water supply. They had managed to find three balloons to bring along, none very large: the *Scout* (7,000 cu. ft), the *Fly* (5,000 cu. ft) and the venerable *Sapper* (5,600 cu. ft). Like their comrades in the south, they had also brought a supply of hydrogen in cylinders – some 22,000 cu. ft, an amount which would not leave much over were each balloon to be filled just once. For transport, they had a single wagon, complete with winch, but when it came to motive power, no provision had been made and Templer was obliged to borrow four horses from another company.

Conditions were far from ideal: they had been sent to one of the more inhospitable parts of the world, a land of scrub-covered desert, where daytime temperatures habitually climbed through the nineties, where unpleasant odours filled the air and where disease was wont to carry off more men than enemy action. Not that the latter were idle. Throughout the night, the cries of nervous sentries disturbed the tented lines, sometimes needlessly, sometimes for good reason, in the latter case when small parties of Dervishes, slipping past the defences under cover of darkness, wrought confusion amongst the ranks, while volleys of rifle fire, aimed more often at shadows than at the elusive enemy, punctured the night and murdered sleep.

For another fortnight, the army's preparations went forward, as more vessels arrived to swell the growing force and equipment was piled up or distributed, while all the time the place bustled with the constant coming and going of the assembling host. Finally, on 19 March, all was ready for the campaign to begin, that day seeing a short, armed reconnaissance of the nearby desert, followed the next day by a much larger foray, when a large force advanced some six miles westwards across the desert. Near the village of Hasheen, in the foothills of the mountains, the first serious clash with a strong enemy force took place. After a day's heavy fighting, with casualties on both sides, the Imperial troops disengaged and returned to their base at Suakin, not having achieved very much. On neither of these days was the balloon required to take part, being either unready for action or overlooked by the army's planning staff. The infinitesimal size of the little detachment in that bustling multitude would hardly have helped to remind the staff of its existence.

Two days later, one hour after first light on Sunday 22 March, another large force, numbering over 3,000 men, marched out under the command of Major-General Sir John M'Neill VC. Its principle components consisted of the 1st Battalion the Berkshire Regiment, a battalion of the Royal Marine Light Infantry, three battalions of the Indian Army, a detachment of Royal Engineers and a squadron of the 5th Lancers. There were also four Gardner machine guns, manned by men of the Royal Navy. Once more, the balloon detachment was left behind, a decision which, with hindsight, would appear to have had unfortunate consequences. The ultimate objective of this new initiative was Tamai, some 14 miles inland, where the main enemy forces were supposed to be mustered. On this first day, however, M'Neill's orders were to advance only about half that distance and then halt to construct a staging post, in the shape of a *zeriba* (a camp whose defensive perimeter was constructed of the tough and thorny mimosa bushes, cut down for the purpose and which grew abundantly in the region). Since the *zeriba* was to be stocked with stores, this meant that the party also included a large number of non-combatants, mainly Indian camel-drivers. With the country outside Suakin largely controlled by Osman and his warriors, the British force was constrained, for its own safety, to march in the traditional defensive square formation which had served the British Army for a century or more. This procedure, although a wise precaution in the circumstances, ensured only a ponderous rate of progress. Even so, it was quite early in the day when the expedition halted at a place called Tofrek, where it was decided the staging post would be built.

All around, the aforesaid mimosa bushes were growing particularly thickly, covering a wide area and sometimes reaching heights of six feet. While this made for an abundance of convenient material for the construction of the *zeriba*, it also furnished excellent cover through which an enemy could approach unseen. Under these circumstances, the force was allowed to fall into a vulnerable condition: many men were scattered about, their arms piled, some cutting and carrying bushes to build the *zeriba*, while others were stood down for dinner. A thinly spread cavalry screen then proved incapable of detecting the presence of large numbers of the enemy and hence of preventing a strong Dervish attack from slipping through and falling with little warning upon the ill-prepared defenders. Many were caught either in the open or sheltering behind defences which were no more than half-finished, as some of the attackers broke into the *zeriba* itself, spearing both soldiers and any unarmed and terrified camel drivers who had the misfortune to stand in their path. After a short, but at times desperate and bloody engagement, the enemy were beaten off, British discipline and Martini-Henry rifles taking a heavy toll of the attacking hordes. Nevertheless, with the defenders suffering casualties of well into three figures, the affair could hardly be counted a success for modern European troops against poorly armed, albeit brave and tenacious natives.

The question thus arises: would matters have turned out better had a balloon observer been present, searching the bush from an altitude of several hundred feet, rather than – or at least in support of – the cavalrymen, working from the mere ten feet or so afforded by their saddles? Viewed from this distance in time, it would seem that the balloonists were denied a valuable chance of demonstrating, in dramatic fashion, the critical contribution they might be able to make to success or failure.

Over the next two days, further supply convoys were sent back and forth from Suakin in support of the garrison at Tofrek, at which point it still lingered. These contingents were also sent out without the balloon detachment, although they were provided with a substitute of sorts. This, borrowing a concept from the navy, was something called the Crow's Nest – essentially an observation platform raised above the ground at the end of a thirty-foot pole. While this certainly had the merit of providing an enhanced view of the surrounding country which any elevated viewpoint can confer, the use of such a rudimentary device, when ten times its height could have been obtained from the latest technology waiting at Suakin, appears little short of risible.

On the second day following the affray at Tofrek, the supply convoy, still in square formation, was once more engaged by considerable numbers of Dervishes as it was returning to Suakin, with one man killed and some 20 wounded. It was on the third day, 25 March, that Osman's warriors roaming the area were surprised and some perhaps perplexed to see a strange bulbous shape rising up to the heavens above the enemy and glinting in the sunlight, as he once more advanced towards them. For on the previous day Templer had at last received the order for which he had been waiting. That evening, as the light began to fail and the fierce sun of the day had diminished to a yellow disc hanging above the western hills, *Scout* was unpacked and laid out. Over the course of several hours, as dusk fell and quickly darkened into desert night, the little party steadily transferred the gas brought out from Chatham, until an inflated *Scout* was floating like a giant onion a few feet above the ground at the end of its tether, ready for a dawn departure.

A few hours later, as night retreated once more and the first outlines of the eastern horizon began to take shape in the cool half-light of a new day, the convoy was already assembled in the now-habitual square, awaiting the order to advance. This time, the usual commissariat camels and supply carts clustered within the four protective lines of soldiers had found themselves joined by an additional and novel companion. With Major Templer holding the balloon wagon's reins, the latter's function was rendered unmistakeable by the spherical mass hovering above it, catching the early sunlight and throwing its shadow across the pale sand in a long ellipse. As shouted orders set the convoy on its journey, the cable was gradually paid out until Lieutenant Mackenzie, perched in the balloon's basket, was floating 400 feet above the marchers. While the temperature quickly climbed once more to its accustomed level and the air began to resemble that of the interior of a furnace, Mackenzie was the most comfortable man in the force. Aloof in his unique and privileged post far above the dust cloud raised by the thousands of boots and hooves toiling uncomfortably across the scrub- and boulder-strewn plain, he swept the horizon round. To the west, he could see a body of horsemen moving among the Red Sea Hills, while to the east lay the sparkling sea, on whose shore a number of Arabs were clearly visible rounding up the many stray camels which had bolted from the *zeriba* in the heat of the action three days earlier.

These two photographs show balloons being operated in Africa, but whether in the Sudan or in Bechuanaland has not been recorded in either case. (Museum of Army Flying / Science Museum – SSPL)

Elsewhere, other groups of Dervishes, some as close as 400 yards from the convoy, were picked out and reported. For he was pleased to find that from his vantage point the bush, which covered so much of the desert on either side, now appeared much less dense than it had seemed at ground level, enabling him to detect any movement amongst it. Thus he was able to keep the force's commanders advised of all the enemy's movements, by means of messages which from time to time he sent down the cable. Templer had the more taxing assignment; with the wagon continually shaken by uneven ground, he was hard-pressed to keep his team moving at a steady pace, attended by the constant fear that a particularly heavy strain might snap the balloon cable, leaving the balloon and its occupant to drift perilously away from the safety of the square to a landing somewhere in the desert and an unfriendly reception from its bloodthirsty inhabitants.

After an airborne vigil lasting for eight hours, Mackenzie was relieved by Sapper Wright, who stayed on watch for a further two. The young lieutenant, alone in his basket, had had ample time in which to ponder his fate, should their formidable enemy attack in force and succeed once more in breaking into the square. He afterwards said that, in the event of such a calamity, he had decided that he would descend to 50 feet from the ground and defend himself from there. Fortunately, he was not called upon to test the merits of this dubious scheme in practice, for the convoy was left completely unmolested, from the time it left Suakin until its return that same evening.

When, on 2 April, Graham finally marched a strong force to Tamai, hoping to confront the main enemy host, the balloon detachment was again included. But, as before, its contribution was not to be tested in actual battle. Osman, realising that he could not challenge his well-armed enemy in the open field without sustaining further heavy casualties, had withdrawn to the hills, where he was safe, but from where he could still mount guerrilla attacks on the invader. On this trek, Major Templer took his turn aloft, but was forced to descend prematurely when the wind became too strong. As the balloon reached ground level, it was caught by a gust and snagged against a mimosa bush, whose thorns caused tears which led to the balloon's subsequent collapse – an unfortunate accident, not only resulting in a loss of precious hydrogen, but one which will have done nothing to diminish prejudices concerning the inherent limitations of this new arrival in the ranks.

Frustrated in its attempts to eliminate Osman, the expedition now turned to its second task, the laying of a railway to Berber. In the course of the next few weeks, this enterprise slowly advanced across the desert, accompanied by escorting troops, with whom the balloon detachment, now operating the smaller *Fly*, was sometimes associated. At different times, a couple of friendly Arabs were sent up, whom Templer rated highly for their keen eyesight. (Templer reported one of them as singing throughout the ascent, though this may only have been the poor man's way of keeping his spirits up – a subtlety which would have been lost on the unfeeling Templer – since on his return to *terra firma* the Arab lost no time in reporting how little he had enjoyed the experience.)

In any event, these later activities bore only a limited relationship to the real *raison d'être* of military ballooning while, with Gordon dead and Khartoum lost, the campaign gradually petered out for lack of any objective supported by the home government, which had never evinced any great enthusiasm for the project anyway. In May, the entire expeditionary force was withdrawn, the partly built railway was abandoned, Sudan was surrendered to the Dervishes and Gordon was left unavenged for another thirteen years.

2

Watchers in the Sky

So Templer, Elsdale and their companions returned home to Chatham, to resume their normal peacetime occupations of training and balloon manufacture and at the same time to ponder the lessons which had been learnt from these first two active-service deployments. Of one thing all were in agreement: ten men was too small a number for the successful manning of a balloon detachment!

They will also have been wondering whether the embryonic air arm might now be viewed in a more favourable, perhaps more enthusiastic light by the higher command, now that it had seen active service on two expeditions. Unfortunately, in Bechuanaland there had been no military action, while in the Sudan, though there the fighting had been real enough, the campaign with which they had been associated was hardly a triumphant one and their own part far from noteworthy. Nevertheless, analysis of that campaign would at least have made it possible to argue that the presence of the balloon had prevented another bloody attack like that launched against M'Neill at Tofrek, by providing earlier and fuller information about the enemy's movements – perhaps even deterring him from approaching nearer by the sight of the strange and mystical object guarding the skies above his opponents' heads. On the other hand – and especially for those without the eyes to see – the balloon was only a very small player on a much wider stage. The army's proper strength still issued from the muzzles of its Martini-Henrys – not to mention that *really* impressive offspring of modern technology, the Gardner machine gun, which, along with the Maxim, had also made its presence felt in the Sudan. How many Dervishes had the balloon managed to kill? There was another shortcoming too, about which there could be no argument: in winds above about 20 mph, the balloon had to be pulled down, or could not be launched. Perhaps the most they could hope was that they had advertised their existence a little more widely within the army as a whole. (In Bechuanaland, the force commander, himself a former Royal Engineer, had been numbered amongst those who, by ascending in the *Heron*, had experienced for themselves the extended view of the countryside which altitude confers.) Finally, looking back from today's standpoint, we should not fail to identify one other feature of these events which marks a particular point in aeronautical history: leading the still-swelling parade of the hundreds of thousands who were to follow him, Lieutenant Mackenzie holds an unassailable place as the very first British airman to perform his airborne duties in the presence of the enemy.

As the nineteenth century moved towards its end, domestic matters, notably Irish Home Rule and industrial unrest, formed the major preoccupations of successive British governments. While foreign governments quarrelled and sometimes came to blows over different matters such as the control of the Balkan lands which formed the European part of the crumbling Turkish Empire, Britain contrived to remain aloof. Not that there was a lack of campaigns to be fought. In Africa the next decade saw several small wars, including further campaigns in Africa, fought to subdue the Ashanti and the Matabele, while the defence of the north-western frontier of the Indian Empire demanded excursions every now and then to quell the troublesome tribes of that mountainous region, as well as a full-scale war in Afghanistan. For none of these operations was any reason found to involve the balloonists and they were not called upon to engage in any more foreign adventures. Even in 1896, when Kitchener returned to the Sudan and began the great logistical enterprise which took him a thousand miles up the Nile to Khartoum and his triumph over the *Mahdiyya* at Omdurman, no balloon figured in that campaign. Railways might be laid across deserts and small navies might be built and sailed many miles up the Nile to the very walls of Khartoum, but no invitation to attend was delivered to Templer and his colleagues. Throughout these years, the balloonists were left in peace to continue expanding and developing their *métier* as far as their limited budget allowed them.

On 1 April 1887, Templer was appointed 'Instructor in Ballooning', his pay in this post being set at £600 per annum. This official recognition of his own efforts was encouraging, but the following year, impatient with the continuing inadequacy of the facilities at Chatham, he took matters into his own hands and, at his own expense, acquired some land at Lidsing, halfway between Chatham and Maidstone, to provide a much-needed open space, unavailable at the depot, where proper training exercises could take place. It was at some time during the balloonists' tenure of Lidsing that Lord Wolseley himself came on a visit and was taken up. This ascent apparently elicited the observation from his Lordship that, 'had he been able to employ balloons in the earlier stages of the Sudan campaign, the affair would not have lasted as many months as it did years', which seems, on the face of it, to be an incongruous assertion given Templer's presence at Suakin. However, perhaps one should admit the possibility that Wolseley, with all his preoccupations, as he tried to accomplish the well-nigh impossible task with which the politicians had landed him, was unaware of the existence of the tiny balloon unit within his overall command, remote as it was from the theatre of operations which mattered most. On the other hand, he – or his staff – might have been all too well aware of the inadequacy of the contribution that the tiny Balloon Section could have made.

If military ballooning itself was going through a tranquil period, James Templer, on the other hand, was to find himself for a short time sailing through stormy skies, for in February 1888, the leading figure in British military aeronautics was placed under arrest. He was then forced to endure an uncomfortable wait, while the case was being prepared, before, on 5 April, he was summoned to appear before a General Court Martial which assembled at the Royal Engineers' Brompton Barracks in Chatham, accused of 'scandalous conduct unbecoming an officer', in that he made false statements to his superior officers, Major Elsdale and Colonel Durnford, and that, worse, he divulged to third parties secret information concerning the construction of the government's balloons.

The case centred on the manufacture by a private company in Birmingham of a

Some of the men of the Balloon Equipment Store, photographed at Lidsing in 1888. (Royal Engineers Museum)

balloon, which, it appeared, so closely resembled the British Army's own balloons in its detailed design, including the use of goldbeater's skin, that suspicions were aroused that a serious leakage of official secrets had taken place. Moreover, such secret information was supposedly known only to a very few persons, of whom Templer was naturally one. When witnesses were found to declare that Templer, despite his denials, had been seen on a number of occasions in a former dance hall in Birmingham, where the balloon was being constructed, the inference was drawn that it was he who had given away the information which had enabled the company to devise a balloon with features so similar to those incorporated in the British Army's balloons – information which was both confidential and of national importance. For Templer, matters began to look very black. The fact that the balloon under construction was intended for a foreign power, namely Italy, only made it worse, introducing the suggestion of that gravest of crimes – treason.

Opening its case, the prosecution lost no time in producing its star witness. This was the twenty-three-year-old wife of the hall's caretaker, Sarah Ackland, who asserted that she had seen Templer in Birmingham on several different days, with not only the head of the company, a Mr Howard Lane, but also some 'foreign gentlemen', while the balloon was being assembled. Her husband, called next, confirmed his wife's statements, after which it was the turn of Henry Elsdale. That officer's evidence, while confirming that the Birmingham balloon was very similar to those operated by the army, in its general tone could hardly be said to have conveyed any impression of belief in his colleague's innocence.

Nevertheless, as the case unfolded, weaknesses in the prosecution case began to appear, which the defence counsel proceeded skilfully to exploit. He began, during his cross-examination of Sarah Ackland, with character assassination, by extracting from her the admission, seemingly irrelevant but allowed by the Court, that, a few days before Christmas, she had been fined a matter of ten and sixpence by the local magistrates for being drunk and disorderly and for assaulting the police. To this was then added the admission by her husband that, having left his job as caretaker, he was now in receipt from 'the Treasury' of a regular payment of £1 per week, allowing counsel to float an inference – which he was careful to leave as such – that Ackland was being bribed to give false evidence.

However, once the defence opened its own case, it soon became evident that such dubious manoeuvres were hardly necessary since, for all of the dates on which Templer was alleged to have been in Birmingham, witnesses were found to affirm that he was, on the contrary, at Chatham. No less a person than Major-General Edwardes CB, lately the Commandant of the School of Military Engineering there, gave evidence that, on 26 November, Templer was his guest to lunch. Next, the MFH of the local hunt was able to confirm that, on 12 November, another of the alleged dates, Templer, far from being in the smoke of Birmingham, was with him, riding to hounds in the Kent countryside. Others followed, all of impeccable character, who were able similarly to swear that they had been with the accused, in or near Chatham, on one or other of the days in question.

The prosecution's case had been founded almost wholly on the Ackland couple's identification of the Birmingham visitor as being Major Templer. By the time that the last defence witness had given his evidence, it was clear that they had been mistaken and the prosecution's case collapsed. At the end of a trial which had lasted four days, all the charges against Templer were withdrawn and his two-month ordeal ended with an honourable acquittal. As he left the courtroom, he was first warmly congratulated by a number of his colleagues and then emerged on to the barrack square to loud cheers from a large crowd of other ranks who had assembled on hearing the welcome news.

In 1889, balloons were again included in that year's manoeuvres at Aldershot. A favourable report on their contribution to these activities was submitted by the GOC Aldershot Division, Sir Evelyn Wood, as a result of which the following year saw the greatest step forward for military aeronautics since the creation of the Balloon Equipment Store. This was the formation of a permanent Balloon Section of the Royal Engineers, with an establishment of three officers and thirty-one other ranks, under the command of Lieutenant H. B. Jones RE. At last, a unit had been created specifically charged with the operation of balloons in the field. The other ballooning activities – effectively the manufacture of hydrogen and the provision of the balloons themselves and other equipment, still referred to as the School of Ballooning – remained under the direction of the perennial James Templer. At the same time, it was decided that both these units should henceforth be based at Aldershot. There, the balloonists' new home, which came to be known as Balloon Square, consisted of a roughly rectilinear parcel of land, some 2½ acres in extent and bounded on two of its sides by the Farnborough road and the southern bank of the Basingstoke Canal respectively. It included workshops, a number of storage gasometers and, for the first time, a balloon shed, within which several inflated balloons could be accommodated. One regrettable omission, however, lay in the matter of horses. Although the Balloon Section's equipment necessarily included wagons, for the transport both of the balloon itself and of the spare hydrogen cylinders indispensable for operations in the field, its establishment failed to include the horses needed to draw them. This inexplicable oversight meant that the Section was still obliged to beg or borrow these on an *ad hoc* basis from some other convenient unit in its vicinity. As it happened, this omission was partially alleviated by another contribution from the ever-resourceful Colonel Templer (as he now was). In addition to being a leading campaigner for military ballooning, Templer was also an enthusiastic advocate of the use of steam traction engines. By fair means or foul, he managed to acquire one or two of these machines, which came in very handy on many occasions, although even here the balloonists could sometimes find themselves obstructed by reactionary forces, since those were the days when such creations of the devil were required, when on public roads, to be preceded by a man on foot bearing a red flag, as occurred, for example, on the journey from Chatham to Aldershot in 1889, when the convoy of wagons, with its unwelcome guide in the lead, took three days to get as far as Guildford, after which horses took over.

The concentration at Aldershot, the army's major home base, undoubtedly also assisted in further focussing attention on the aeronautical Cinderella, although not everyone was impressed by the upstart. Aldershot, after rather low beginnings, had by then developed into a somewhat genteel town whose streets echoed with the ring of hooves and the low rumble of carriage wheels; a town where officers, with their ladies, might on fine evenings be seen strolling along Queen's Avenue, while a regimental band played popular airs outside the Officers' Mess. Thus, to some, the erection of the balloon shed, in workaday corrugated iron, with its accompanying gasometers and workshops, sat ill with the elegant façades of the 'best' part of Aldershot and indeed represented the intrusion of a somewhat brash and low-class modernity. Such reactions could only be reinforced by Colonel Templer's unfortunate habit of taking his wife into town, perched on a trailer towed behind one of his noisy and smoky traction engines.

With the balloonists free to devise and introduce further developments and improvements, one such which benefited from a more attentive study was the provision of an adequate supply of hydrogen of a suitable quality. That this was one of the most critical considerations affecting ballooning as practised by the Royal Engineers needs no emphasis. It was also a feature which was ripe for change. The original technique for the production of hydrogen, exemplified by the abandoned furnace at Woolwich, involved the passing of steam across red-hot iron. In the course of time, this exciting procedure was replaced by another, described earlier and only slightly less stimulating, in which sulphuric acid was poured on to zinc. Both processes

Members of the Balloon Section gathered at Aldershot in 1893. James Templer, with stick and gloves, is at centre-front, while glimpsed behind is one of his steam engines. (RAF Museum)

were not only potentially hazardous to the operators, but also carried the drawback that the gas thus produced included a certain amount of acid vapour, which tended to attack the balloon skins. Templer, rising once again to the occasion, pressed for the adoption of the much more efficient and cleaner electrolysis process and in 1896 succeeded in persuading the War Office to purchase such a plant from Messrs Siemens of Woolwich, which was duly installed at Aldershot. The new method then gradually supplanted the zinc/acid process, although the latter continued in use for some time.

As the status of military ballooning had gradually advanced from unofficial toleration to that of official recognition, the different activities concerned had correspondingly and naturally evolved into two different sectors, as has been described above: on the one hand, the operation of balloons, both for training purposes and in the field, which was the duty of the Balloon Section, now under the command of Captain G. M. Heath RE; on the other, the technical development and manufacture of balloons, of the necessary hydrogen and of what in a later age would have been called the ground equipment. In 1897, this was recognised by a further change of name, with the School of Ballooning taking the more appropriate name of Balloon Factory, to deal with the latter activities. (The years were to bring further changes of name; in an attempt to clarify a rather complex progression, the different appellations are summarised in Appendix I.) Colonel Templer, with his long experience in the design of balloons, their ancillary and all-important ground transport and the equally important business of the manufacture and storage of hydrogen, remained in charge, with the title of Superintendent, with, as Assistant Superintendant, the erstwhile guardsman Francis Trollope.

It is appropriate at this point to insert a brief description of the balloons which were used for military purposes in those days. Although the hydrogen balloon as used by the British Army differed little in principle from all those which had sailed the skies for a century or more, the years at Chatham and Aldershot had seen the introduction of certain improvements. The most important of these concerned the material of which the envelope was made, as has already been described. In detail, the envelope was built up from a number of narrow strips of goldbeater's skin, known as gores and joined together by the Weinlings' famous and secret method. The gores tapered to a point at each end, so that, when brought together along their lengths, the resulting envelope took up the form of a sphere. At its base, this spherical envelope ended in an open neck, or tail, through which the balloon was filled and through which excess gas could escape, to maintain equilibrium when the atmospheric pressure fell as the balloon ascended, or if the hydrogen was heated by the action of the sun. For tethered work the neck would usually be tied up to prevent undue loss of precious gas, while conversely, for free runs it was normally left open, to cope with the greater variations in atmospheric conditions likely to be met with on such voyages. A second aperture was located at the apex of the envelope, in which was fitted the 'top valve', normally held closed by springs. This valve could be opened, against the springs, by pulling the 'valve line' which, hanging down inside the envelope, ended within the aeronaut's reach. The top valve was used during free flights to decrease buoyancy by the release of gas and thereby maintain or reduce the balloon's altitude, or to bring about its descent during the landing approach at the end of a flight.

The balloon envelope was enclosed completely within a net, which was draped around its outside, with the lower edge of the net attached at a number of points around the circumference of a ring, or hoop. From this hoop, in turn, was suspended the balloon's payload, in other words, the basket with the crew inside. The weight of the basket was thus supported by the upward thrust of the low-density hydrogen within the envelope bearing against the net and transferred thence to the hoop.

As for instruments – on free runs the balloon pilot was usually furnished with a barometric altimeter, a rate of climb or descent indicator and a compass. A grapnel, for lowering during the descent to catch on some suitable point on the ground, and sandbags, to perform the opposite function to that of the top valve, by being jettisoned to lighten the balloon if necessary, completed the main essentials of a balloon's equipment.

For the operation of a tethered balloon in the field, the ancillary but essential transportation equipment consisted of six standard army-pattern wagons, horse-drawn and suitably modified for their special purpose. One, the balloon wagon itself, was fitted with a drum, holding the appropriate length of wire cable and fitted with a brake and two winding-down handles, one on each side. Four other wagons were each fitted up for the carriage of thirty-five gas cylinders each, connected to a copper-lined manifold, through which the balloon was filled. The sixth wagon was used for carrying various other pieces of equipment.

When it came to the inflation and launching of a balloon, the Royal Engineers had by that time reduced this practice to a fine art, which was laid down in detail in a *Manual of Military Ballooning* compiled by Captain B. R. Ward RE, who had replaced Captain Heath as Officer Commanding the Balloon Section. This being the army, the procedure was defined by a 'drill', which ensured that the work was performed in a manner which was closely controlled and efficiently carried out.

To begin with, the balloon party, which numbered sixteen men led by two NCOs, was fallen in in two ranks, and ordered to 'number off'. The odd numbers were the 'balloon men', the first four even numbers 'tube men', and the last four 'sandbag men'. If, as should have been the case, all the members of the squad had been trained in the full drill, the whole procedure could then be accomplished by means of a series of commands, with each man performing the particular task corresponding to the number assigned to him. Thus, for example, on the command 'Mount', each 'number', knowing his function, would climb on to the appropriate wagon. On the command 'Dismount', certain men would then move to the filling area, carrying with them the necessary equipment, such as the balloon itself or its basket, while others stationed themselves at the tube wagons, ready to control the delivery of gas. All these movements would be carried out at the double. 'Lay out' would see, first, a protective ground cloth being laid out, following which the balloon itself, with its net, would be unpacked and rolled out onto the ground cloth. Then, once all was ready, inflation would commence through the neck of the balloon ('Turn in'), while completion of the filling was signalled by 'Turn off'. Although today such parade-ground formality can sometimes attract a degree of condescending amusement, in a very different army and in very different times, it was no bad thing when it concerned a task which involved the handling of a balloon made of a somewhat delicate material while also attempting to fill it with an easily combustible gas – all the more so for work which, at times when it really counted, might well have to be performed under fire.

Above right and middle: Men of the Balloon Section preparing a balloon for launching. *Above:* On the command 'Lay out', the ground cloth is spread, to be followed by the balloon itself. *Below:* On the command 'Turn in', the gas valves are opened and the balloon begins to inflate. (Jean Roberts)

With the drill completed, the now-inflated balloon is ready to be launched. (Author's collection)

Work at the Balloon School in 1895. The men appear to be in the act of filling a small 'pilot' or weather balloon. Half-hidden by the man in the centre is what looks like a barograph. Second from the right looms the unmistakable figure of James Templer. (RE Museum)

With the earlier, more haphazard days thus consigned to the past, the Balloon Section was now a regular participant in training exercises, particularly on the artillery ranges at Okehampton and Lydd. At the former location, the balloons were used for observing practice firing, while at the latter their assistance was invoked in connection with experimental firing of siege-guns and the effects of explosives on buildings. The wind velocity on these occasions remained a significant and restrictive factor, its effect often rendering the work of the observer uncomfortable and difficult, as he found himself trying to focus his field-glasses on a distant object, from a basket which not only swayed around but which also tended to rotate in one direction and then twist back again. To quote a description in the *Royal Engineers Journal* for 1 November 1897:

> The experiments were frequently interrupted by the weather, as experience would appear to prove that a captive balloon is of little service for military purposes with the wind at a strength of over 20 miles an hour. [...]
> On calm days the inflated balloon can be transported from place to place, while still at its required height, by the simple means of moving the wagon. In general practice, however, if it has to be moved more than a few hundred yards, it is hauled down and towed along close to the ground by the wagon horses or by the men of the detachment alone. This operation, if it has to be carried out against a strong wind, is very tedious; but in calm weather, or with the wind, the balloon can in open country be moved many miles without difficulty, and can easily keep pace with troops on the march. [...]
> Nervousness also has to be overcome, and above all things the interior economy of the passenger must be educated to accommodate itself to the motion. The work in rough weather is indeed no joy and *mal-de-mer* is frequent even with the best sailors.

Military ballooning had advanced considerably in the couple of decades since its inception, but considerations such as those referred to above still hampered its effective use and probably limited its more widespread acceptance by the military hierarchy. However, the time was nigh when it would be called upon to undertake its most extensive active-service deployment so far, albeit a deployment which coming aeronautical developments would ensure was also its swansong.

3

South Africa

In South Africa, quarrels between the British authorities at the Cape and the Dutch farmers on the veldt were never far below the surface and in 1899 matters once more reached a critical point. In October, the negotiations which had been taking place between the Government of Cape Colony and the independent Boer republics of the Transvaal and the Orange Free State finally broke down and hostilities opened in the Second South African War. Though this is not the place for a lengthy description of the history of that war, some general account of events is necessary, in particular, those in which the Balloon Sections found themselves involved.

The war began badly for Great Britain, which during the early weeks was baffled to find that its professional soldiers were being worsted by the amateur but hard-riding and sharp-shooting Boers who flocked from their farmsteads to defend their two republics. Boldly, the Boers lost no time in going on to the attack and invading the British colony of Natal. The defenders fell back in some disarray, and by the beginning of November, the town of Ladysmith, with a large number of British troops inside, was cut off and besieged. To make matters worse, two other bodies of Imperial troops were also trapped in Kimberley and Mafeking, towns on the borders of the Boers' own homelands. As if this were not bad enough, the relief columns which then marched northwards to drive the Boers back found themselves obliged to fight a series of engagements, gaining ground only slowly and at the cost of heavy casualties.

The nadir of British fortunes was reached in early December. On the 10th, Sir William Gatacre failed to eject a Boer force from Stormberg Junction, well inside Cape Colony, whilst losing some 600 men killed, wounded or captured. On the following day, the Kimberley relief column under Lieutenant General Lord Methuen, having after a hard fight managed to get across the River Modder, was utterly routed two or three miles further on, at the foot of the kopjes of Magersfontein. In Natal, to the east, the second relief column, striving in a similar manner to reach Ladysmith, had found itself brought to a complete halt before the strong defensive positions which the enemy had set up in the steep-sided hills on both banks of the River Tugela – itself a barrier of some significance – from which it was completely unable to dislodge him. On 15 December, this force, led by the Commander-in-Chief South Africa himself, Sir Redvers Buller VC, met with another costly reverse when it failed to force the crossing of the river at Colenso, thus completing the trio of woes which were to acquire the mournful epithet of 'Black Week'.

All these events caused consternation at home, the press in particular being unstinting in its disapproval. The end result was the dispatch of two of the foremost soldiers of the day, Field Marshal Lord Roberts and, as his chief of staff, Major-General Lord Kitchener, fresh from his victory over the Dervishes at Omdurman, to take over the running of the campaign.

When the war had begun, the Balloon Section, being by now a recognised part of the army in the field, had been one of the many units which found themselves aboard the troopships carrying the 'gentlemen in khaki ordered south'. As is so often the case, the demands now placed upon it by the arrival of a real war were greatly in excess of the resources it had hitherto been allowed to develop in peacetime and it was obliged to undergo a rapid expansion. Officers with previous ballooning experience were recalled from other duties and the single Balloon Section was in time expanded to four. That the initial expansion was achieved with commendable dispatch may be judged from the fact that the first Section to arrive reached Durban on 26 October 1899.

Before then, whilst they were still upon the high seas, the balloonists had managed to score a certain moral success, albeit a fleeting one, over the somewhat unworldly Boer farmers. While the latter's amateur soldiers were advancing confidently into Natal, there was by contrast great trepidation in Pretoria – inspired perhaps by the novels of Jules Verne – that these aerial craft, which it was known the English were intending to deploy, would be used to mount a bombing raid on the Transvaal capital. Orders were issued to all telegraph stations that all balloon sightings were to be reported. In an interesting fore-echo of the UFO 'sightings' of a later age, daily reports of the approach of these alarming assault ships, sometimes singly, sometimes in whole squadrons, often flashing lights, were duly transmitted, before calmer counsels indicated that such an apocalyptic contribution to the conflict was not to be feared.

No.2 Section, under the command of Major Heath, assisted by Captain W. A. Tilney, 17th Lancers, and Second Lieutenant C. Mellor RE, was the first to land and was immediately ordered to Ladysmith, arriving there on 27 October, in time to be trapped and to share the privations of the siege which commenced shortly afterwards. It was soon in action. Ladysmith lay in a depression commanded by hills on all sides, on which the Boers were busily installing their artillery. Early on 30 October, Sir George White, in command, mounted a large-scale assault, in an effort to dislodge the enemy guns, which were already beginning to bombard the town. A balloon was put up and was successful in locating the positions of some of the latter, while directing the fire of its own. On the ground, however, the action was an unmitigated disaster for the British, who were forced to retire after heavy casualties, leaving the enemy in control of the heights, from which, throughout the siege, he continued to shell the town. For its part, the Section continued to launch its balloons and carry out useful work, observing Boer movements and directing artillery fire. Occasionally, members of the defending force were taken up, such as Lieutenant Colonel Sir Henry Rawlinson of the Coldstream Guards, who was pleased to find that he was 'not a bit sea sick but inclined to hold on very tight'. However, despite having a fine view of the surrounding country, like so many, he reached the conclusion that it was 'difficult to spot guns ... as it rocks about so and keeps revolving round so much that one cannot keep ones glasses steady'.

By late November, the Section had exhausted all the hydrogen which it had managed to bring with it on its hasty journey to Ladysmith and, being cut off from any further sources of supply, was obliged to cease operations for the remainder of the siege. Shortly before that time, though, it had contributed briefly to the morale of a little knot of Britons who, a couple of miles to the south-east, were trudging northwards, bound for imprisonment in Pretoria. Among them was the young Winston Churchill, captured in the course of his celebrated adventure with the armoured train and who later related how their spirits were temporarily uplifted by the sight of the balloon, catching the sunlight above the town and flashing a defiant signal of freedom to the downcast prisoners.

The Royal Navy was also present during the siege, a contingent of naval guns having turned up just before the town was cut off, adding some much-needed power to the defence. Naturally, the balloon observers sought to assist with the sailors' gun-laying as they were accustomed to do for the army. Unfortunately, their efforts appear to have met with some disdain from the Senior Service. Today's reader of some post-war exchanges on the subject cannot but detect in them a whiff of inter-service

This picture is described as the balloon camp in Ladysmith, during the siege. It therefore seems fairly safe to assume that the figures are those of No.2 Section's three officers – Heath, Tilney and Mellor. (RE Museum)

rivalry ... In a report to the Committee on Military Ballooning in 1904, Commander A. W. Heneage wrote:

> I have the honour to report that I have no recollection of the balloon at Ladysmith being of any material assistance to the naval guns. This, I think, was mainly due to the balloon having to be removed so far in rear of the guns that the officer in charge could not see as well as we could; also to the fact that we had a powerful telescope on a fixed platform, and that we, being accustomed to the use of telescopes at long ranges, could accurately mark our own shots.
>
> I do not recollect any signals being taken in from balloons, but I remember at the engagement of 30th October a message being telephoned from it saying that our shooting was excellent, and that one of our shells had hit the 6-in gun on Pepworth Hill. This was before the balloon was moved back.

The second paragraph suggests a certain selectivity in the Commander's recollections. Was he offered and did he take the opportunity to see for himself how the scene of conflict could be revealed from a balloon, compared to his 'fixed platform'? A second report by Commander M. H. Hodges gives the aeronauts even less credit:

Whilst in charge of a 4.7 gun, during the siege, I did not receive any assistance from
the balloons in correcting the fire etc., and the only communication I received from
them was a message on one occasion which read: 'I think your last shot knocked out
Long Tom,' referring to the Long Tom mounted on Pepworth Hill.

Such innuendoes from the navy could not be allowed to pass unchallenged and the
President of the Royal Engineers Committee was constrained to send the following
memo to the Director of Fortifications and Works (DFW) at the War Office:

The R.E. Committee have noticed in the final report of the Committee on Military
Ballooning, 1904, reports by Rear Admiral the Hon. H. Lambton & Commander A.
W. Heneage, which give an erroneous impression of balloon work in Ladysmith in
connection with Naval guns.
    Lieutenant Colonel Heath (President of the balloon Sub-Committee) who was
commanding the Balloon Section at Ladysmith, wishes to point out that the balloon
was placed about a mile on the right flank of the 4.7" Naval gun, firing against
'Imbulwana' and not in rear as stated by Commander Heneage. The bursts of shells
both over & under the target could be very clearly observed, and were for some days
communicated by telephone to the Naval Battery by the officer in the balloon.
    A message however was received one morning by the O.C. Balloon Section which
seemed to indicate that the assistance offered was not appreciated, so no further
communications were made, and the work of the Balloon Section was confined to the
mapping down of positions of Boer camps, noting daily movements on the part of the
enemy, and communicating this information to the Head Quarters Staff.

With No.2 Section trapped behind the enemy lines in Ladysmith, General Buller to the
south had been left without any balloon support, as he strove to advance and relieve the
town. In an effort to remedy this, another officer with ballooning experience, Captain
G. E. Phillips RE, took it upon himself, shortly after Black Week, to put together an
improvised detachment, by assembling what balloon equipment and personnel he could
lay his hands on – mainly that which had been fortuitously left behind by Major Heath.
Numerous ascents took place, notably during January 1900, while Buller was still trying
and failing to dislodge the enemy from the Tugela hills. In the course of these, the balloon
(the *Thames*) was holed and Phillips himself was wounded, but the hilly country in which
the Section was attempting to operate made it easy for the enemy to conceal himself,
even from the elevated viewpoint of the balloon, and its contribution was on a minor
scale. Nevertheless, it attracted the favourable comment from one of Buller's subordinate
commanders, Major-General N. G. Lyttleton, that 'useful work in investigating the Boer
position and in directing our fire was done by the Balloon officers'.
    No.1 Section, meanwhile, under Capt Jones, accompanied by Lieutenants A. H. W.
Grubb RE and R. G. Earle RE, had landed at Cape Town on 22 November from the
SS *Kildonan Castle*, equipped with a total of eleven balloons, mostly of the 'T' 10,000
cu. ft class. Before moving northwards to join the 1st Division under Lord Methuen,
it spent a fortnight in the Cape Town area, sorting out its equipment and setting up a
depot and gas-making plant at Fort Knokke.
    On 5 December, the Section was ordered north and conveyed by train as far as
De Aar, some 100 miles from the front. Leaving a substantial part of its stores and
wagons there to be brought on later, the rump of the Section finally reached the River
Modder by rail on 9 December, during Black Week and as Methuen was completing
his plans for the disastrous attack on the Boer positions at Magersfontein to the north
of the river. As was so often the case, the first problem to be overcome was the finding
of motive power for the wagons. It was past noon on the 10th before the Army Service

Corps had been persuaded to provide sufficient mules, horses and oxen to make up two teams, a mixed one for the balloon wagon and oxen for a single gas-tube wagon. Strong winds, followed later by pouring rain, then prevented any ascents that day, thus depriving Methuen of the valuable information concerning the disposition of the enemy's defences which Jones, aloft in his basket, might have provided. As it was, when the first attack, by 4,000 men of the Highland Brigade, was sent in shortly before dawn on the 11th, it had to advance over open ground with its commanders lacking all idea of just where the Boer marksmen might be. They were still groping their way forward in the half-light when the enemy opened fire at short range from his positions hidden amongst the Magersfontein kopjes. The Scotsmen, caught in open ground, suffered grievously and the attack was halted in its tracks.

At eleven o'clock, with the remnants of that first attack, both dead and living, still lying where they were stopped, the Gordon Highlanders were ordered to launch a second assault, which met with equal defiance and equal failure. At the same time, with the weather having cleared, the balloon *Titania* was at last ordered up. Captain Jones, as he rose, found himself gazing upon a battlefield littered with prone kilted figures, the living clinging to what little shelter they could find from the remorseless rifle fire, while many others lay unmoving in the stillness of death. Beyond this melancholy scene, Jones was actually able to detect and report a gap in the enemy's defences on his eastern flank, but by then the failure of the attack was complete and Methuen was unable to exploit the situation before the gap was closed. The balloon also sent down useful though unwelcome news of the arrival of Boer reinforcements from Abon Dam and Spytfontein – information whose value was acknowledged by Methuen in his dispatch after the battle. But the day had been effectively lost before the attack began, for want of adequate intelligence concerning the enemy's positions. The next morning, the British commander acknowledged defeat and fell back to the Modder. Two days later, Buller met his bloody repulse at Colenso and Black Week was complete.

For the next two months, with Methuen stalled at the Modder, fighting was no more than sporadic. Although many ascents were made, not always without damage to the balloons, brought on partly by squally weather, including the occasional dust-storm, and partly by the poor condition in which some of them were to be found, any action by the Section of a warlike kind was restricted to observation of enemy positions and an abortive attempt to direct the fire of a naval 12-pounder gun. The Section's efficiency at this time was not helped by its own share of the endemic sickness which was beginning to pose as much of a peril to the army as the Boers themselves. Of the Section's three officers and thirty-four other ranks, Lieutenant Earle and eight men were at that time in hospital.

On 10 January 1900, Roberts and Kitchener landed at Cape Town to begin their task, too late for their arrival to prevent the further tragedy of Spion Kop on 22–23 January – the last and greatest reverse for the Imperial Forces. On 8 February, as Harry Jones himself was joining the sick list, the two generals arrived at Methuen's camp on the Modder and almost immediately the tide began to turn. On the 12th, watched by an observer in the basket of the balloon *Elsie*, the army recrossed the river and started to move east, away from Magersfontein, on a wide outflanking movement. In the van, the British cavalry, under Sir John French, having crossed the Modder at Klip Drift, burst right through the Boer positions and, in a wild day's ride, reached the gates of Kimberley that same evening, thus lifting the 123-day siege.

This new-found energetic action on the British side transformed the situation. While the besieging Boers around Kimberley hastened to inspan their wagons and begin a retreat to the northward, Piet Cronje, commanding the Boer army at Magersfontein, yielded his positions there, hitherto so stoutly defended, and started to withdraw eastwards up the Modder Valley. This manoeuvre proved to be unsuccessful when,

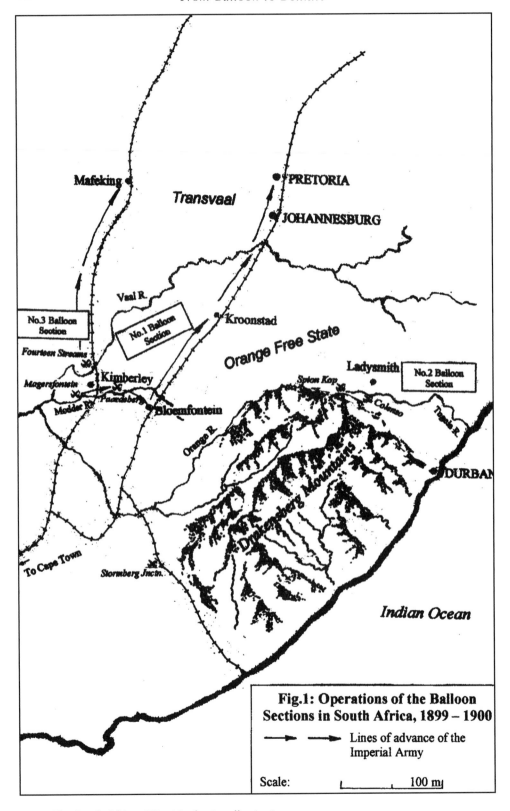

Fig.1: The South African War. (Author's collection)

on 19 February, the Boer general found himself trapped and surrounded on the north bank of the river at Paardeberg, some 30 miles from Magersfontein. No.1 Balloon Section, coming by a different route, reached the Paardeberg area in the early hours of the 22nd. It set up its position on the south bank, some thousand yards from the forward enemy trenches, and at dawn on 23 February, the *Duchess of Connaught* was filled with hydrogen. A turbulent breeze precluded any ascents until the afternoon, when Lieutenant Grubb was able to go up and make some rather shaky sketches of the Boer positions as he was tossed about in the capricious air. (He later reported that 'it was very difficult to persuade officers to go up and see for themselves and I think only three or four availed themselves of going up for short ascents during the period'.) Over the next few days, as the wind dropped, many more ascents were made, usually accompanied by a fusillade from the enemy's rifles, which had little immediate effect: by the time the balloon reached its operating altitude of 1,000 feet, the Boers seemed to lose interest and it was left unmolested by the opposing marksmen. During these ascents, the observer's time was divided between the sketching of the enemy's positions and the direction of artillery fire, communication with the batteries being by means of signal flags. On the 27th, Cronje surrendered, marking the first major setback suffered by the Boers since fighting began. This reverse was due in no small measure to the remorseless pounding his positions had received from the Imperial Artillery, which itself owed much to the guidance given by the reports of the fall of shot transmitted from the balloon.

With the dark days of Black Week well and truly behind them, the Imperial Forces were now set on a steady advance into the Boer heartlands. There was much foot-slogging to be done before the ultimate objective – Pretoria – was reached and numerous actions would have to be fought against a doughty and by no means demoralised foe, but the contributions of the aeronauts would be on a diminishing scale. On 7 March, No.1 Section had moved with the Cavalry Division to Poplar Grove, 10 miles beyond Paardeberg, expecting to confront the Boers who had entrenched themselves on a group of kopjes. By then the 11,500 cu. ft *Bristol* had replaced the battle-scarred *Duchess of Connaught*, which was leaking badly, some of the enemy's shots at Paardeberg having found their mark. Little useful work was done, however, since the enemy prudently chose to withdraw before battle could be joined. During the day, Capt Jones, fit once more, returned and reassumed command.

The next fight, some twenty miles further on at Driefontein, was a hard one, with 100 Boer dead and nearly as many British, but the *Bristol* had been deflated and took no part.

On 13 March, Roberts entered Bloemfontein, the Orange Free State capital, unopposed. Here, logistics, rather than the enemy, obliged him to pause. He was now astride the main railway line which ran from the Cape all the way to Johannesburg and Pretoria and which formed his essential supply line. While the army was revictualled and rearmed, the Balloon Section, too, was re-equipped. Amid the mountains of food and fodder, remounts and replacements, which were offloaded from the trains which steamed in daily, the balloonists, who had gone into camp outside the town, found a most welcome fifty cylinders of hydrogen. Later on, the arrival of more balloons, bringing the total complement up to at least five, kept the Section busy. While the new arrivals, some rather old, were prepared for action, not without misgivings in some cases, the damaged *Duchess of Connaught* was unrolled and smeared with glycerine, as protection against deterioration.

On 1 May, the great march northwards was resumed, advancing on a broad front and using the railway line as its axis. The Balloon Section was included in the main force, although delay in collecting up all the necessary oxen meant that it did not move off until late afternoon. However, after a night march beneath a star-filled sky, it succeeded in rejoining the army at Karee Siding at eight o'clock the next morning.

This sketch depicts a balloon which, having been kept inflated, is being manually transported during the campaign in the Transvaal. (Paul Chapman)

At Smaldeel on the 6th, the *Bristol* was refilled and towed to the Vet River. With the enemy still falling back, No.1 Section kept up with the main army as it probed forward, seeking to determine where the Boers proposed to make their next stand. They were found gathered in force along the line of the Zand River, towards which the advance accordingly continued. On the evening of the 9th, the *Bristol* was at Welgelen, where, in calm conditions, it was sent up to look for signs of the enemy positions. The next morning, at first light, the Section moved off again, with the *Bristol* aloft and towed along at the end of its rope, while its observer continued to send down reports. By midday the enemy was once more in retreat and within days Roberts was in Kroonstad, having advanced some eighty miles in ten days, although, with the enemy keeping his distance, fighting had been limited and the Section's contribution of small significance.

After a pause for fresh supplies, the drive towards Johannesburg continued. With the crossing of the Vaal River on the 27th, the conquerors entered the second of the erstwhile independent republics. On that day, the *Bristol* was emptied, having been kept continuously inflated for three weeks – a tribute to the gas-tight qualities of goldbeater's skin. Three days later, the governor of Johannesburg formally surrendered the capital of the goldfields to Roberts. As the Section marched through the town and past Lord Roberts to its camp five miles further on, one last objective remained – Pretoria, the political capital of the Transvaal, which lay another fifty miles further north. However, with the Boers' days of triumph well and truly over, this last stride was unlikely to prove a difficult one.

Nevertheless, on the whole, the three-month campaign had been a strenuous one, not least for No.1 Section, as they strove to keep up with the head of the advance, hampered as they were by the sluggish progress of the lumbering oxen which, by

Hobson's choice, they had been obliged to use to draw their train of wagons, along roads which were frequently poor and across many rivers, large and small, which lay in their path. Probably their most taxing day came towards the end of their trek: hardly had they set off that morning when they were brought to a halt at a river bridge which had failed to bear the weight of one of the heavy naval guns which were accompanying the column. By the time their brother engineers had effected the necessary repairs, the sun was already descending, with the greater part of their journey still to be accomplished, over roads which deteriorated from poor to very bad and which, well before they reached their destination, had to be negotiated in darkness.

After a couple of days, the advance on Pretoria was resumed, but met only light resistance and observers who ascended found little to report. On 4 June, the balloonists were treated to a last moment of excitement when an enemy shell burst uncomfortably close just as Capt Jones was preparing to ascend in *Task*, but no damage or injury resulted. Continuing with the launch, Jones found little to report and returned, Lieutenant Grubb going up in his place. However, the latter too lost no time in coming down again, reporting that the balloon appeared to be leaking badly. *Torpedo* was thereupon unpacked and inflated by transferring the hydrogen from *Task*, which was later burnt as unfit for further use.

On the 5th, Pretoria capitulated. With the Boers driven from the field and the war apparently reduced to 'mopping-up' operations, there was really nothing more for the Section to contribute. As present victory overlaid sad memories of past defeats and fallen comrades, a lighter mood prevailed and the balloonists found themselves making ascents to give joyrides to various visitors who, with time now hanging on their hands, tended to turn up, curious to examine at closer quarters the aeronauts and the 'gasbag' which had been bobbing up and down amongst them since the Modder.

No.3 Balloon Section disembarked at Cape Town on 30 March 1900, under the command of Lieutenant (temporary Major) R. B. D. Blakeney RE (the same who had escaped the perils of the lightning strike in 1894), accompanied by Captain B. A. Warry, Essex Regt, Lieutenant A. H. Bell RE and thirty-two other ranks. By then, Mafeking, far to the north, was the only town still under siege, while the main British force under Lord Roberts was preparing to resume its advance towards Johannesburg. Simultaneously, a secondary column, under Lord Methuen, had been detached some 100 miles to the west and was also moving northwards, along the branch of the South African railway which led to Rhodesia and passed through Mafeking on its way.

Leaving some 100 cylinders of hydrogen behind as backup, to be drawn on as necessary, the Balloon Section caught up with Methuen's force on 23 April at Warrenton, a few miles south of the point where the railway crossed the Vaal River, at the place called Fourteen Streams. Here they found the column temporarily held up, with the enemy occupying the north bank in considerable force. The balloonists were soon in action. At six o'clock next morning, in a gusty wind, *Thrush* made the first of many ascents, as from his basket its observer was able to send down reports giving the positions of the enemy's artillery. He was also able to provide the useful reassurance that there was no sign of any attempt on the enemy's part to mount an attack from the flank. As the weather gradually improved, the balloon was able to continue its work throughout the day, until sunset brought it to an end.

During the following days, the Section was fully employed throughout the daylight hours, making observations of the enemy dispositions, as well as reporting the apparent extent of the damage which had been suffered by the bridge across the Vaal, information which scouts on the ground had not been able to obtain. At Fourteen Streams, as at Paardeberg, artillery played a major role, with the balloon rendering valuable assistance by directing the fire of the British guns. At this juncture, a 6-inch gun mounted on a railway wagon was brought up from the south to provide increased firepower and range. Two of the targets chosen for its attention were not visible from the ground, so

A rather cumbersome-looking method of signalling by semaphore, which was devised by the civilian balloonist Coxwell and which was used during the war. (Paul Chapman)

its fire too was directed from the balloon, the latter's wagon being drawn up alongside – an arrangement which enabled the balloon observer to shout down to the battery commander his estimates of the errors in the fall of shot. On the following day, gun and balloon were moved a mile closer to the Boer positions, bringing them within range of the enemy's own artillery. Although the positioning of a balloon alongside its associated gun greatly enhances the efficient collaboration between observer and gunner, a disadvantage of this arrangement lies in the fact that the balloon acts as an admirable target marker for an enemy who possesses the means of response. Such was the case here and the British gun itself came under fire. However, Captain Warry, who was aloft at the time, immediately identified the enemy positions responsible and the wrath of the 6-inch was turned upon them. A dozen rounds sufficed to silence them for the day and although the following morning the duel was resumed, the end result was the same and this time final.

On 7 May, the enemy positions were attacked by infantry and cavalry. By the end of the day, all resistance had collapsed and once more the Boers were in full retreat. On the 9th, with no immediate prospect of further engagements, the balloon was deflated. One week later, the relief of Mafeking took place and scenes of wild rejoicing were witnessed back at home.

Following these operations, No.3 Section was first of all sent away to join the 1st Division at Boshof, in the Orange Free State. No sooner arrived, however, than it was turned round and sent back to the 10th Division, which was at Vryburg, occupied in repairing the railway around Mafeking, whilst preparing to march south-eastwards into the Transvaal. It set off on 26 May, with the balloonists in its train, proceeding by way of Lichtenburg and Ventersdorp. By the time it reached Potchefstroom on 11 June, it was clear to Blakeney that, in any subsequent operations, the army would find no use for the aeronauts, whereas the railway thereabouts was being operated in a fashion which, in Blakeney's opinion, was less than satisfactory. Railway work was certainly an activity in which the Royal Engineers could claim expertise and No.3 Section was not without men who could offer such experience. Blakeney accordingly volunteered its services, which were duly accepted, and for the remainder of their time in South Africa, the men of No.3 Section abandoned their profession of balloonist and turned to that of railwayman.

The other Sections found themselves in a similar situation, No.1 getting the job of building a redoubt on the crest of a kopje to the east of Pretoria. During the morning of 11 July, heavy firing was heard to the northward and early the following day the Section was stood to arms, but the alarums remained offstage and it was soon able to resume its work. Then, a week later, it found itself returned for a while to active campaigning, when it received orders to join the 11th Division, which was marching about in the country to the east, seeking the elusive Boer. By then Lieutenant Grubb had left, having in June received orders to join the Mounted Infantry, and Capt Warry and Lieutenant Bell from No.3 Section had been posted in in his stead, as that unit was being run down. For the next fortnight, No.1 Section's train of ox-drawn wagons, with a full strength of three officers and thirty-eight men, accompanied the 11th Division as it roamed the countryside, vainly looking for an enemy to fight. No such consummation ensued, the balloon remained unfilled and unlaunched and by early August the Section was once more fully employed in more traditional sapper's work.

Despite Roberts's triumph in the field, the war was, of course, far from over and due to continue for two more long years, as the still-defiant burghers, changing their strategy, continued their struggle by guerrilla tactics, to the renewed bafflement of an army trained only to fight a similarly trained army on a 'proper' battlefield. It was a situation which left the balloonists redundant and on 29 November orders were finally received to send all balloon stores to Cape Town, for shipment back to the UK. The history of the Balloon Sections in the Boer War had come to an end.

It had been a packed year and one which was not without its satisfactory side. If the

A couple of Templer's steam traction engines on active service during the South African War. (Author's collection)

balloonists represented only a very small part of the total force which had been in the field, they had on one or two occasions lent significant and material assistance to that force's eventual victory. Furthermore, they had done so while contending with factors which sometimes hampered their full effectiveness.

Transport was one of these: obliged to compete with other arms, which perhaps were sometimes looked on with more favour, the necessary means of locomotion could often be hard to find and, when found, unfitted to the task. For a unit which, to perform its duties, needed to be in or near the van of an advance, a slow-moving team of oxen was not ideal.

The balloonists' other impediment arose from the topography of the country in which they were campaigning. For one thing, the fight was being waged on the High Veld, which tends to lie at altitudes of 4,000 feet or more. Since the lifting power of a balloon diminishes with height, it follows that the balloonists in South Africa sometimes found themselves unable to ascend as high above the local ground level as they were used to at home. It was a drawback which was of greater moment in hilly country, such as Captain Phillips found at the Tugela, where the Boers could occupy the reverse slopes and lie safely concealed from any aerial observation.

The absence so far in this account of any reference to the presence in South Africa of the almost-indispensable Colonel Templer may have been noted. Perhaps, it might be conjectured, he had remained in England, continuing to run the factory and provide support to the units in the field. Not so. He too had been ordered south, as early as November 1899, being temporarily replaced at the Balloon Factory, first by Brevet Lieutenant Colonel J. R. L. Macdonald CB RE and then, when Colonel Macdonald went abroad, as is narrated below, by Major Trollope, Elsdale's assistant in Bechuanaland fifteen years earlier. Perhaps Templer was at the depots then, applying his expertise to the all-important hydrogen production? Again no. Surprisingly perhaps, Colonel Templer took no part in the ballooning in South Africa, having been appointed to command the RE's 45th Steam Road Transport Company. It was apparently decided that his other field of expertise, that of traction engines, wielded a higher priority – being probably rarer at that time – than his ballooning experience.

While most of the RE's balloonists had been mobilised and sent to the Cape to confront the Boers, it had still been found possible to form one more Section, as well as a small detachment, which had also left these shores, though bound for quite different regions, and intended for quite different duties.

The British Empire, with its preoccupations, interests and responsibilities scattered across all corners of the globe, often found that, while a conflagration was being overcome in one spot, it had to send a fire-engine to deal with a blaze which had broken out in another. Even as the Boer War was beginning, trouble was stirring in China, in the shape of the Boxer Rebellion, a popular revolt against what was seen as foreign domination. The rebellion was marked by considerable violence, especially against Europeans with, in particular, the murder of a number of Christian missionaries.

By June 1900, as Roberts was entering Pretoria with his victorious troops, the 'Boxers' had overrun Peking (now Beijing) and were besieging the legation quarter, where the Europeans lived. By then, however, a multi-national force, from the various nations whose citizens were in peril, including the USA, had been assembled and was fighting its way to their relief. That British military aeronautics was at last here to stay may be judged by the fact that measures were taken to send a Balloon Section out from the UK, for inclusion in the expeditionary force.

When the trouble arose, No.4 Section was already in the course of formation, having been originally intended for service in India. With the emergence of a more urgent demand further to the east, these plans were now put on hold and the Section, under the command of Lieutenant Colonel Macdonald, embarked in the SS *Bombay* and on 11 August sailed for China. Only three days later, with the *Bombay* no further than the Bay of Biscay, Peking was relieved and the rebels were driven out. However, the country was yet to be pacified and as the *Bombay*, making a stately 10 knots, sailed steadily eastwards and the men of No.4 continued on their way, hopes might still be cherished that the whole show would not be over before they arrived. On 14/15 September, the *Bombay* reached Singapore and then turned northwards up the China Sea, putting another 2,700 sea miles behind its stern, as it also called in at Hong Kong and Shanghai, before, on 3 October, reaching its final destination, Wei-hai-wei on the shores of the Yellow Sea, fifty-four days and 11,000 miles after leaving England. There, Second Lieutenant T. E. Martin-Leake RE and six men were disembarked, with orders to set up a gas-making factory. The rest of the Section, not yet done with travelling, transferred to another ship, the *Nevasa*, and continued on its weary way. At last, on 9 October, after two months spent mainly at sea, the balloonists reached the end of their long voyage. Once on dry land, a few hours' train journey brought them to Tientsin, where they began unloading their stores, while Colonel Macdonald handed over command to Capt A. H. B. Hume RE, on the former's appointment as Director of Railways. Hume had scarcely time to settle in before the Section received further marching orders, this time to Peking itself. This move required the wagons and gas cylinders to be loaded as deck cargo on to junks, which were not very suitable for the purpose. After a further tiresome journey by river and road, which, though uneventful, was accompanied by the noise of much firing in the surrounding countryside, the Section finally arrived at its quarters in Peking on 28 October, eleven weeks after setting out from England.

With the Boxers defeated, the balloonists had, after their long odyssey, turned up after the final whistle. Like their comrades in Africa, they were now redundant and were obliged to accept other sapper tasks of a more mundane nature to perform. For No.4 Section, this turned out to be the installation of electric lighting at Peking railway station. The only plant available for this purpose was currently installed at the

Summer Palace, outside Peking, so Hume's first task was to take a party of men out to the palace, to dismantle it all and bring it back to the city.

This was accomplished in a week, but for some reason the reinstallation work did not commence immediately and the Balloon Section was allowed a short while in which to indulge in its proper work, though perhaps only unofficially, since it could scarcely make any useful contribution thereby, now that the 'war' was over. Nevertheless, on 13 November, the *Tugela* was filled and a number of ascents were carried out, during which all personnel managed to get into the air. Strong winds then intervened to prevent any further ballooning for a couple of days, before the return of calmer conditions allowed activities to be resumed. *Tugela*'s skin had suffered some deterioration to its skin due, it was thought, to the dryness of the local air, and had been further damaged by the boisterous wind. The second balloon, *Teviot*, was therefore brought out and filled with the gas transferred from its sister. However, little in the way of serious ballooning was accomplished – indeed, what little that had been done could scarcely be justified – and by 20 November, the Section had once more been diverted to more useful engineering work, including the completion of their work at the railway station.

In the New Year, it found a little more in the way of excitement. The recent upheavals had left the countryside outside the city in a state of lawlessness, so in this situation a request was received from the village of Tanjadun, not far from the balloonists' temporary quarters, asking for protection against a gang of looters. The gallant men of No.4 Section were happy to oblige, in an operation which resulted in the capture of fifteen of the gang, who were handed over to the authorities to be dealt with.

In March, the Section turned to the laying of railway track inside the city but, with order being gradually restored, no reason for its presence in China any longer existed, and in May, Capt Hume and seven of the Section's personnel, together with the factory (which had not been called upon to produce any gas anyway), proceeded to India to fulfil the original intention, while the remainder of the Section was taken back to Aldershot by Lieutenant Martin-Leake.

In India Captain Hume formed an Experimental Balloon Section, based at Rawalpindi and intended for use on the North-West Frontier, although it never saw action in that mountainous region. The unit was later transferred to the Bengal Sappers and Miners and was largely manned by men of that corps, command being assumed by Captain W. A. Stokes RE. A hydrogen manufacturing plant was established at Rawalpindi and balloons, including the *Venus* (11,500 cu. ft) and the *Achilles* (13,000 cu. ft), were operated experimentally for some years, until the Section was disbanded at the end of 1910.

Finally, in January 1901, a small detachment (it was not large enough to constitute a full Section) was sent to Australia, under the command of Second Lieutenant T. H. L. Spaight RE, for the solely ceremonial purpose of attending the celebrations in connection with the inauguration of that nation's advance from the status of colony to that of Commonwealth.

In 1901, the Balloon Factory also supplied two balloons to Captain Robert Falcon Scott, for use on his forthcoming expedition to the Antarctic. No RE personnel accompanied the expedition and the balloons were operated by naval ratings, under the direction of Lieutenant E. R. Shackleton. Whether due to their handlers' lack of experience, the extreme environmental conditions, or for some other reason, the balloons were not a success and earned from Captain Scott the unflattering epithet of 'an unmitigated nuisance'.

4

Ballooning Twilight

By the time that the aeronauts had returned once more from Africa, a new century had dawned and a new monarch had ascended the throne. The Victorian Age was over, the twentieth century had begun and the Age of Progress had dawned, fired by the expanding technology of the previous century's industrial revolution and bringing with it new and exciting novelties such as the internal combustion engine, the motor car and the telephone. There were some – not yet very numerous – who were sure that they would soon be joined by the aeroplane. To them, balloons belonged, with the crinoline and the horse-tram, to the nineteenth century.

However, for the moment, the powered aeroplane had no more substance than the many paper schemes and earthbound projects which were continually being devised; for the purposes of actual aerial navigation, it was still the lighter-than-air craft which reigned supreme. Ballooning had indeed become quite popular with fashionable society. Meetings were regularly held at Hurlingham and Ranelagh, thronged by crowds which rivalled Ascot in their elegance.

In the more sternly practical military world, it was recognised that the current situation of army aeronautics needed to be re-examined and its future needs determined, particularly in the light of the valuable experience which had recently been acquired in South Africa. To this end, a Committee on Military Ballooning was set up in June 1903, under the chairmanship of Colonel P. T. Buston DSO RE, to receive reports from some of the participants in the recent conflict and to consider a number of questions which now required attention. The committee's secretary was Brevet Lieutenant Colonel J. E. Capper CB RE, who had just been appointed to the command of the Balloon Sections – a replacement, by an officer of his rank, of the junior officer previously in the post which itself reflected the enhanced status which army ballooning had now acquired. For Capper himself, the posting represented a return to military ballooning: as a young subaltern in the early 1880s, he had spent some time working alongside Templer in the School of Ballooning.

Of the subjects tackled by the committee, the interconnected problems of the stability of the basket and of the limiting effect of the wind speed on operations generally were probably the most vexing. Numerous references can be found to the basket's propensity for not only swaying from side to side but also rotating first one way and then the other. Under these conditions, the observer, whilst possibly experiencing nausea from the former effect, would be finding both of them a great hindrance to him as he tried to focus his glasses on a distant patch of ground, in order to determine what it might conceal. The effect of this was that it was generally allowed that, in wind speeds above 20 mph, military ballooning was not practicable.

Other concerns dealt with the desirable size of the balloon establishment, both in peace and in war, with the training of the officers and other ranks of the Balloon Sections and with what that training should comprise. The expansion enforced by the war was largely retained, with an establishment of five Balloon Sections, one cadre section and a depot. The strength of a Balloon Section under war conditions was

A balloon winch and its crew in 1906, as military ballooning lingered on through its sunset days. (Museum of Army Flying)

The last moments of a balloon launch. The Long Valley at Aldershot, well away from the public gaze, was much used by the army for a range of activities over many years. (Author's collection)

A well-dressed crowd attending a balloon meeting at Ranelagh in 1906. (Author's collection)

recommended to be as follows:

Officers	3	
Dismounted men:		
	NCOs	8
	Sappers	22
	Buglers	1
Mounted men:		
	NCOs	3
	Shoeing smiths	1
Drivers	27	

For peacetime conditions these figures were reduced somewhat, but in practice the Sections were always chronically under strength and for training purposes had to combine together, so that usually no more than two full-strength Sections could be put into the field at any time.

A third question was the all-important one of transport and its motive power. Although, as has been noted, the traction engine had entered the field, instances of its use are unlikely to have been many – and those few probably due only to unofficial action on the part of James Templer. In South Africa, the Balloon Sections were certainly never in a position to profit from their erstwhile leader's current duties and had been obliged to use beasts of whatever species they could lay their hands on. Oxen were widely employed for supply trains during the war and the balloonists also used them quite frequently, but they offered only a ponderous rate of movement to a unit which could often be summoned to be at the forefront of the fight and to keep up with the artillery as it moved forward. In the action at Driefontein, balloons had not been employed, simply because their wagons, harnessed to oxen, had not been able to match the speed of the advance. At Warrenton, No. 3 Section had employed a team of mules, which were more satisfactory, but under normal circumstances the horse was still the usual and most satisfactory means of locomotion. For these, the following war strength was recommended:

Horses, Officers' Riding	6
Horses, Public Riding	4
Horses, Draught	42

Some thought was also given to the question of dress. With the introduction of khaki for the fighting on the veld, the British Army had acknowledged that, in modern war, practical considerations must take precedence over traditional military pomp. In ballooning, this pragmatism was every bit as applicable as anywhere. In his 1903 annual report, Capper observed that:

> The equipment of officers and men is entirely unsuited to ballooning. Generally every effort should be made to do away in dress with anything that can catch in the net or tear the skin of the balloon.

He maintained that 'belts should be abolished, an officer in a balloon does not want to carry a revolver, and he has to take off his belt and revolver before entering the car, with every prospect of losing it'. As for spurs – they 'should not be allowed near a balloon. They should only be used when mounted for horses that actually need them, but as far as possible Balloon officers' horses should not need spurs.'

Yet another consideration was the problem of communication with the ground. Balloon cable was designed to incorporate a telephone cable in its core, but at that stage of technological progress, this mode of communication had too often suffered from breakdowns. In South Africa, more old-fashioned methods were used, such as semaphore, as suggested by the illustration on page 46, while at Warrenton we find the observer disdaining anything suggestive of modern technology by leaning out of his basket and shouting. At Paardeberg, where Grubb was too far from the guns for such sociability, signal flags were used (although, since he afterwards admitted to an almost complete lack of practice in the art, it is to be wondered whether the results achieved were always satisfactory).

Whilst committees pondered, the practical work went on. In the factory, there was the manufacture and compression of hydrogen, to replace that lost in the field. The zinc/acid process was still in use, although more than two-thirds of the output was now produced by the electrolysis method. As for balloons, five were made during 1903 – three of 13,000 cu. ft capacity and two of 11,500 cu. ft. These two sizes, known as the 'A' and 'V' Classes respectively, represented, together with 10,000 cu. ft (the 'T' Class), the three standard sizes of balloon. A list, necessarily incomplete, of the balloons known to have been operated by the British Army can be found in Appendix II.

The Balloon Sections, meanwhile, spent much of that 1903 summer on training work. Until the end of June, they carried out these duties at Aldershot, after which they moved to Bulford for a month, No.1 Section returning to base in early August, while No.2 moved on to Tidworth, finally arriving back at Aldershot in late September. For both Sections, the season ended with participation in the autumn manoeuvres.

During this training period, the aeronauts did not always restrict themselves to tethered ascents. On a number of occasions, once the necessary authorisation had been obtained, the more extensive preparations which a free run demanded, would be made. Barometer, grapnel and map would be stowed in the basket with, in addition if the crew were wise, *Bradshaw's Railway Guide* for the unavoidably earthborne return journey. Launching would be preceded by the release of a small 'pilot' balloon, to gauge the likely direction which the wind would ordain for the course their craft was to follow. Finally, with the cable released, the dull routine of observing and reporting the results of artillery fire would be exchanged for the more carefree delights of sailing downwind many miles over countryside and town, to end in a bumpy landing in a field, perhaps two or three hours later. To complete the exercise, the balloon had then to be deflated and packed up, following which, suitable transport having been found, it would have to be conveyed to the nearest convenient railway station, for the journey back to base of both it and its crew.

During the winter of 1903/04, two Sections were sent overseas, No.1 to Malta, under Lieutenant T. H. L. Spaight RE, and No.2, commanded by Lieutenant P. W. L. Broke-Smith RE, to Gibraltar. The ascents on Malta began in early January 1904, with the launching of the 10,000 cu. ft *Trusty* to a height of 600 feet. Over the next two months, many ascents were made, some in strong winds, using in addition to *Trusty* three other balloons, *Vestal* and *Vega* (11,500 cu. ft) and *Throstle* (10,000 cu. ft). During this period, the opportunity was taken to experiment with aerial photography – resuming work which had been started by Major Elsdale more than twenty years earlier. Some successful films were taken, but the effects of that balloonist's bugbear, the wind, resulted in many blurred images. In an effort to stabilise the balloon and its basket on such windy days, experiments with a 'Storm Guy' were also carried out. This arrangement consisted of three auxiliary guy ropes, fastened at the top to the net enclosing the balloon and at their lower ends to the balloon cable itself, by means of an attachment which incorporated a device borrowed from the navy called a 'selvagee'.

The Section which travelled to Gibraltar was embarked in a destroyer, from the deck of which it launched its balloon and tested the possibility of detecting mines, or even submarines, below the surface of the sea, but little of any real value was accomplished.

In 1904, the Committee on Military Ballooning issued its final report. Having considered the results from the deployment of balloons in the Sudan, in South Africa and in China, it recommended that

Endeavours should be made to obtain:
(a) A captive balloon capable of ascending in all weathers.
(b) A kite capable of taking a man up when the wind is too strong for a spherical balloon.
(c) A reliable dirigible balloon.

If (a) represented a fond but forlorn hope for the apostles of gentle buoyancy, (b) opened the door to its competitor, the brute force of aerodynamics, in the form of kites, which were soon to reveal their viability; (c) aimed to keep the lighter-than-air school in business, with renewed interest in the old vision of a balloon with an engine, enabling it to be propelled through the air, thus becoming 'dirigible'. It was in France and Germany that most work had been done in this field, which as an incidental derivative had also produced the so-called kite balloon. In this development, the traditional spherical balloon envelope became horizontally elongated, the effect of which, associated with a 'weathercock' tail, was to keep the balloon heading into wind, thus enhancing its stability.

In 1904, as the longer days and better weather returned, the Balloon Sections resumed the work of training, with a class of eight officers from other regiments and corps assembling at Aldershot to receive instruction in the handling and control of balloons in the field. After this, the Sections went their separate ways, to Lydd in Kent, to Rhayader in Wales and to Larkhill on Salisbury Plain – the last place being destined to figure strongly in the later annals of British military aeronautics. At each of these locations, the work consisted of observing the fire of the artillery units which were also camped there to carry out their summer training. The Section which went to Rhayader, in addition to its artillery spotting work, also carried out an experiment to test the vulnerability of a balloon to ground fire – a subject which was quite often considered in the abstract, but which had been explored little in practice – although on a number of occasions in South Africa a certain amount of experience had been acquired on an involuntary basis! A 10,000 cu. ft balloon was sent up to a height of 700 feet and a number of shots from a 5-in gun were fired at it. The ninth shot sufficed to bring it back to earth, although, since it had not been found possible to move it about as had been intended, the gunners had no doubt found rather easier target practice than they should have done.

During its stay at Rhayader, the Section was joined on attachment by an officer of the 15th Hussars, Lieutenant F. H. Sykes. On 10 August, before returning to his regimental duties, he accompanied Lieutenant G. F. Wells RE on a 28-mile free run of the balloon *Veritas*, marking the debut of a career in military aeronautics which, in later years, would see him rising to a prominent position in that field.

With the training season reaching its close, it was time once more for the annual manoeuvres, which began near Colchester on 7 September. No.1 Balloon Section, commanded by Lieutenant Broke-Smith and with a strength of three officers and sixty-six other ranks, joined the defending Red Force and encamped at Middlewick. At 11.15 on the opening morning, a 11,500 cu. ft balloon was filled and sent up from Abberton, a few miles south of Colchester, for the purpose of detecting a possible seaborne landing by the invading Blue Force at the mouths of the Blackwater or Crouch rivers. No landings were observed, but the invading fleet of transports and accompanying warships was seen off Clacton, some twelve miles to the east, and this sighting, together with the absence of any sign of the 'enemy' in the vicinity of the two rivers, was duly reported to the GOC. By then, the opposing force had landed near Clacton and was advancing inland. Unfortunately, the countryside through which it was moving was well wooded, allowing its movements to be completely hidden from the balloonists.

On the following day, adverse weather precluded any ascents and by the time a balloon was sent up at first light on the 9th, things were going badly for the defenders, who were falling back in a south-westerly direction. After an enemy cavalry vanguard was spotted approaching, the balloon was quickly hauled down and as quickly deflated. The Section then lost no time in whipping up its horses to escape the clutches of the advancing foe, finally arriving in camp just outside Braintree at 8.00 p.m.

Thus far, the Section had been able to contribute little of note. However, on the following morning, with it now becoming Blue Force's turn to retreat, a free run was ordained and Broke-Smith, accompanied by Lieutenant Wells, ascended from the village of Black Notley, near Braintree, intending to observe the enemy's progress in the direction of Colchester and to report it by telegraph. As matters turned out, the plan was frustrated by the treacherous wind, which for the purpose should have been blowing from the west. Unfortunately, disobeying the weather forecast, it slipped too far round to the north and the two aeronauts found themselves being haplessly carried off south-eastwards, in the direction of Maldon, at the head of the Blackwater estuary, while the battle zone on which they were vainly attempting to focus their field-glasses remorselessly receded ever further away towards the distant horizon to the north.

On Monday the 12th, supplies of hydrogen had dwindled to the extent that it was possible to fill only one small balloon, of 4,500 cu. ft capacity, but this craft, even when relieved of its basket, could not be persuaded to rise higher than 200 feet. Faced with such reluctant buoyancy and with the wind strengthening towards 20 mph, any further intentions of taking to the air were abandoned. The Section returned to camp and remained there, leaving the last two days of the manoeuvres to be conducted without any further assistance from the sky. On the 15th, the Section packed up and returned to Aldershot, part by road and part by rail, able to claim only a minor contribution to the events of the previous ten days. If, in the army as a whole, there remained those who doubted the relevance of military aeronautics, the events of the previous week had exposed limitations which could only support such prejudice.

In 1905, a Balloon Section was again sent to Gibraltar. Commanded by Lieutenant Wells, its mission was to pursue the trials, begun the previous year, aimed at the detection from above of the presence of mines below the surface of the sea. For this purpose, the Section was embarked once more in a destroyer and in the course of two days made a number of ascents as the ship cruised across the prepared minefield, the mines (inert, needless to say) having been laid at different depths, varying from 70 to 6 feet. Results were once more inconclusive, the turbulent conditions produced by the wind gusting around the Rock making for difficult observation; sometimes a mine could be detected, while others remained completely hidden, particularly when the surface was broken up by ripples, or if there was no sun to aid visibility.

Meanwhile, on the administrative side, more changes took place. Balloon Square was clearly far from ideal for the launching of balloons and, more recently, kites. Not only was its limited space cluttered with various buildings, but it was also uncomfortably close to two public roads. One of these, lined with houses and trees, was no more than twenty yards from the doors of the balloon shed itself, making the withdrawal of a balloon from its shed a hazardous business, if there was anything of a wind. The result was that balloons were frequently kept in the open some distance away, where they were at the mercy of the elements and, if left unguarded, of malicious hands as well.

For these reasons, the decision was taken to find a more practical location for the army's ballooning centre and during the winter of 1905/06 it removed from Aldershot, to take up its new home two miles to the north at South Farnborough, thus initiating a famous aeronautical association which still continues today, albeit sadly diminished. The parcel of land which the balloonists adopted lay on the northern edge of Farnborough Common and adjacent to the Farnborough Road. Here, balloons could be walked out of the balloon shed, directly on to the nearby Common, where there was virtually unlimited space in which to deploy them. This was followed in April 1906 by another name change, as Colonel Capper became Commandant of what was henceforth to be known as the Balloon School.

The succeeding month saw the end of an era, when Colonel Templer, having celebrated his sixtieth birthday, retired and relinquished his position at the centre of the stage which he had dominated for little short of thirty years, although the manner in which it came about was not of the happiest. For the second time in his career, James Templer was to find himself a major figure in the proceedings of a court martial, although on this occasion it was not he who stood accused.

It happened that certain irregularities appeared to have been discovered in that most sensitive of areas, the handling of funds, in this case those of the Balloon Factory, and the man responsible, Templer's warrant officer clerk, was arrested and charged. The case actually concerned the factory's hydrogen production, or more precisely, the oxygen which was a by-product of that process. The clerk, Jolly by name, seeing that the unwanted oxygen was going to waste, had conscientiously suggested that it should be sold on the open market, thereby benefiting the public purse. Templer, although harbouring certain initial reservations, had after consideration given the go-ahead and an agreement had been entered into with a private company, the negotiations for which had been left entirely to Jolly. However, the resulting arrangements were of a somewhat casual nature and involved the passage of the cash payments for the oxygen, not in the usual way by official channels, but informally through Jolly's own hands. It was generally agreed in court that there was no suggestion of personal corruption, that all the money had ended up in the proper place and that, furthermore, Jolly had, at some personal inconvenience, been motivated solely by the best interests of the Balloon Factory. Nevertheless, by handling public funds as if they were his own, even

Fig.2: This 1909 revision of the Ordnance Survey map of Farnborough Common and its environs shows many features of interest, including: the emergent Balloon Factory; the heavily wooded nature of most of the nearby land; a part of the Aldershot military lines; and the Basingstoke Canal, on the south bank of which the RE balloonists set up their home in 1890. Woodlands Cottage is also marked – on the east side of the Farnborough Road, immediately opposite the 'Swan Inn Plateau'.

John Capper. (Paul Chapman)

temporarily, the court was obliged to conclude that he had acted improperly and he was therefore found guilty, with loss of seniority, under that useful catch-all clause in King's Regulations, Conduct Prejudicial to Good Order and Discipline.

That ended the legal aspect tidily enough, if hardly to the satisfaction of W/O Jolly, but the matter was then carried onward by the GOC-in-C Aldershot, Lieutenant General Sir John French, who chose to see in the affair a failure by the accused's commanding officer, namely Templer, to exercise sufficient control over his subordinate's work. Furthermore, Sir John was inclined to blame this error on the fact that Templer was 'only' a militiaman and not on the army's Active List. While it might be argued that, despite Sir John's prejudices, it was precisely Templer's alleged lack of familiarity with 'proper' military procedures that had contributed much to the successful management and advance of military ballooning over the years, it was difficult to deny that, in this case, his undue use of informality had been at the root of the matter. So he had to go, Colonel Capper assuming the post of Superintendent of the Balloon Factory in his place and in addition to his command of the Balloon School. Templer, however, was not immediately made to disappear into full retirement. In a move which paid tacit tribute to his great expertise, he was retained for two more years as 'Advisory Officer', for a fee of £1,000 per annum. Like the proverbial old soldier he was, he gradually 'faded away'.

The balloons of which he had for so long been the champion were set to do the same, as the dirigible, with its power to challenge the supremacy of the wind, to which its forebear had been subordinate, began to emerge. For the moment though, that time was yet to arrive; a practical dirigible was still a little way off and for a while longer balloons continued in service unchallenged. However, their last days were not to pass without a final drama.

Although the war in South Africa had claimed many soldiers' lives, none of the balloonists, although not infrequently exposed to the enemy's fire, had been called upon to pay the ultimate price. Now, in more peaceful times, the arm of tragedy reached out and touched them too. It was the afternoon of 28 May 1907; at Aldershot a military review, attended by King Edward VII and Prince Fushimi of Japan, had just come to an end. As the clock approached half-past four, the 10,000 cu. ft balloon *Thrasher*, crewed by Lieutenant T. E. Martin-Leake RE (whom we last saw serving in China, several years earlier) and Lieutenant W. T. McC. Caulfeild RE, ascended from Cove Common, at the start of a free run. A steady wind from the east offered the chance of a good long flight before darkness or the proximity of the sea required a return to earth.

It was also a day of poor visibility and very soon the balloon had disappeared into the haze, leaving the watchers below to turn their minds to other matters. It would be some hours before the usual telegram arrived at the Balloon School, reporting their return to earth, probably somewhere in the West Country.

No such communication arrived that night and when the following morning came with still no message, mild concern increased to intense anxiety and enquiries were dispatched to coastguards, while telegrams were sent to the two aeronauts' next of kin. Fears were briefly allayed when a message came in from the Weymouth coastguard, relaying a wireless call from the Isles of Scilly, reporting 'balloon picked up all safe'. On the following day, however, this message turned out to be completely erroneous and it was necessary to dispatch further telegrams to the anxious relatives, cruelly dashing the hopes which had been raised earlier. Two days later, *Thrasher* was found floating in the water, some miles out to sea. There was no sign of its late occupants and hope sank further.

The available details of *Thrasher*'s last voyage are no more than sketchy, gleaned only from the testimony of a few witnesses on the ground, interviewed later, and the balloon's own log, not all of which was recovered. The first three hours of the craft's journey passed uneventfully, as the wind bore it steadily along on a track of about 240°. Its altitude varied considerably: at one time it rose as high as 1,700 feet, whilst on another occasion nearly touching the ground. By a quarter to eight, the balloon had passed Blandford Forum and was once more low down – low enough for the two aeronauts to exchange a few shouted words with people on the ground. The visibility was still very poor and that, combined with their very low altitude, would have made it difficult for them to determine their true position. They may well have thought that their course was somewhat more northerly, which would have sufficed to keep them over land for many more miles. In fact, they were now headed directly for Chesil Beach and no more than five miles from the sea, in the shape of Lyme Bay – the scene of that other ballooning tragedy, twenty-six years earlier, when *Saladin* was carried out to sea, with its hapless passenger. Near Winterbourne Abbas they actually called down to two men, asking them to seize their rope, which was trailing, but this proved unsuccessful and they were carried onwards and out of sight.

There was now little time to spare, as they neared the end of dry land. Probably still unsure of their precise whereabouts, they were passing over ground which lies generally about 500 feet above sea level, but which falls steeply down to the beach and the water's edge. When that moment came and the surf line suddenly appeared before them out of the mist, they would have had little time to react. Despite valving hard, they had no time to lose their unwanted height before they were swept on and over the sea. The Abbotsbury coastguard and another witness saw the last moments of the flight: some distance offshore the balloon was seen to strike the water and then immediately rise again, after which it disappeared into the murk.

As the days went by, with no further news, hope for the two young aeronauts, already slim, sank lower. The last spark was finally extinguished, a month after the tragedy, when their two bodies were also recovered from the sea, leaving the precise reason for their deaths undetermined. One possible theory, mooted at the time, is that both men were thrown out of the basket by the impact as the balloon struck the sea. This would certainly accord with the report that it then rose up again, as it would do when relieved of the two men's weight, but neither the inquests nor the army Court of Enquiry was prepared to reach any positive conclusion and the precise reason for the tragedy was left, in Capper's words, 'a complete mystery'.

Although by 1908 it was becoming clear that the thirty-year reign of the military balloon was coming increasingly under threat from its big brother the airship (even from the aeroplane, some said), that year actually saw the formation of a new unit dedicated to balloon operation. In the previous year, the Territorial Force (TF), manned by part-time volunteers, like the old Yeomanry Companies it replaced, had been created. A few enthusiasts, led by a certain Harold Holtorp, of Dulwich in South-East London, now proposed that the new Force should include a balloon section. Though it met with some initial and inevitable apathy from higher levels, persistence found its reward and a unit, based on the capital city and called the London Balloon Company (LBC), was born. It was, also inevitably, a poor relation of the regular balloonists and, throughout its life, although it attracted a respectable number of recruits, it was severely limited with regard to any practical ballooning it was able to enjoy. In this respect, the LBC itself did not help matters by locating its headquarters and training site in premises in inner London, where the possibility of actually launching a balloon was non-existent. In those circumstances, the Balloon School, when approached, could hardly be expected to donate any of its best equipment and that which the LBC did acquire ('scrounge' might be a better word, one suspects!) tended to be the Balloon School's cast-offs. It was given a couple of old balloons (one of which had a *silk* envelope) and two kites, but none of them was suitable for practical use.

Like the rest of the TF, the company paraded regularly in its drill hall on a given weekday evening, where they were able to practise the handling of what equipment they possessed. Nevertheless, such indoor activities, totally earthbound and lacking any aerial culmination, although useful for familiarisation purposes, must have been somewhat dispiriting for men who had been inspired to join by a vision of sailing amongst the clouds. They would have looked forward impatiently to the usual annual summer camp, when for a while at least the real thing would be to hand.

Unfortunately, there were disappointments awaiting them there too. The camp would naturally be held at Farnborough, with training given by the permanent staff of the Balloon School, where real balloons and kites would be launched and where some members of the LBC, at least, might hope to go up in them. However, when the time came in 1908 for the first camp to be held and with the infant company only precariously established, arrangements to cater for it were anything but clear. At Farnborough, John Capper, in receipt of no firm orders on the subject and with only the grapevine to go on, wrote in some perplexity to the Chief Engineer, Aldershot Command, seeking clarity and instructions:

> I forward herewith copies of a letter sent by Mr H. E. Holtorp to the Secretary of the Aero Club, and of a circular sent by the same gentleman, which has been sent round to various gentlemen of my acquaintance.
>
> Beyond the publication of the fact that a Balloon Company is to be formed in the Territorial Army, and having been asked to recommend two non-commissioned officers for the permanent staff, I have had no information as regards this Company. You will observe that it is mentioned the Company will proceed to Aldershot this summer for training with the Army Balloon School. This is news to me.
>
> No arrangements have been made as regards the equipment of this Company; nor is it possible to train a Balloon Company as is proposed by an Annual Training in camp of 'not less than 8 days nor more than 15 days', with one evening drill during a fortnight. The result cannot be expected to be satisfactory, neither officers nor men would get more than the merest smattering of balloon work, whilst I would not on any account entrust them with the duty of sending men up into the air with the

Officers and men of the London Balloon Company assembled on Jersey Brow in 1909. (Paul Chapman)

kites.

May I be instructed, please, as to what course, if any, should be taken as regards the London Balloon Company.

Holtorp, at his end, was equally confused, believing, even at the end of June, that the LBC still lacked official recognition and, in the absence of precise orders, being unsure whether or not there would be any summer camp anyway. In the end, the administrative muddle resulted in a last-minute order for the company to go into camp, not at Farnborough, but Arundel, where they spent a frustrating fortnight training to be ordinary earthbound sappers, designated a 'Telegraph Company' and far from any means of levitation.

By the time that the following summer came along, sufficient time had passed for their credentials to be fully established, and at the end of July 1909, they arrived at Farnborough ready, as budding aeronauts, to spend a fortnight in camp on Jersey Brow. Their world was still an imperfect one however, since the greater part of the Balloon School had, as was usual at that time in the summer, departed elsewhere on its own summer camps, to places like Lydd and Rhayader, with only a minimum of regular staff available to pay attention to the visitors. Nevertheless, they were at least in the right place, gaining practical experience and knowledge in their chosen role. By the time they struck camp on 7 August, they had participated in ninety-six ascents by balloon and seventy-one by kite.

As the LBC gained acceptance, it was able gradually to draw more profit from its association with the regular balloonists and thus enhance one of its TF functions as a useful reserve of trained personnel. Under these conditions, it remained an active unit of the Territorial Force for some years, only ending its life when the basis of its existence, the balloon, itself became obsolete. As this day approached and it became ever clearer that the balloon would soon be supplanted by the aeroplane, a handful of the LBC's members turned their attention in that direction and supplemented their lighter-than-air work by learning to fly, albeit at their own expense. By April 1912, when the Royal Flying Corps came into being, five LBC members had been granted Royal Aero Club (RAeC) certificates. Thus the LBC, like its regular cousin, acted in a small way as an early seedbed for a few of the many aviators which the RFC would later need.

In August 1910, the Balloon School decided to explore another possible military function of aeronautics, one which had been much talked and written about, but without any practical outcome, namely aerial bombing. In experiments which were as primitive as they were impractical, a small team led by Broke-Smith tried dropping missiles from tethered balloons. A cloth target was spread on the ground and for the next couple of days the aeronauts took turns in hurling missiles, in the shape of sandbags, at the target a thousand feet below, while the balloon was being moved towards it at walking pace. Little would seem to have been gleaned from the tests, unless it was an idea of how difficult it is to hit a target on the ground from the air. All the shots missed, some by only a small distance, others by as much as a hundred feet or more.

Rather more useful work was carried out, a few days after the bomb-dropping exercise, with experiments in the new field of wireless telegraphy, which clearly had promising implications for the improvement of the all-important air-ground communications. On 26 August, the 13,000 cu. ft balloon *Andes* was launched from Cove Common on a free run into a westerly wind, under the command of one of the erstwhile bomb-aimers, Lieutenant R. A. Cammell RE, accompanied by Captain H. P. T. Lefroy RE, who commanded the RE Wireless Experimental Section. Lefroy had brought along an early wireless set weighing nearly as much as himself and, as *Andes* climbed and bent its path to the south-east, he began sending and receiving signals between *Andes* and the ground station at Aldershot, while Cammell attended to the balloon's navigation. As they were carried slowly across the Home Counties, communications were successfully maintained until they had passed Leatherhead, representing a transmission range of some fifteen miles. That was the end of the main purpose of their ascent but, not to be done out of the pleasures of a more lengthy trip, they continued their voyage until, after two and a half hours in the air, the approaching Kent coastline indicated the need to return to earth, which they did at Sittingbourne.

Balloons were certainly a long time dying. Even in February 1912, when heavier-than-air machines had become firmly established, Major Sir Alexander Bannerman, commanding what had by then become the Air Battalion, was urging the *retention* of captive balloons, by making the following submission to the Aerial Navigation Standing Sub-Committee of the Committee of Imperial Defence:

The observer in a captive balloon or kite can be situated, 1500 feet up in the air, 1000 yards away from the battery to the rear and to a flank, and can be in direct telephonic communication with the battery commander the whole time. The result of every shot can be reported immediately it is fired and has struck. Artillery have been ranged on invisible targets with striking success, and the results of the fire as reported from the air, when compared with the results as reported by the range officers near the targets, have proved to be most remarkably accurate both as to distances under and over the target and as to distances to the right and left. [...] An aeroplane observer can not be in telephonic communication with the battery commander.

It would seem that all he can do is to report the general effect of the firing, and returning [sic] to the battery to drop his reports. He cannot presumably conduct the actual ranging in the efficient way in which this can be carried out by the stationary observer who is in constant and complete communication with the artillery commander.

Bannerman also proposed the use of free balloons at the soon-to-be-founded Central Flying School (CFS), for training pupils in cross-country aeroplane flying, on the grounds that map-reading and navigation would not be 'easily taught in an aeroplane, as the attention of the flier, particularly while learning to fly, is engrossed in the management of his machine'. Bannerman was himself at that moment taking lessons at Brooklands, gaining his pilot's certificate (No.213) on 30 April, and so could claim that he spoke from first-hand experience. Although his views as expressed above seem, with hindsight, somewhat reactionary, when war came he was in fact to find, on the former point at least, vindication of a sort: despite the triumph of the aeroplane, the observation balloon was to find itself reborn and widely used, as kite balloon observers shared the task of artillery cooperation with the crews of the RFC's RE8s and BE2s.

5

The Dirigibles

As we have seen, not all the army's ballooning had been restricted to tethered ascents; training activities had always included a certain number of free flights, justified by the need for the aeronauts to be able to cope should the tether carry away, and also, though less convincingly, by the proposition that balloons in free flight could be used for reconnaissance – or even the dropping of explosives. The next logical step, therefore, was the addition of an engine and propeller, thus making the craft 'dirigible' – the term being derived from the Latin *dirigere*, to turn or direct – and giving the hapless balloonist some chance of becoming master of his own navigation. In conjunction with this, control of his movement through the air would clearly be assisted by adopting the elongated shape of the kite balloon, rather than the traditional spherical form.

The best work on the subject had been done in France, beginning shortly after the Franco-Prussian War with the work of a naval architect by the name of Stanislas Charles Dupuy de Lôme. The envelope of the craft which he built was 118 feet long, 48 feet across at its widest point and contained approximately 120,000 cu. ft of hydrogen, but was hampered, in those early days, by the lack of a suitable engine. His solution was to fall back on human muscle, supplied by a team of eight sailors. These worked in alternating teams of four to turn a capstan which was connected by a shaft to a two-bladed propeller, 30 feet in diameter, mounted at the rear.

In late January 1872, the craft had been finished and was ready for the inflation of its envelope. This took a further three days before, on the morning of 2 February, she was ready for her first ascent. At 1 p.m., the balloon, as it was still called, ascended from Vincennes into a strong southerly breeze, carrying fourteen persons (including the eight stalwarts). By strenuous efforts, the vessel was induced to advance at a speed of some five or six miles per hour, which allowed her to respond to the rudder when experimental changes of heading were tried, demonstrating at least that the principle was sound. Although she stayed aloft for two hours, that ascent proved to be the beginning and end of her useful life and the skies saw her no more.

The next important advance came in 1884, when two army officers, Capitaines Krebs and Renard, built and flew a dirigible, somewhat larger than de Lôme's, which they named *La France* and which was powered by a 9-hp electric motor. Favoured in this way, she outdid her predecessor's sweating crew by clocking a speed of about 14 mph.

Later on, at the turn of the century, a dapper little Brazilian named Alberto Santos-Dumont became the toast of Paris by flying over its rooftops with nonchalant ease, in his one-man semi-rigid 'airships', which by then were able to call upon the petrol engine for their power source. In Germany too, and at the other end of the dimensional scale, Count von Zeppelin had begun to give signs of the success he was later to achieve, with his massive rigid airships. In both those countries, as well as in Great Britain, much thought was being devoted to the effects on future conflicts which these different lighter-than-air craft were likely to have. Although, for the time being,

Dupuy de Lôme's dirigible. (Author's collection)

the balloon remained the only means available to soldiers of ascending into the third dimension, there were many who now believed that a successor was imminent and that that successor would be the airship.

That the desirability of this path of progress was recognised by the Committee on Military Ballooning in 1904 has already been reported. Both James Templer and John Capper would have needed no further encouragement. Unfortunately, their ambitions were greatly hampered by the usual lack of funds. In 1901, Templer himself had paid a visit to Paris to see Santos-Dumont and, on 2 January 1902, wrote to the Inspector-General of Fortifications (IGF), the War Office Department which, somewhat incongruously, was responsible for ballooning:

> The dirigible Balloon has now, by the prowess of M. Santos-Dumont, been so advanced that I shall have the honour to be in a position to recommend that certain experiments be carried out in Dirigible Balloon work by this Department.

But, even while he was in Paris talking to Santos-Dumont, he had known that the financial estimate for the following year which he had submitted to the IGF had been halved to the modest sum of £6,000. This money was, in any case, only intended to cover the production of further spherical envelopes, needed to allow the Balloon School to continue its normal duties, with no consideration being given to the implied costs which would be incurred by the significant technological advance involved in the construction of an elongated 'dirigible balloon'. Nevertheless, Templer, with his habitual disdain for his masters' intentions, doggedly initiated work in the Balloon Factory on a non-rigid envelope of goldbeater's skin, with a capacity of 50,000 cu. ft, which reached completion by early 1903. When, later that year, the Committee on Military Ballooning came to his aid, with its own recommendation for the acquisition of a 'dirigible balloon', more badly-needed funds were unlocked, but these were limited, there was still much to be achieved, and time was slipping by. Most importantly, an appropriate and reliable engine had to be found and acquired, while neither the complete assembly of an airship nor its operation could be seriously contemplated unless a suitable airship shed, in which she could be housed, were to be built. This latter was itself a major undertaking and would naturally require the further allocation of a not-inconsiderable amount of cash.

Alberto Santos-Dumont. (Author's collection)

To Templer, such obstacles were fit only to be ignored and he pressed stubbornly on, not only pursuing his own work within the Balloon Factory, but also directing his gaze further afield to the private sector, where several individuals were attempting to build their own versions of a dirigible. Some of these were investigated, but none demonstrated any practical suitability. In July 1905, Templer, now joined by Capper, repaired to Alexandra Palace, in North London, to witness the first flight of one such airship, which had been designed and built by a Dr F. A. Barton and his assistant Mr F. L. Rawson. This craft was about 190 feet long, had a non-rigid envelope of oiled silk filled with 190,000 cu. ft of hydrogen, and was propelled by a 50-hp Buchet engine. That afternoon, at about half-past four, in gusty conditions, she was walked out of her shed, but was soon found to be incapable of rising whilst carrying her proposed load of 1,000 lb of ballast and five passengers. After the removal of some of the ballast and one of the passengers, the airship managed to float successfully upwards, but it then became apparent that, with the engine working at its full power, she was unable even to hold her position against the fresh breeze which was blowing. Before the eyes of the watching crowd, the craft began to move slowly backwards, gradually drifting downwind and dwindling in size until she finally disappeared from their gaze. Forty-five minutes after she had taken off, she returned to earth at Romford, Essex, some 11 miles downwind, and was wrecked in the process. Colonel Capper, in his report, made no bones about it:

> The ship is of no practical utility whatsoever. The gas bag is inferior and will not hold gas. Some of the rigging broke when she swayed on the ground, and would give way could she push against a heavy wind, and the fans are quite incapable of driving the large mass through the air at more than a snail's pace.

Meanwhile, 1905 saw the Balloon Sections fully occupied in the business of removing from Balloon Square at Aldershot to their new home at South Farnborough; not only that, but in the previous November, sanction for the necessary airship shed had been received from the Director of Fortifications and Works, who had now replaced the IGF, and its erection went hand in hand with the move to the new site.

The shed became available for use in the following April, but another two and a half years were to pass before, on 10 September 1907, the elongated envelope begun by Templer in 1902 finally emerged through its doors as a complete airship, ready to take to the air as a navigable craft. Bearing the proud name of *Nulli Secundus*, she was seen to be cylindrical in shape, with hemispherical ends, and measured some 120 feet long by 25 feet in diameter. Her appearance was made distinctive by the four light-coloured bands, made of silk, which ran over the top and down the sides of the envelope and from which was suspended the tubular structure bearing the car containing the crew and the engine. The flying controls, which underwent a series of changes, were many and varied: for lateral stability, two stub-wings were mounted amidships (they were

Cody tending *Nulli Secundus*'s Antoinette engine. (Jean Roberts)

Nulli Secundus sailing triumphantly over St Paul's, before its downfall. (Jean Roberts)

The wreck of the *Nulli Secundus* at the Crystal Palace. (Jean Roberts)

later moved further aft); a single large rudder provided directional control; two twin assemblies, derived from the tried and tested box-kite, were slung below the envelope, for pitch control; lastly, for the later flights, a low aspect-ratio elevator was added above the rudder. For motive power, a French 50-hp Antoinette of eight cylinders had been obtained, which was mounted at the front of the car and which drove two contra-rotating propellers, one on either side. This installation had been largely designed and built by an American, long domiciled in England and now in the employ of the Balloon Factory. His name was Samuel Franklin Cody, whom we may leave in silhouette for the moment. We shall hear much more of him very soon, when he strides to the centre of our stage.

Before a large crowd of spectators, the *Nulli Secundus* was walked out on to the Common by an RE ground crew. From there, after preliminary tests, with Colonel Capper at the helm, Samuel Cody attending the engine and Captain W. A. de C. King RE, the Balloon School's Chief Instructor, making a third, she made what was not only her own maiden flight, but the first by any British military airship. *Nulli Secundus* indeed. The craft was then returned to her shed while luncheon was taken, after which a second flight took place with Capper and Cody once more at the controls. On the ground, Colonel Templer was present to witness the culmination and pinnacle of nearly thirty years work on behalf of British military aerostation.

So far, the new craft had been cautiously kept within the bounds of her home ground. In the ensuing days, however, in the course of two more flights, the airship was boldly taken on excursions around the local area. Not only the residents of Aldershot and Farnborough, but those living as far off as Camberley and Frimley were given what must have been their first sight of an airborne craft moving under its own power, as she made her unhurried progress before their uplifted gaze. These were followed on 5 October by the *Nulli Secundus*'s most celebrated flight, albeit marred by an unfortunate epilogue. Taking off from Farnborough Common in mid-morning and once more crewed by Capper and Cody, she set off in a north-easterly direction and was soon giving the people of Frimley a second view of this startling novelty looming above them. And this time, as she gave no sign of diverting from her course, it slowly became apparent that she was embarked on a voyage which would take her much further afield than before. On she went, passing over first Staines and then Brentford, her steady progress marked by more upturned faces as she sailed majestically on, her rounded nose pointed purposefully towards the centre of the capital. At an altitude of only a few hundred feet, her flight became a tour which took in Buckingham Palace, Whitehall and Trafalgar Square, before circling St Paul's and finally turning southwards to cross the river and pass over the Oval.

An hour had now passed since take-off and the wind, ever the potential enemy of the early aeronaut, was ready to interfere once more. From a gentle breeze it had strengthened to a fresh westerly, blowing from the starboard bow and which *Nulli Secundus*'s maximum forward speed of 16 miles per hour was insufficient to overcome. Capper and Cody, instead of returning in triumph to Farnborough, had no choice but to concede defeat and land at Crystal Palace, in South-East London, where they were obliged to abandon their aerial conveyance and make their way home by old-fashioned land transport – actually Cody's motor car, which had followed them from Farnborough. Five days later, the wind, encouraged by its earlier success, now increased even more in strength, causing the airship to threaten to break free from her mooring. The NCO left in charge, one Corporal John Ramsey, was obliged to slash the envelope open with a knife tied to the end of a pole, thus saving the craft from total destruction. In recognition of his presence of mind, Ramsey was promoted to sergeant, but for *Nulli Secundus* the incident marked the end of her short season of success.

She was rebuilt in the following year, being designated in her new form *Nulli Secundus II*, a terminological solecism over which we will pass as swiftly as possible.

Although her envelope retained the same shape as formerly, in other ways she incorporated a number of detailed changes of some significance. Firstly, the entire envelope was given a second skin, of silk, apparently as water-proofing but at the cost of a weight penalty of some 330 lb. Perhaps the most obvious feature distinguishing the new model from the old was the addition of a long fairing beneath the main cylindrical envelope, triangular in cross-section, and running nearly the whole length of the craft, this additional space being used to house a reserve supply of hydrogen. A third change concerned a major redesign of the control surfaces. The single rudder was replaced by twin surfaces, one on either side of the centre-line, and the two stub-wings had disappeared, though the elevator remained. It was at the front that the greater changes were apparent: the two sets of box-kites had gone completely and, instead, there was a second, large-span elevator mounted below and just forward of the new fairing. In this form, *Nulli Secundus* emerged from her shed at about six o'clock in the evening of 24 July 1908 and resumed her airborne career, watched by a large crowd. Crewed by Capt King, Captain A. D. Carden RE, the Balloon Factory's Assistant Superintendant, and Lieutenant F. C. Westland RE, the pride of the Balloon School left the ground, only to return to it again with some force, apparently caused by the ground-handling party failing to release her mooring ropes. Recovering from this embarrassment, the airship set off on a short return flight across Cove Common and as far as the Long Valley. The return flight yielded more excitement when, while the crew were coping with the shedding of a propeller drive belt, *Nulli Secundus* was allowed to pitch nose-down, so that she once more struck the ground, rebounded into the air and finally hit one of the Common's many trees, resulting in damage which kept her in her shed for several weeks.

On 14 August, she flew again, crewed by the old firm of Capper and Cody, but this time the flight was cut short by a burst petrol pipe. The next day saw another brief flight, once more curtailed by a broken pipe, this time in the engine cooling system, but it was also to be her last. *Nulli Secundus*, with little accomplishment to her name, was deemed to be of no further use and was broken up.

Though all too short, she had known her day of triumph, when the novel and impressive sight of her ample form cruising serenely above the City of London had brought a surge of pride to the watchers below, as well as, less vividly, to the nation as a whole. This unprecedented event, assisted by somewhat disingenuous articles in the press, seemed to bring reassurance that the British Empire could continue to claim its habitual leading position, no less in the new world of the sky than in the old one on the seas and on land. Only a relative few, less sanguine and better-informed, knew that the achievement was modest compared with that which was being achieved on the other side of the North Sea. In Germany in particular the giant rigid airships of Count von Zeppelin had been going from strength to strength. On 30 September 1907, shortly before Capper's one-way excursion to London, LZ3 had made a flight of nearly eight hours duration. By the following summer, while the British airship was still being prepared for her brief second career, the next Zeppelin, LZ4, with a length of over 400 feet and a volume of 530,000 cu. ft – ten times that of *Nulli Secundus* – had been built and had extended that record to twelve hours, covering a distance of 240 miles. Nor was the Count alone. Major August von Parseval was just beginning to produce a series of successful non-rigid airships, while in a couple of years Professor Johann Schütte, in association with Karl Lanz, would begin building the rigid airships which, when war came, would join the Zeppelins in releasing their bombs on a defenceless London.

In the Balloon Factory ambitions were of a considerably lesser magnitude. There, a second airship was being built, smaller yet than *Nulli Secundus*, which attracted the name of *Baby*, for her capacity was no more than 22,000 cu. ft. Apart from her small size, she differed greatly from *Nulli Secundus* in shape, having a pointed nose which

Top: *Nulli Secundus II* emerging from her shed, watched by a large crowd. (Jean Roberts)

Middle: Out and ready to go, looming impressively over the heads of the waiting onlookers. (Jean Roberts)

Bottom: On her way to circumnavigate the local area. (Paul Chapman)

swelled to maximum cross-section at about quarter-length, then gradually diminished again to a point at the tail. This early example of streamlining was somewhat undermined by an aspect ratio of little more than 3:1, which gave *Baby* a distinct appearance of portliness. She had a non-rigid envelope of goldbeater's skin and was initially powered by two 8-hp three-cylinder Buchet engines mounted one behind the other and driving a single propeller. The car housing the two engines and the two-man crew was slung from the envelope by cables. For stability in the pitching and yawing planes, there were two horizontal and one vertical inflated fins, the vertical one being later removed. The control surfaces, comprising port and starboard elevators and a rudder, together with a fixed fin, were mounted on the car, which betrayed a marked resemblance to the fuselage of one of the aeroplanes which were now suggesting themselves as the dirigibles' challengers.

Baby was taken out for her maiden flight on 11 May 1909 and thenceforth flew intermittently during the rest of the year. She suffered chronically from directional stability problems, which gave rise to numerous experimental modifications, notably the removal of the vertical inflated fin and its replacement by a silk sheet, triangular in shape and stretched between the underside of the envelope and the rear of the car. The flights were also plagued by engine failures and in August the Buchets were replaced by a single 25-hp REP air-cooled engine, named after its designer, the Frenchman Robert Esnault Pelterie, and arranged to drive two contra-rotating propellers, one on either side of the car – a similar arrangement to that on the *Nulli Secundus*. This engine proved no more reliable than its predecessors, and for *Baby*'s final flights, a British-built 35-hp Green was used.

If the engine problem had been alleviated, the directional instability had not and the decision was taken to enlarge the envelope by the insertion of an additional middle section to increase the overall length to 104 feet and the capacity to 33,000 cu. ft. The controls were improved by the replacement of the two remaining plump fins by three flat plate ones, with a rudder hinged to the rear of the vertical one. At the same time she was given the new name of *Beta*, Latin scholarship being now superseded by the Greek (*Nulli Secundus* being considered as *Alpha*). In her new form, the enlarged *Beta* demonstrated much improved handling qualities, making a number of successful flights in the course of that summer.

In June 1910, Colonel Capper took her on a night flight to London, expunging the memory of his previous attempt in *Nulli Secundus* by completing the round trip and returning successfully to Farnborough. A similar voyage was made in July, this time in daylight and under the command of Lieutenant Broke-Smith, now the Balloon School's adjutant and chief instructor. Late in September, Colonel Capper took *Beta* to Salisbury Plain, where she took part in the annual manoeuvres. In January 1911, *Beta* became the first of the army's airships to be equipped with wireless. Under the direction of the wireless expert, Captain Lefroy, the tests which had been begun in balloons were continued during a number of cross-country flights. Signals were successfully transmitted and received at ranges of up to thirty miles, although this achievement was somewhat diminished by the need to stop engines and drift when signals were being received.

In the course of the next three years, *Beta* was joined by two more airships named, in natural succession, *Gamma* and *Delta*, and then by a fifth called, for some reason, *Eta*, which happens to be the seventh letter in the Greek alphabet. All of them continued the design policy of non-rigid envelopes which had derived naturally from the ballooning years. However, the fabric of *Gamma*'s envelope marked a departure from the well-tried goldbeater's skin which had stood British military balloons in such good stead for so many years. Although still a marvellous, well-nigh impermeable material for balloons, when it was used for airships, difficulties were encountered in attaching to it the framework and car carrying the engine and crew. Construction

Baby seen in her earliest days, with the three inflated fins with which she was born, but which did little to overcome her inherent instability. (IWM Ref. RAE-0 453)

Beta outside her hangar. The section inserted to lengthen the craft can clearly be seen, while *Baby*'s plump fins have been replaced by more practical flat plates, including a moving rudder. (Author's collection)

An early picture of *Gamma*, when she still had her 'tailbags', with the 'new balloon shed' also prominent. (Jean Roberts)

of the envelope was therefore sub-contracted to the Astra company in Paris, which produced one of rubber-proofed fabric, 152 feet long and with a capacity of 75,000 cu. ft. In shape she continued *Beta*'s attempt at streamlining, and this became the norm for all later airships. She was distinguishable by the incorporation at the tail of two inflated stabilising bags, one on either side and reproducing in miniature the shape of the main envelope itself. Pitch control was provided by pairs of flat-plate elevators, mounted at the front and rear of the framework car, which was slung below the envelope. This, as well as providing the crew accommodation, also housed an 80-hp Green engine, driving two four-bladed propellers. In a novel departure, the latter were able to swivel through 90 degrees in either direction, a feature which was of great assistance during landing and take-off.

Although her name placed her third in the list, *Gamma*'s first flight, in February 1910, took place three months before the enlarged *Baby*, under her new name of *Beta*, returned to the skies. That spring, *Gamma* made a number of flights of an experimental nature and then spent the remainder of the year mostly undergoing various modifications. The front elevators were removed, as were the stabilising bags, to be replaced by flat-plate stabilisers, while the Green was replaced by two 45-hp Iris engines (designed by a certain Geoffrey de Havilland, of whom more later). Later on still, in 1912, the craft was given a new and larger envelope of 100,000 cu. ft, with which, in April, she then made what seemed to have become the mandatory run up to central London, making a circuit around St Paul's and showing the flag above Whitehall, before returning safely to Farnborough. In the autumn, she further emulated *Beta* by taking part in the autumn manoeuvres.

Delta was completed early in 1912 and, at 160,000 cu. ft, was the biggest of the Farnborough-built dirigibles. She began life as a semi-rigid dirigible, by virtue of two longitudinal girders being fixed to the underside of the envelope, from which the car was suspended. When the girders buckled under load, this became another short-lived experiment. The girders were removed and *Delta* reverted to the non-rigid form, like her sisters. Like *Gamma*'s, her envelope was of rubberised fabric; goldbeater's skin had finally become a thing of the past. Nevertheless, the new material was not without its problems: *Delta*'s envelope was found to be leaking badly, which considerably delayed first flight, so that by the time autumn had arrived, the airship was still languishing in the hangar, undergoing one pressure test after another, as leaks obstinately persisted. In the end, a solution was found in the form of a flexible nitro-cellulose dope, developed by the factory chemist, Dr Ramsbottom, and applied to the complete hull.

Once this problem had been overcome, *Delta* at last made her maiden flight in September 1912. Profiting from the *Gamma* experiments, four flat-plate stabilising planes, two horizontal and two vertical, were fitted at the rear. For pitch control, an elevator was hinged to each horizontal plane, while the lower vertical plane carried a rudder. For propulsion, two White & Poppe engines had been chosen, developing between them a total of 220 hp, which provided the airship with a respectable maximum speed of 42 mph. Having at last taken to the air, *Delta* was just in time to join *Beta* and *Gamma* in the manoeuvres which opened soon afterwards. Perhaps insufficiently air-tested, it was unfortunate that she then broke down whilst on her way from Farnborough to the manoeuvre area and had to return to base.

Eta, the last of the army's airships, joined her sisters in August 1913. Made of the now-standard rubber-proofed fabric, her 118,000 cu. ft envelope made her similar in size to *Gamma* in her later form. She was powered by two 80-hp Canton-Unné engines, which allowed her to match *Delta* for speed.

To return to the earlier years: even by 1910, *Beta* and *Gamma* were still the only means available to the Balloon School for effective aerial navigation, and to many in influential positions, the airship was the craft which seemed to possess a brighter future than the late-maturing aeroplane. Plans had therefore been laid to supplement

Gamma in later days, with her attendant handling party. The original balloon shed lies in the background, with the top of the original airship hangar (in the course of extension) visible behind it. (Author's collection)

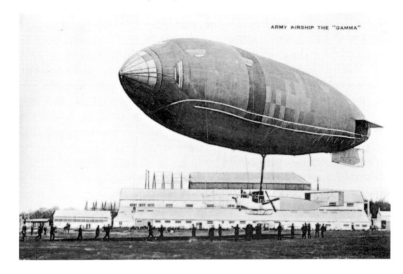

Delta floating just outside the second airship hangar to be built at Farnborough. It was known as the 'Lebaudy', since this was originally the home of that unfortunate craft. Next to it, *Delta*'s own shed is under construction, while beyond that stands the so-called 'portable hangar'. (IWM Ref. RAE-0 355)

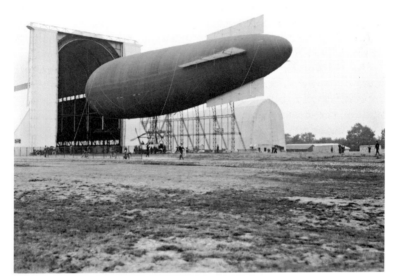

Last of the line: *Eta*. (Author's collection)

the home-built dirigibles by the purchase of two French-made airships, from the
companies Clément Bayard and Lebaudy Frères respectively. Funds for the purpose
were, as ever, limited, so while public money to the value of £18,000 was made
available for the acquisition of the former, in the case of the Lebaudy, the lead was
taken by private enterprise, with an appeal launched by *The Morning Post* in its issue
of 21 June 1909, declaring its objective of raising the sum of £20,000. The National
Airship Fund, as it was called, was aimed at all the newspaper's readers, high and
low, and met with a response which was both patriotic and air-minded. Every day
the paper published a progress report, with every day an impressively long list of the
latest subscribers – sometimes as many as thirty or forty in a day. They came from a
wide spectrum of society, with contributions which mostly ranged from a couple of
guineas to a shilling, the latter from 'Two Schoolboys'. Another contribution came
from the widow of Colonel Elsdale, specifically in memory of that early stalwart of
British military ballooning. Many remained modestly anonymous, concealed behind
such pseudonyms as 'The Bungalow', 'A Poor Widow' and the intriguing 'An Old
Parson Adrift'. On the day that *The Morning Post* reported Louis Blériot's flight across
the English Channel, it was also able to announce the gift of a thousand pounds from
a member of the Waldorf Astor family, which enabled the fund to pass the £10,000
mark.

Yet this manifestation of public enthusiasm for military aeronautics was to be
rewarded only by disappointment. Both imports, after suffering considerable delay in
delivery, proved in the end to be failures and contributed nothing to British military
aeronautics. The Clément Bayard was the first to arrive, crossing the Channel to a
landing in London on 16 October 1910, where another newspaper, the *Daily Mail*,
had provided a shed at Wormwood Scrubs in which she could be housed. She had a
capacity of 227,500 cu. ft and, propelled by two 120-hp engines, had averaged 33
mph on the voyage, helped by a light tail wind. But her envelope was leaking badly
and, after being dismantled and taken to the Balloon Factory, she was deemed to be
beyond economical repair and was never flown again.

The saga of the Lebaudy was more protracted but no less inglorious. At 353,000 cu.
ft, she was somewhat larger than the Clément Bayard and over twice the size of *Delta*,
with two engines rated at 135 hp each. Ten days after the Clément Bayard's arrival,
the Lebaudy too was flown across from France, in the hands of her French crew. Also
on board was Brevet Major Sir Alexander Bannerman RE, who had just taken over
command of the Balloon School from Colonel Capper. Another airship shed had been

THE MORNING POST LEBAUDY AIRSHIP   Nº2.

The Morning
Post Lebaudy
airship, having
arrived at
Farnborough,
is just about
to enter into
the argument
with her shed.
(Author's
collection)

specially erected at Farnborough to house the new arrival (at last some meaningful sums of money were being allocated to service aeronautics!) and she was flown directly there. Her successful arrival, however, was to be followed only by misfortune, her troubles beginning from that moment.

Some confusion seemed to have arisen about the relative dimensions of the shed and its proposed occupant, with the result that the top of the airship appeared to be rather higher than the shed entrance. The officer in charge of the handling party, Captain Broke-Smith, noticing the apparent discrepancy, halted the docking operation in order to investigate. Unfortunately, before he was able to pursue his intentions, they were frustrated and countermanded by the interference of a senior officer who was present among the welcoming throng. This individual, whom Broke-Smith darkly and, one suspects, aggrievedly describes in his subsequent account as 'an officer of high rank in uniform', took it upon himself to order the docking to continue, whereupon the airship duly entered into an argument with the top of the shed entrance, as feared, causing her envelope to be punctured and then collapse, resulting in further damage.

Repairs were put in hand, but took some considerable time, so that six more months elapsed before, in the evening of 4 May 1911, the airship was ready to be relaunched. Misfortune once more attended her test flight, still in the hands of her four-man French crew. In a light westerly wind and with Major Bannerman again on board, she cast off and began what became an erratic flight around Farnborough Common. After a short time in the air and with the clock well past 7 p.m., the pilot judged it time to land before the light failed. He began an approach towards the landing ground, where a party of 120 men under the command of Captain Broke-Smith was waiting. On board, Major Bannerman needed all his British phlegm as the craft pitched and yawed in a manner which suggested that she was scarcely under control, while, according to Bannerman, the co-pilot 'began to pull rather wildly at the various valve lines hanging within his reach'. Although the airship was making very slow progress into the wind, she nevertheless failed to lose height sufficiently quickly, being still some 500 feet up when she arrived above the heads of the landing party, with the two guide ropes which had been dropped hanging far above their reach, leaving them with no occupation but to gaze upwards at their departing quarry, as she now veered away to the north, trailing her ropes and followed below by her would-be attendants in hot but vain pursuit. With more altitude now belatedly shed and the wind pushing the craft further to the east, the ropes began to entangle themselves, firstly in a nearby copse of trees and then amongst the roofs of the Balloon Factory. The effect of this was to pull the airship's nose around to port, while adding to the severe pitching and yawing motion which she was still displaying and which the two pilots were having difficulty in correcting. The craft had now taken on a southerly heading, coming lower and lower and moving at a much higher ground speed, while the ropes, having freed themselves from their previous entanglements, had swung round and begun to trail through the crowd of onlookers which had collected to watch, fortunately without causing any injury. The airship was now very low indeed and seemingly uncontrollable: although the pilot was desperately applying full right rudder, trying to regain the open space of the Common, she continued to turn obstinately to the left and crossed the Farnborough Road, carrying away a line of telephone wires as she did so and running through the tops of some trees. With her envelope now punctured, one propeller was torn off, spinning its way though the branches, while the flight finally ended with the wreckage draped across the roof of Woodlands Cottage, occupied by a Captain and Lady Follett, providing a startling interruption to the latter's preparations as she dressed for dinner. The occupants, still in the car, came to earth on the Folletts' front lawn, but happily there were no injuries, either to those on board or to anyone on the ground.

Wrecked beyond repair and of no further use to the aeronauts, the airship became

Above and below: The garden of Woodlands Cottage, adorned by the Lebaudy, well and truly wrecked. (Author's collection)

of interest to the lawyers. Claims for compensation were lodged by the National Telephone Company and by Colonel H. L. Jessep, the actual owner of the Folletts' dwelling, whilst a plaintive plea for some sort of recompense also came from *The Morning Post*, which was intending to return to its airship fund subscribers all the contributions which they had made, accepting liability for the £12,000 which had already been paid to the manufacturers in France. Settlement was delayed by the nice point as to whether Lebaudy or the War Office was accountable. The former, from its Paris offices, denied all responsibility, maintaining that, although it was their crew which was in command of the airship, they were at the time acting in accordance with general instructions from the British Army representatives on the spot. For its part, the Army Council, having debated the matter, concluded that the outcome was too problematical to justify further argument and surrendered to its fate. It agreed to bear the maker's charge for the repairs from the first accident, while *The Morning Post*, whose patriotism and forbearance must surely be applauded, agreed to write off its own losses and even to shoulder the cost of Colonel Jessep's claim. One can only speculate on the feelings, ranging perhaps from sadness to anger, of Mrs Elsdale, the Poor Widow, the drifting Parson and all the other patriots, to see their hopes embodied in the Airship Fund thus vanish with the Lebaudy into the scrapyard.

On 18 May, just a fortnight after the Lebaudy debacle, *Beta* also found itself in difficulties, in the same patch of sky. She made one flight that day which was uneventful, although her pilot, Captain Carden, reported that she was 'very hard to get down' and that the rear steering wheel was 'extremely awkward and puzzling to use'. She then took off again, commanded this time by Lieutenant C. M. Waterlow RE, accompanied by QMS Fewster and Sergeant Bourne. The wind was very light from the north-west. After climbing to a height of 1,000 feet, they adopted a heading which took them over Stanhope Lines in Aldershot, from where Waterlow prepared to return to the Common and land. It was from that point that his troubles began, as he started to experience for himself the problems to which Carden had alluded. He began to discharge gas in order to shed height, but the gas pressure was, it seems, already lower than it should have been and this manoeuvre met with such limited success that, on arrival above the landing point, he found himself still at 200 feet, with his mooring ropes (which were in a tangle anyway) well outside the grasp of the handling party. To avoid straying over the built-up area to the east, he decided to turn to the right and remain over the open Common while he sorted himself out. He now found himself beset by another difficulty, for unfortunately:

Owing to the rear steering wheel acting in a reverse direction, my hard-a-starboard really resulted in hard-a-port, with the result that the balloon headed straight for the Farnborough Road. Unable to correct this error in time, I opened the front ballonet valve at once and shifted myself and Serjt. Bourne back as far as possible and accelerated in order to get a quick rise and if possible to clear the telegraph wires with the rope. This failed and the rope caught and at once upset the steering with the result that I was unable to get the ship turned round until I [was] nearly up to the Alexandra Road.

... the rope was now too much caught up and the strain pulled her head round and I had to stop the engines and wait to be freed. The ropes were caught finally in the trees by Woodlands Cottage. I dropped the grapnel at this point and the men seized it and after cutting the tow-rope free succeeded in manoeuvring across the telephone wires. The damage, as far as I know, is confined to the telephone wires, grapnel and tow ropes.

It later transpired that the rear steering wheel was connected to act in the opposite sense to the front one – a design fault which seems astonishing to the modern way of thinking. Although *Beta* emerged relatively unscathed on that occasion, one wonders whether the local inhabitants – not least the Folletts in Woodlands Cottage and the management of the National Telephone Company – might not have been starting to become a little anxious about the new monsters which had begun to circulate over their heads!

Beta was to contribute little of note for the rest of the summer. Five days after the latter incident she was returned to the factory, deemed to be in an unsatisfactory condition. Reissued on 1 June, she survived for a fortnight before the soldiers sent her back again, for further overhaul. Two months later, she reappeared, and this time it was found possible to keep her in service for the remainder of the training season. All the same, both *Beta* and *Gamma* were now showing signs of considerable wear and tear and spent a great deal of time in the factory in an unserviceable condition, prompting Bannerman, in a long report to DFW on 19 February 1912 concerning the lack of availability of his dirigibles, to complain:

> The envelopes of these vessels have undoubtedly seen their best days, and it seems probable that unless something is done in the matter we may find ourselves left without any airships at all, and whatever may be the opinion held as to their use on active service, of their value as a means of training in aerial reconnaissance there can be no doubt. In the matter of the Gamma especially, old rubber fabric does not inspire confidence in those who have to navigate the vessel.
>
> As regards the Delta, past experience does not lead one to count much on her proving an addition to the training fleet, in any case during the coming season. Moreover, unless our strength is increased, I shall not have men enough to handle her.

As a consequence, both *Beta* and *Gamma* were given new envelopes (an enlarged capacity of 42,000 cu. ft earned the former the name of *Beta II*), thus extending their useful lives. As for *Delta*, given the prolonged delay in her first flight occasioned by the stubborn tendency to leak from which she was suffering at that time, Bannerman's gloomy predictions about her future usefulness may be forgiven, but in the end, as has already been related, Dr Ramsbottom's dope proved her saviour and she was able to join her sisters in the sky.

Although the home-built dirigibles had their problems, they certainly enjoyed more fortunate service lives than the two imports from France and made numerous successful flights during the next few years. They all, with the exception of *Nulli Secundus*, took part in the yearly manoeuvres, often using wireless to report back their observations of the troop deployments – activities which made their own contribution to the army's dawning awareness of the changes which aeronautics was slowly bringing to the conditions under which future battles would be fought. On 18 October 1913, *Delta* was used for an early parachute jump, Major E. M. Maitland descending successfully from an altitude of 1,800 feet.

On another occasion, *Beta* was proceeding on one of her missions around the countryside when the sapper at the engine was surprised to find that the officer in command was manoeuvring to land. The reason for this began to emerge when the former realised that they were coming to earth in the grounds of a country house, where he could see that some of the servants had been assembled, ready to provide the landing party, indicating that their visit was not unexpected. An entertaining picture is induced of a team of gardeners and footmen (under the command of the butler?) tentatively seizing mooring ropes, their efforts encouraged by shouted advice from above. On this occasion, it certainly worked, for their craft was safely secured and the aeronauts were escorted to the house for a few hours' pleasant diversion from the rigours of aerial navigation, the officer above stairs, while the sapper was entertained in the servants' hall. There seem to have been other occasions when nominally serious training flights were similarly diverted to such more sociable and pleasurable applications; however, one must of course assume that such events were no more than intermittent pleasures, seized to lighten the rigours of an otherwise dedicated professional existence.

There were indeed other times when incidents of a less enjoyable nature took place, such as Waterlow's steering difficulties in *Beta*, already described. Another occurred during an ascent by the same craft in the course of a local flight during the previous summer, with the unfortunate Waterlow again in command, assisted by Lieutenant Cammell and a civilian mechanic named Cox who manned the engine. An oil leak began their troubles, which so preoccupied Cox that the engine was allowed to stop for lack of fuel pressure. Although power was soon restored, that bugbear of lighter-than-air vehicles, longitudinal stability, next claimed the captain's attention and both crew and ballast had to be moved forward in order to hold the nose down. Following this, the engine stopped for a second time, due to the fracture of the pipe which connected the fuel tank to a bicycle pump (!) which was being used to maintain the pressure. Farce now began to show his mischievous face, for it then emerged that restarting had been removed from their list of options, since the starting handle, which had been placed upon the floor, by persons unknown, had unfortunately fallen overboard. Cammell and Cox then attempted to turn the propellers over by hand, but perhaps fortunately for them, the engine refused to respond. Bereft of any means of propulsion, *Beta* was now being carried northwards away from Farnborough Common and Waterlow decided it was time to return to mother earth. All might now have gone well, had not the landing area which presented itself consisted, not of open fields, but a wood, where the grapnel, having been lowered, obediently but unhelpfully performed its function by fastening itself on to one of the trees, while gusts of wind caused *Beta* to become caught ever more firmly amongst the branches.

These events had inevitably attracted a crowd of curious locals, drawn both by the arrival of such a novel visitor and by the always enjoyable sight of some fellow human beings in a predicament. More usefully, a sapper ground party, having been summoned, also turned up to assist in salvage operations. In order to lighten the craft, Cox was instructed to abandon ship and he climbed down to earth via a suitable tree trunk. Then, with no little difficulty, those below began gradually to haul the airship, her envelope now punctured, free from its encumbrances, directed by Cammell from the command post he was now occupying in a tree, having followed Cox overboard. Waterlow, as captain, naturally obeyed tradition and remained with the sinking ship until she was extracted, somewhat the worse for wear, and conveyed back to her base.

Many other events, both exploits and misfortunes, befell these leviathans in their stately journeys across the peaceful skies of southern England, but none were marred by serious disaster or fatality and their crews enjoyed what they must in later, darker years have recalled as halcyon days. On 1 January 1914, the army ceased to operate lighter-than-air craft and all four dirigibles were transferred to the Royal Navy. By then, the gentle buoyancy of gas had largely been supplanted by the employment of another, more aggressive means of defeating gravity, namely the generation of an aerodynamic lifting force by the relative movement of air across a flat or curved surface – wings!

Beta in 1910, sailing serenely over the balloon shed and the airship hangar alongside it. (Author's collection)

II

KITES – FLYING BUT STILL TETHERED

'Stop, Crosbie! Come down!' The officer with the megaphone and the other Royal Engineers around him gazed upwards with increasing anxiety at Lieutenant Talbot-Crosbie, perched perilously on his seat in the car suspended below the Man-Lifting Kite flying 200 feet above their heads. Talbot-Crosbie, of the Royal Garrison Artillery, who was one of a number posted on attachment to the Balloon School for a course of instruction in kiting, seemed to be climbing rather higher than Captain King, the Balloon School's Chief Instructor, felt was wise for his inexperienced pupils. And now, far from obeying the latter's order, Crosbie was continuing his upward path, as his Kite, drawn by its own lift, ran on up the cable which was being held taut against the sky by the train of lifter kites flying high above it, in amongst the puffs of cloud scudding past in the stiff breeze.

'Come down, Crosbie! Pull your down line!' called Captain King again, as the trainee aeronaut, now some two or three hundred feet above the ground, showed no sign of responding. King turned towards the soldier manning the winch and ordered him to be ready to apply the brake from the ground. As he did so, a general shout went up of 'the cable's gone'. Spinning round, King was in time to see the car and its occupant coming down at a great rate, followed by the lifter kites higher up, which were swerving sideways out of control, while the cable fell slack and uselessly downwards. Having soared upwards at a high speed, the inexperienced Crosbie, in response to his instructor's calls – and his own feelings of alarm – now seemed to have pulled his 'down line' as enthusiastically as previously he had the 'up line', with the present disastrous result.

With a thud, the car hit the ground on its side, even as King and the other members of the RE Kiting Detachment were running up to assist its now unconscious passenger. The latter, although he soon regained his senses, was sufficiently badly injured to be placed upon a stretcher and borne off to the Connaught Hospital, while the Balloon School prepared itself for the inevitable Court of Enquiry, which duly assembled eight days later.

The date was 20 October 1909 and the place Cove Common, Aldershot. The Man-Lifting Kite, or War Kite, beneath one of which Talbot-Crosbie descended so unceremoniously that day, represented another method by which the British Army at that time was attempting to equip itself with aerial observation platforms. It had been adopted to supplement the tethered balloon, when the wind speed was too high for the latter to be launched. It might be said that the Man-Lifting Kite represented a brief transitional phase between the heyday of the 'gasbag' and the final triumph of the aeroplane, replacing as it did the former's use of the buoyancy of hydrogen gas with the latter's reliance on the brute strength of aerodynamic forces, whilst, however, sharing the balloon's disadvantage of lack of mobility over and beyond the battlefield.

It seems to have been in China, in ancient times, that the earliest kites made their appearance. In Europe, they have certainly been made and flown for several centuries.

So far as their use for warlike purposes is concerned, it was in 1876, when balloons had yet to enter into service with the British Army, that a civilian balloonist named Simmonds made what he called a 'Parakite', which was designed to 'raise the weight of a man and to remain in position at such an elevation as would allow of observation being taken of a military position not otherwise capable of being seen'. It was tested at Chatham, but suffered from instability in flight and was not a success.

After that, it was not until 1893 that the story of the Man-Lifting Kite really began for the British Army, when Capt B. F. S. Baden-Powell, temporarily forsaking balloons, began experimenting with kites on an unofficial basis. He designed them in a hexagonal form, made from cambric stretched over a bamboo frame and measuring about 500 sq. ft in area. His first successful trials were carried out at Pirbright Camp, on 27 June of the following year, when he managed several times to lift a man off the ground, limiting the height to some ten feet, for safety reasons. The following year, he changed his approach somewhat, using smaller kites of some 100 sq. ft in area, flown in trains – i.e., a series of such kites attached at intervals along the rope. With these, he and others made ascents to heights of around 100 feet, with a parachute rigged above the aeronaut to guard against any sudden and untoward loss of lift.

It has nevertheless to be recorded that his efforts received scant encouragement from his seniors. During the South African War, in which he served, he advocated the addition of a kiting detachment for service in the field and asked permission to take a set of kites out from England. His enthusiasm was defeated by a War Office ruling which cunningly allowed that he could certainly do so, provided that the kites formed part of his personal baggage, relying no doubt on the knowledge that this was limited to 150 pounds. Despite this obstructiveness, he did manage to get some kites out to the Cape, disguised, rumour had it, as medical stores. This scheming was not sufficient to see their use in active operations, although he was able to fly them on numerous

Above left: Captain Baden-Powell's War Kite. (Paul Chapman)

Above right: Baden Baden-Powell. (Paul Chapman)

occasions, albeit only for experimental and demonstration purposes, including aerial photography and the elevation of aerials for wireless telegraphy.

It was round about the same time that a second voice began to be raised, to add to Baden-Powell's in extolling the virtues of kites for military purposes. It was at first greeted with even less enthusiasm than the latter's, but this second campaigner was the one who would in the end prove to be decisive.

For it is at this point that we find the colourful figure of Samuel Franklin Cody, whom we glimpsed earlier aboard *Nulli Secundus*, clamouring for our full attention. He was probably unique among the early aeronautical pioneers in that a number of years before he turned to working with kites – and later with aeroplanes – he had become quite well-known to the theatre-going public for his activities as a showman, earning his living by presenting and appearing in theatrical entertainments based first on the 'Wild West' and then later on the Alaskan 'Gold Rush'. To this end, he tended to dress the part, off stage as well as on. His habitual headgear was a wide-brimmed hat, from beneath which long hair flowed down to his shoulders. These tresses were complemented by a black beard and a luxuriant matching moustache, the tips of which were waxed into flamboyant points. The story of his earlier life supported his theatrical persona. He had apparently been born in Texas, probably in 1861, and while still a child had survived an attack by Red Indians on his log cabin home, in which his parents were killed. Later, he became an accomplished horseman and rifleman, riding the range as one of the cowboys of western legend and driving cattle hundreds of miles across the plains to market. Tiring of these adventures, he then took himself further north, joining the crowds of fortune-seekers when the Gold Rush erupted in the Yukon.

Such was the romantic history of his early life, which was widely accepted, both during his lifetime and for many years afterwards. Tiresomely, more recent investigators seem to have discovered that much of this agreeably exciting tale lacks the basis of fact. We are now told that he was born in Davenport, Iowa, some six or seven miles to the north of the border with the fabled Lone Star State, that his family name was Cowdery, rather than Cody, and that a certain degree of doubt hovers over his exploits on the prairies. At the time, however, the legend formed a valuable backdrop in support of his theatrical activities, while the implied relationship to the famous 'Buffalo Bill', assisted by his exotic appearance, enhanced the value of his undoubted prowess as a horse rider and crack shot, around which his shows were designed.

About his later years on this side of the Atlantic, however, and in particular his activities in the aeronautical field, we can be more confident. He arrived in England in 1890 and it is during that last decade of the nineteenth century that we find him deriving a comfortable living as well as a certain popular fame from his theatrical extravaganzas. It was probably just before the century's end, while he was presenting and acting in another of his melodramas, this one being based on the Yukon Gold Rush itself and entitled *The Klondyke Nugget*, that he began experimenting with kites, which he hoped would be capable of raising a man into the air. By 1901, he was sufficiently confident about the performance of his creations to approach the army with a commercial proposal. With the latter still heavily preoccupied with a difficult war in South Africa, it is not altogether surprising that, like Baden-Powell, he was not on this occasion rewarded with a positive response.

Cody continued with his main occupation, entertaining the public with dramatic tales of villains, heroes and maidens in distress, while, in his spare time, undeterred by official disinterest, he kept on experimenting with his kites, gradually incorporating improvements. On 6 February 1903, he tried again, this time choosing the Admiralty as his target, with a letter offering a 'superior design of kite'. This approach too was not immediately successful, eliciting the reaction from the navy that 'Major Baden-

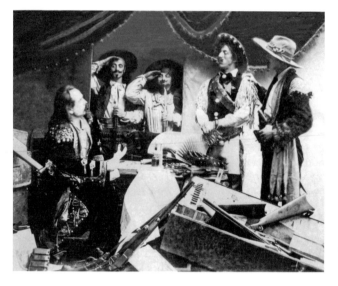

The Cody theatre company. (Jean Roberts)

The vintage Cody, with flowing locks and moustache waxed into extravagant points. (Jean Roberts)

A poster advertising Cody's melodrama *The Klondyke Nugget*. (Jean Roberts)

Powell recognised the difficulties of flying kites from on board ship and is thinking over the matter. Mr Cody has probably no notion of these difficulties and would only waste our time.' The disingenuous Cody had perhaps not assisted his own case by writing his letter on notepaper which was headed 'The Klondyke Nugget Co.' and giving his address as the Grand Opera House, Liverpool, where the show was then appearing. However, if he appeared – erroneously – to the author of the above comments as frivolous, he was also persevering.

A month later he tried again. This time his letter had been dispatched from the Royal Artillery Theatre, Woolwich, and contained an invitation to a demonstration of his kite which he intended to give on Woolwich Common. This event went off most successfully and an officer who attended, impressed with the practical evidence with which he was confronted, returned a favourable report, as a result of which Cody was invited to carry out further demonstrations, both on land and at sea. These duly took place but, despite their manifest success, the subsequent negotiations were unsuccessful, with the Admiralty declaring its opinion that such devices would serve no useful purpose at sea and Cody finding himself once more rebuffed.

Turning aside for a moment from the martial sphere, he found another means of testing the merits of his kites, by entering the Kite Competition which the Aeronautical Society held at Worthing, on the South Coast, on 25 June. There were only three other contestants, one of whom was his stepson, Leon (an enthusiastic kite-flyer in his own right). After numerous flights had been made by all the four entrants and the results had been assessed (based on the average of all the heights achieved), it was found that the elder Cody had been beaten into second place by a certain Charles Brogden, indicating that the American was not alone in his successful pursuit of this particular branch of aeronautics.

Transferring his energies to the application of kites for a totally different purpose, Cody now conceived the idea of demonstrating their viability as a source of motive power. His scheme was to harness a kite to a canoe, which would then be pulled along by the force of the wind acting upon the kite – so long, of course, as the wind continued to blow ... Naturally, Cody's sense of showmanship required that the attempt, when made, should include an element of the spectacular. He therefore proposed to test his novel craft on the waters of the English Channel, across which his kite would tow him to a landing on the shores of France. Naturally, also, the newspapers were kept fully informed. In October 1903, Cody embarked at Dover in conditions which supplied him with the northerly wind he needed, but one which also gave him a rough sea to sail upon. This first attempt failed when the wind veered and he was reduced to paddling back to his starting point. A few weeks later he tried again, this time in the other direction, setting out from Calais in the chill of a November evening. He made good progress at first, but as the night wore on, the wind once more sulked and threatened the same failure as before. For hours he lay becalmed in mid-Channel, wet and frozen in his open boat and quite alone. However, with the dawn, the wind relented and, as it strengthened, he was borne triumphantly to a landfall in Dover Harbour, after a voyage which had taken him thirteen hours to complete.

The following year, Cody decided to try his luck in the military field once more and once more approached the army. By now, the 1904 Report of the Committee on Military Ballooning had, as we have already seen, recognised the potential usefulness of kites to supplement balloons – particularly in winds too strong for successful ballooning, when the kite, on the other hand, comes into its own. It should come as no surprise, therefore, that on this occasion Cody was rewarded by an invitation to bring his 'apparatus', as it tended to be called, along to Aldershot and there to demonstrate its capabilities.

On 6 June, with all his gear, he arrived at Aldershot station, to find awaiting him on the platform a party of sappers from the Balloon Sections, led by Lieutenant R. V.

Before venturing upon the deep, Cody tested his conveyance in waters both calmer and safer. (Jean Roberts)

The kiting canoeist, safely ashore, addresses his latest audience. (Jean Roberts)

Samuel Cody hangs suspended beneath his Man-Lifting Kite, while at the same time, ever obliging, he provides a usefully detailed view of the latter's construction. (Jean Roberts)

D. Holwell RE. Everything was carried off to Balloon Square and matters were set in train with such dispatch that the first launches were made the very next day, assisted by a recorded wind strength of 17 mph. During the next ten days, in winds generally varying between 13 and 20 mph, some twenty ascents were made, Colonel Capper and ten other members of the Balloon Sections taking turns to trust themselves to the American's contrivance, the highest altitude recorded being 1,000 feet. On 13 June, there was some excitement when a pilot kite was carried away by a gust, whereupon the whole train became unstable and started to descend, but at so slow a rate that the aeronaut concerned, Lieutenant Holwell himself, came gently to earth and emerged completely unharmed.

On the 16th, Cody and Capper went up in the basket together, demonstrating a useful payload. On 25 June, the trials came to an end, with a further five ascents which passed off without incident, although probably quite excitingly, the wind speed at 1,000 feet having risen that day to a stiff 40 mph (nudging Beaufort Force 8, or Fresh Gale). Capper was quick to issue an approving report, which was duly accepted. An order was placed for three sets of kites plus three spares, at a cost of £100 per set, while Cody himself was appointed to the Balloon School as 'Chief Kiting Instructor', at a salary which, after some rather lengthy bureaucratic procrastination, was set at £1,000 per annum. He was also allocated free fodder for his horse – an early sort of mileage allowance, one might suppose. It is perhaps worth remarking that Cody's employment by the military authorities, despite what could be described as a somewhat inappropriate background, might well be produced as evidence that the army of those days was not as hidebound and unimaginative as is sometimes implied.

At this point, there may be some virtue in describing in more detail the kite system which Cody had developed and which was put into service by the Balloon School. A decade earlier, the Australian aeronautical pioneer Lawrence Hargrave had produced a design in a double box-kite configuration, which he flew with some success. Box-kites had also been flown in America, both at the Blue Hill Observatory, Massachusetts, for meteorological work, and on Governor's Island, in New York Bay, where a Lieutenant H. D. Wise of the US army ascended to a height of forty feet below a train of four kites.

Cody's own kites were based on this form, but to enhance their stability he had added extensions – known as bat's wings – at top and bottom on either side. For launching, a standard balloon wagon was used, with its winch suitably adapted. At the start of operations, the wagon was aligned with the wind direction and anchored thus by having its trail staked to the ground. When all was ready, a small 'pilot' kite, attached to a light line, of piano wire, was first deployed from the winch drum and then allowed to ascend to a convenient altitude, say two to three hundred feet, from which point it began to pull out from the drum the main, heavier cable. It was then the turn of a train of larger 'lifter' kites – the number dependent on the wind strength – to be sent up. Each of these lifters was fitted with a ring, or 'fairlead', by which it could be threaded on to the cable. When each lifter was released, it was drawn up the cable under the effect of its own lift, until it was arrested by a stop, or 'bulb', which was fixed to the cable and which was of too large a diameter to allow the fairlead to pass over it. These bulbs were spaced out at intervals along the cable and were of diminishing diameters, the largest being at the top and the smallest at the bottom. Since, correspondingly, the fairleads on each kite introduced on to the cable were also of diminishing diameters, each in turn was able to run on over the smaller bulbs without being halted, until it was brought to rest by that one which corresponded to its own fairlead. By this simple but ingenious means, a train of lifter kites would be established at intervals down the cable, which itself had meanwhile been drawn further out from the winch and was being held up in the sky by the lifting power generated by those same kites. Then, once a suitable altitude had been reached, further extension could be halted by application of the winch's brake.

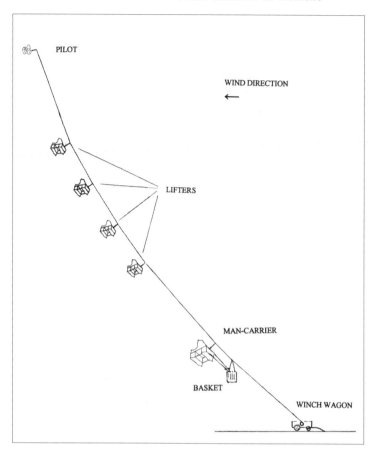

PILOT

WIND DIRECTION

←

LIFTERS

MAN-CARRIER

BASKET

WINCH WAGON

Fig.3: Illustration
of the principles of
a Cody kite train.
(Author's collection)

When all the lifter kites were thus flying satisfactorily, the pull on the cable was measured by a dynamometer on the winch. If the officer in charge of kiting deemed this value to be sufficiently high, the large man-lifting kite itself was assembled on to the cable, free like the lifters to slide along it on its own fairlead, but drawing behind it a steel trolley, which also slid along the cable, and from which was suspended the object of the whole exercise – a chair, or better, a standard balloon basket, containing the observer. The latter was furnished with 'Up' and 'Down' lines attached to the 'Man-Lifter' kite, by means of which he could alter the attitude of the latter's surfaces to the prevailing wind and hence the aerodynamic lift it was able to develop. Thus, when he increased the lift generated by the Man-Lifter by pulling on his 'Up' line, he was able to make his conveyance rise along the 'Jacob's Ladder' in the heavens above him. Conversely, by using his 'Down' line, he could make it descend. Finally, he was also provided with a 'brake', or means of clamping the trolley to the cable (there was no corresponding bulb in the case of the Man-Lifter), which enabled him to stay at any desired altitude (usually between 1,000 and 2,000 feet), while he concentrated on his observations. All this, Cody, a man with no training in science or engineering, had developed by rule of thumb, brain-work and painstaking experiment. He was, it could be said, an outstanding example of the old adage – that genius is 5 per cent inspiration and 95 per cent perspiration!

Once the Royal Engineers had acquired their kites, and with them the services of their energetic inventor, they continued to operate them, in training and on manoeuvres, for some years, although history and their eventual supersession by the aeroplane denied them the opportunity of exploring and demonstrating their utility

Cody shows off
some of his kites.
(Jean Roberts)

A very long train
of kites, assembled
for show perhaps.
It would be most
unusual for as many
Lifter Kites as this
to be needed at one
time. (Jean Roberts)

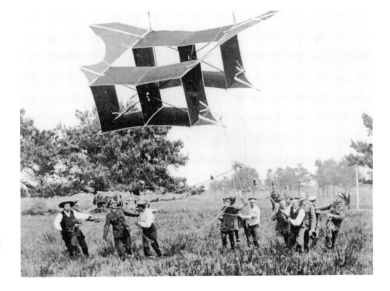

The Man-Lifter gets
airborne, under the
watchful eyes of
Samuel Cody, on
the extreme left and
readily distinguished
by his Stetson. (Jean
Roberts)

on any battlefield. While they endured, they provided a significant extension to the wind conditions in which the Balloon Sections could carry out their aeronautical duties: in light winds, when the kites could not develop sufficient lifting power, the well-established balloons remained supreme; when the wind was stronger and balloons could not be launched, the kites were literally in their element and took their place. Under normal circumstances, an observer would ascend to an altitude of between 1,000 and 1,500 feet, although a record altitude of over 3,000 feet was established in 1905, which must have been a sight to behold. The intrepid occupant of the basket that day was Lieutenant Broke-Smith, but it is unfortunate for us that, in his laconically short report of the event, he modestly fails to include any account of his own emotions as he swayed about, high above his comrades on the far-off ground, his connection with them and the promise of his safe return amongst them provided only by a flimsy-looking cable, curving a very long way backwards and downwards to the winch below.

As with all devices which are designed to be operated by man, skill and experience were essential attributes. Turbulent conditions, particularly likely near the ground, could destabilise the train and required swift action to overcome their effect. If the wind strength was marginal, the officer in charge of kiting needed to be particularly alert for any drop in the wind velocity and be ready to order the flight of kites to be hauled down before loss of lift brought them down out of control. Inevitably, the occasional exciting incident took place, Lieutenant Holwell's first unceremonious descent being followed from time to time by others such as Lieutenant Crosbie's rather more serious accident which introduced this chapter. Nevertheless, despite the apparently precarious situation in which War Kite aeronauts were required to place themselves, no really serious injury, let alone death, was ever suffered during those years. Whenever anything untoward did occur, the carrier kite always demonstrated an ability to descend to earth relatively gently, acting rather like a parachute.

The degree of confidence which the soldiers had in the safety of their kites may be judged from their willingness to let even civilians go up on them. At a public 'open day' in 1907, ascents were offered to all comers for ten shillings (50p) a trip (altitude unspecified!). The less daring, to whom such a perch might look unduly precarious, could choose instead an ascent in a tethered balloon, which was also rather cheaper, at two shillings (10p) a go.

Incidentally, in the case of Crosbie's adventure, the Court of Inquiry concluded that the bulb for the top lifter had slipped up the cable, allowing the lifter to rise and damage the pilot kite, depriving the flight of lifters of the latter's stabilising effect. As for Maurice Talbot-Crosbie himself, although he was some time in recovering from his injuries, even at one point contemplating resignation from the army, by the following May, he was able to report to Colonel Capper that he was well on the way to returning to his duties and had even coaxed the sum of £73 10s from a reluctant War Office, to cover the expenditure he had incurred for his medical treatment.

Not long after, Samuel Cody was also to be found engaging in a battle over money with a parsimonious War Office, as he tried to secure what he regarded as his just dues for services rendered. His appointment as the Balloon School's Chief Kiting Instructor was terminated in September 1909, under circumstances which will be related more fully later. At that juncture, he suggested to his former employers that he was entitled to a not inconsiderable remuneration for all his work, which, in the shape of the Man-Lifting War Kites, had placed in their hands a most effective aerial observation platform and which, as it happened, was rather cheaper to operate than the balloons which it supplemented. The reward for this ought, he felt, to be considerably more than the £1,000, which they were at first prepared to offer him. As he put it:

If you wish to present me with a gratuitous gift of £1,000 for my services during the past four years, I shall be most happy to accept. But on the other hand, if you mean this sum to remunerate me for having placed my invention, with the greater part of it protected by patent, at the exclusive disposal of the British Government and for which I quoted you in the first instance – £5,000 with 12 years engagement, or £8,000 without the promise of engagement, I would respectfully point out that I worked solely and exclusively for several years on the subject of man lifting kites, spending over £3,000 of my own money before entering the service.

But Cody was swimming in waters of a murkiness which were unsuited to his straightforward nature. To the pen-pushers of Whitehall, the honest declarations of achievement which seemed perfectly adequate to him were not of the stuff which had the power to unlock the official coffers. There were due processes to be observed; the Whitehall animal must be fed with documents of a suitable nature and which, having been submitted, could then be carefully enclosed in an appropriate file, accompanied by a suitable written minute. Such a file would then be fit for passing on to other interested parties, via a stately circuit of in- and out-trays, attracting further minutes as it did so, until the matter achieved its final consummation. A certain Harris, the War Office official dealing with the business, tried to explain this elegant *modus operandi* to Cody, but appeared to meet with an incomprehension which reduced poor Harris to a state of exasperation, which he was driven to vent in an intemperate note to his opposite number in the Treasury:

> Dear Harman,
>   We have duly warned Cody as to the necessity for legal forms and so on in his claim. But he seems to be a thick headed and ignorant person and has apparently misunderstood or forgotten what he has been told. We are now trying again to explain to him. Meanwhile I think the Treasury had better write as you propose.

Such sentiments concerning Cody's mental abilities would, had they seen them, have excited considerable indignation amongst his many friends at Farnborough. In any event, he wisely engaged solicitors, who would have better understood the 'legal forms' required, to act on his behalf. With their guidance, various affidavits and other records were produced, and in August 1912, he was at last rewarded with the receipt of the additional £4,000 for which he had asked.

However, by that time, the vehicle which had been the cause of his arguments with the bureaucrats had come to the end of its short period of military employment. Both Cody and the Balloon School itself had moved on in step with the changing times. Both, at first jointly and then separately, had moved out of the world of balloons and kites into that of the aeroplane.

III
WINGS

I

Collecting the Breeze

It is said that, some time shortly after the beginning of the second millennium, probably while King Ethelred, known to us as The Unready, was engaged in his losing struggle against the invading Danes, there was living amongst the brotherhood of the Benedictine Abbey of Malmesbury in Wiltshire a young monk of the name of Eilmer. It seems that, when he was not engaged in his devotions or working at tasks set him by his seniors, he was wont to spend his time watching the birds and marvelling at the ease with which they soared so effortlessly around the abbey's tower and swooped over the roofs of the town. Apparently – as with so many others, in the centuries which followed and probably earlier as well – he was seized with the ambition to copy them – perhaps join them in their kingdom of the air. Eilmer was evidently no empty dreamer, for he followed up his observations by embarking on the practical step of designing and making a pair of wings, seeking as well as he could to imitate those of the birds he had been studying. Thus it was, the story goes, that one day young Eilmer was to be found climbing up the tower, carrying his wings with him and determined at all odds to put his theories to the test. Reaching the top, this early pioneer of the skies, whom posterity was to dub the Flying Monk, carefully equipped himself and stepped to the edge, his heart in his mouth. Then, overcoming his fears and stretching out his arms, he boldly cast himself off into the void.

According to the account written some sixty or seventy years later by William of Malmesbury, another monk of that same abbey, Eilmer

> … had fastened wings to his hands and feet, I know not by what means, in order that he might fly like Daedalus, taking the fable as the truth, and, collecting the breeze at the top of a tower, flew for a distance of a furlong or more.

There being available in those far-off days no witnesses in possession of the necessary aeronautical knowledge and experience, we have no expert opinion as to whether the intrepid and inventive Eilmer achieved true flight. We know only that he survived the experiment for, as William goes on to tell us:

> … trembling with the violence of the wind and the turbulence, together with his awareness of the rashness of his deed, he fell, breaking his legs and being forever lame thereafter. He himself used to say that the cause of his downfall was that he had forgotten to put a tail at the back.

He thus became henceforth the Limping Monk. Clearly, as he acknowledged, his design needed further refinements, but there is no record of Eilmer carrying out any further research. Was Man thus denied the gift of Flight, nine centuries earlier than the actual event? Perhaps not. After all, once he had added the necessary tail, thus groping his way a little further towards conquering the mysteries of aerodynamic stability and control, Eilmer would have needed to turn his attention to the small matter of the invention of the internal combustion engine – that essential propulsion unit, the acquisition of an efficient example of which was so often to spell the difference between success and failure for the eventual pioneers. He was, we must take it, somewhat before his proper time.

In the centuries following Eilmer's painful experiment, tales of other hopeful students of flight can sometimes be found, lurking in the half-light betwixt history and legend. We hear of an Arab savant here, a Chinese philosopher there, but only in accounts accompanied by little supporting evidence and less achievement. Roger Bacon in the twelfth century and Leonardo da Vinci in the fourteenth injected some scientific reasoning into the quest, while in the seventeenth century, another Italian, Francesco Lana-Terzi, both priest and professor, designed a 'flying boat' which he proposed could be raised into the sky by a number of metal spheres from which all the air had been exhausted. However, it really belonged to the lighter-than-air school and, in any case, remained no more than a project and, like so much of the earlier theorising, was unconsummated by practical experiment.

It needed the arrival of the nineteenth century for some real progress to be achieved. Sir George Cayley, of Brompton Hall in Yorkshire, was first to show the way. Like the best of the later pioneers, his full-scale experiments were preceded by the study of theory and by practical research. He was nearing the end of his life before, as the culmination of decades of work, he turned to the construction of man-carrying gliders. He was now over sixty years old so, unlike Eilmer, he wisely remained firmly on the ground for their trial flights. For the first test flight, in 1849, a young boy was given the honour of sitting in the machine and being launched a short distance through the air. No record appears to have survived concerning the boy's reactions to his experience – or, indeed, those of his parents. Four years later, a second glider was constructed and, in a more ambitious experiment, Sir George's coachman was detailed to be the world's first, though highly unenthusiastic test pilot. The location chosen for the flight was a small but steep-sided valley called Brompton Dale, to the eastern side of which the glider was borne and from where, accompanied by its obedient occupant, it was launched into the air. The latter, one Appleby, had probably been provided with a simple control, but with little idea of how to use it, one might surmise, was more likely to have clung tightly to his seat as he suddenly found himself riding the unsubstantial airs, deserted by the solid ground and with no earthly support between himself and the bottom of the dale, glimpsed over the side vertiginously far below. He came to no harm, as his master's well-conceived contrivance carried him across the void to land safely on the other side. However, for Appleby, one such experience was enough and he lost no time, tradition has it, in handing in his notice. Sir George himself died in 1857, unaware that, many years after, his work would earn for him the title of 'The Father of Flight'.

Contemporary with Sir George were John Stringfellow and William Henson, of Chard in Somerset, who also took care to remain on the ground. Henson began with high ambition. His proposal for a passenger-carrying 'Aerial Steam Carriage' and a parallel scheme to launch an 'Aerial Transit Company' to operate it, which promised 'Certain Improvements in Locomotive Apparatus and Machinery for conveying Letters, Goods and Passengers from Place to Place', anticipated the first airlines by nearly eighty years. When the reality failed to match his dreams, he turned, with Stringfellow, to the design of a steam-powered model aircraft, which, in 1848, apparently flew successfully, although by that time Henson had emigrated to the USA, thereby abandoning his aerial aspirations entirely and taking no further part in the story of flight.

In 1866, four years after Grover and Beaumont began their campaign for the adoption of balloons by the army, the Aeronautical Society of Great Britain (later 'Royal') was founded 'for the purpose of increasing by experiments our knowledge of

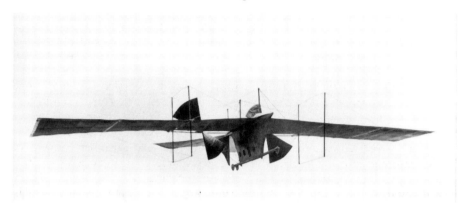

A model of Henson's Flying Machine. (Author's collection (Science Museum – SSPL))

Henson's Aerial Steam Carriage which, ahead of its time, was meant to equip the world's first airline. (Author's collection)

Clément Ader's *Avion III* which was tested at Satory in October 1897. (Author's collection)

Aeronautics, and for other purposes incidental thereto'. That same year, on 27 June, one of the founder members, Francis Wenham, read before the society his paper 'On Aerial Locomotion and the Laws by which Heavy Bodies Impelled through the Air are Sustained'. Two years later, the young society held its Aeronautical Exhibition at the Crystal Palace in South-East London. The seventy-seven exhibits included balloons, engines, kites and model flying machines, but it was the two entries submitted by a now-elderly John Stringfellow which took the palm. His steam-powered triplane demonstrated its ability for sustained flight (albeit along a guide wire), while a separate steam engine which he exhibited in working condition beat all other contenders to win the £100 prize offered by the society for such a device.

By the time Stringfellow died in 1883, the progress which he, Henson and Cayley had begun seemed to have come to something of a halt. The membership of the Aeronautical Society was in decline and, although men such as Wenham and others pursued their studies with undiminished energy, the theories and the projects showed no promise of producing any practical end-product. The balloon and possibly the dirigible appeared to be the sole means of aerial navigation for the foreseeable future. However, as might be expected, there were other actors waiting in the wings. In 1890, a further step forward for the heavier-than-air school was signalled by a French engineer, the forty-nine-year-old Clément Ader. He had designed and built a bat-like monoplane to which he had given the name *Eole* (or in Latin *Aeolus*, the Greek god of the winds) and which was powered, like Stringfellow's models, by a steam engine. That autumn, he took it to Gretz-Armainvilliers, a few kilometres south-east of Paris, where, on 9 October, in the grounds of the local chateau, he coaxed it off the ground and 'flew' for a distance of 50 metres. This 'hop' represented neither sustained nor controlled flight, but it was a welcome advance.

In Great Britain, meanwhile, aviation had also claimed the attention of the well-known inventor, Sir Hiram Maxim. In 1894, he conceived a rather clumsy-looking device – also steam-powered – which was more test rig than flying machine. It had a wingspan of 110 feet and was designed to take off by running along a set of rails. The latter were however matched by a second set, a couple of feet above the first, installed to restrain the great machine from rising further. It duly demonstrated its ability to fly, even to the extent of breaking the upper rail in its eagerness to soar upwards, but this degree of audacity proved its undoing, for it ended by crashing to the ground and was wrecked. With this limited achievement, Sir Hiram seems, rather unambitiously, to have left it there for a while and gone off to invent something else, although he did return to aeronautics later.

For the moment, the baton was returned to Ader, who had attracted a certain amount of official support from the French War Ministry. With their financial assistance, he had been able to continue his experiments with a new machine, for which he coined the name of *Avion*, but which was also unsuccessful. The year 1897 found him trying again, with *Avion III*. This craft was powered by two steam engines, but was otherwise similar in configuration to his previous efforts. Tested at the army camp at Satory, near Versailles, it achieved little more success than the other two, and Ader, with no more government funding forthcoming, retired from the struggle a disappointed man.

Meanwhile, work of a considerably more practical nature had been performed in Germany, where in 1891 Otto Lilienthal achieved successful gliding flight with wings of a shape which, like Eilmer's, owed much to those of the birds. He was followed by the Englishman Percy Pilcher, who also showed promise of success. Both of them had made plans to progress to powered flight when first one and then the other inaugurated the long roll of brave men who perished for the sake of Man's conquest of the air. Nevertheless, the advance to the skies, from being almost moribund, was beginning to stir once more.

Percy Pilcher in the air. (Author's collection)

Maxim's aeroplane on its rails at Baldwyn's Park in 1894. (Author's collection)

In 1900, the distinguished scientist, Lord Rayleigh, expressed his own views on the prospects for human flight. In a cautious review, he 'declined to speak very definitely, though he made it quite clear that he would not limit the possibilities of aeronautical science, and inclined to the view of ultimate success.' His optimism was, however, no more than restrained, since he added that 'even when artificial flight is possible, it may not be a very safe way of travelling, one for instance that may not commend itself to an elderly lady who desires to come up to town from the country to do a day's shopping'. There's something in that.

In America, two men in particular, Octave Chanute and Samuel Pierpont Langley, adopting a more positive approach, were devoting much time and thought to aerodynamics and the theory of flight. Although they both made and experimented with a number of models and man-carrying gliders, it is today by their considerable theoretical contribution to the new science that they are both best remembered.

Langley, in particular, converted theory into practice by putting a great deal of effort into both models and full-sized aeroplanes. Over a period of about four years, beginning in 1894, he built a number of models (which, curiously, he called 'Aerodromes'), based on a tandem-wing configuration and powered, like those of Stringfellow and Ader, by steam. They were years filled with many disappointments, but perseverance finally brought its reward when, on 6 May 1896, his latest model flew for a distance of 1,100 yards. Six months later, with an improved model, he extended this record to ¾ mile.

This achievement marked another major step towards the ultimate conquest of the air and placed Langley in the van of that advance. He now set about the design and construction of a full-sized aeroplane, a project which went hand in hand with work to devise and produce a petrol engine to power it. The new 'Aerodrome' was to the same tandem-wing configuration as the models, had a wingspan of 48 feet and weighed 730 lb. Directional control was to be achieved by means of a triangular rudder set below the aft pair of wings, while an elevator forming part of the cruciform tail unit was to provide control in the pitching plane. At the beginning of October 1903, the machine, with its new engine, was ready for its first test flight. It was to be launched using the same method as that which he had adopted for his models, namely by means of a catapult mounted on a houseboat moored on the River Potomac. The pilot was to be his assistant, Charles Manly, who had been associated with the design of the new engine, but who completely lacked any experience as a pilot. At that point in aviation's progress, this was hardly to be wondered at, although he could have emulated some of the other pioneers, by first acquiring a certain degree of skill, by training himself on a suitably designed glider. Instead, Manly was to be shot quite vigorously into the air and then required, on the instant, to take charge of his craft's trajectory by means of controls whose responses were unfamiliar.

As it happened, this omission turned out to be of no importance, since in the subsequent events Manly remained an entirely passive participant and was not called upon to demonstrate any piloting ability – or lack of it, while the choice of water to provide a relatively soft landing surface turned out to be a wise precaution. For, when the moment of truth arrived and the machine was shot off from the deck of the houseboat, it immediately pitched nose-down and plunged directly into the river. Both Manly and the wreckage were rescued and, after extensive repairs, the team tried again. Once more, their efforts resulted only in a similar failure and a second ducking for the intrepid Manly.

The date of this latter unhappy event was 8 December 1903. At that same moment, on a windy island some 200 miles to the south, two other Americans had nearly completed their own preparations and were within days of the success which Langley had been denied. It had been three and a half years earlier, in May 1900, as the balloonists of the Royal Engineers were lending their assistance to Lord Roberts's steady advance on Pretoria, that Octave Chanute had found himself reading a letter which had arrived from an unknown bicycle manufacturer named Wilbur Wright, writing from an address in Dayton, Ohio, describing the latter's own ambitions to devise a successful flying machine and asking for his help.

Chanute had been studying aeronautics since the 1850s and, by the end of the century, had become well known as the repository of a great source of information on the subject, both practical and theoretical, and was unhesitating in providing Wright with both data and moral support. By the following October, Wilbur and brother Orville had constructed their first glider and were established in their camp at their chosen testing site near Kitty Hawk on the Outer Banks running down the coast of North Carolina. There, taking advantage of the lift drawn from the fresh Atlantic breezes blowing over the sandy dunes, they began to experiment with it, making many flights as they gradually improved both its design and their own piloting skills. When, three years later, Orville and Wilbur made the four flights which guaranteed the two brothers eternal fame, it was only a very small beginning. Further years were to pass before the aeroplane had advanced from an experimental device to a practical vehicle, as the Wrights and others on both continents toiled, learnt, built and – from time to time – crashed.

While the scientifically inclined had been bending their minds to the discovery of the secrets of flight, other intellects, fully confident that these collective efforts would, in the end, be crowned with success, were burning more midnight oil in considering the changes that the aeroplane would wreak on the life of the world when it eventually arrived. Inevitably, the potential military uses of the aeroplane and its effect on future hostilities between nations formed no small part of their thoughts.

Even the poets tried to peer at what might be. As early as 1842, while Cayley and Henson were engrossed in their own studies, Alfred Tennyson had penned his own vision of Man's future in the air, which, while it foresaw a highly beneficial aid to world trade, did not exclude the sombre expectation that it would also provide new scope for human conflict:

For I dipt into the future, far as human eye could see,
Saw the Vision of the world, and all the wonder that would be;
Saw the heavens fill with commerce, argosies of magic sails,
Pilots of the purple twilight, dropping down with costly bales;
Heard the heavens fill with shouting, and there rained a ghastly dew
From the nations' airy navies grappling in the central blue.

Down at that lower, more mundane level which is unknown to poets, a Capt J. D. Fullerton RE, who after retirement from the army in 1905 was to serve for several years as secretary of the Aeronautical Society, had for some time been developing his own theories about the effects which military aeronautics, once developed, would have on future warfare. In 1892, addressing the Royal United Service Institution on the subject of 'Modern Aerial Navigation', he delivered his conclusions:

The success of aerial machines will enormously affect the position of the United Kingdom; in fact, there is no country in the world which will be so much affected. A total change will have to be made in our defensive system; the value of our Navy will be very much reduced, and the 'silver streak' of which we hear so constantly will, for all practical purposes, disappear. An aerial navy of the very first class will be an absolute necessity, if we are to maintain our position as one of the leading Powers in the world.

In 1897, he returned to his prophesies with a paper for *The Aeronautical Journal*, the house magazine of the Aeronautical Society, in which he predicted that:

Future wars will commence with heavy fighting in the air between opposing aerial navies, followed by attacks on marine fleets, and concentrated bodies of troops by the conqueror. Marine navies will especially suffer, and among the land forces cavalry, artillery and all mounted troops will find anything like concentrated action an impossibility.

Fullerton ended with the following deductions:

1st   In the near future, aerial warfare by swift flying air-ships will revolutionize the present methods of war by sea and land.

2nd   Owing to the high rate of speed of the air-ships, all nations will have to maintain themselves ready for war at very short notice.

3rd   The nations most affected by aerial warfare will be those which depend at present for their defence on marine navies.

4th   As aerial ships will be, comparatively speaking, inexpensive, the smaller nations will be able to make use of them.

5th   Owing to the possibility of war at very short notice, a larger proportion of a nation will have to be kept under arms.

6th   Warfare by sea and land, on any extended scale, will only be possible to the nation which has command of the air.

For all that, the day-to-day activities of both the Balloon Companies and the factory at Aldershot still lay perforce with balloons and kites. Nevertheless, Fullerton was not alone in believing that a fundamental change was on the way. A few years later, when John Capper was placed in command of the army's aeronautical service, he was no less interested in the promise offered by the heavier-than-air mode of aeronautics and his years at Aldershot and Farnborough were to find him both initiating and encouraging numerous moves to find practical aeroplanes for the army's use. In the autumn of 1904, he had managed to get authorisation for a visit to the United States, ostensibly for a visit to the World's Fair at St Louis, known also as the 'Louisiana Purchase Exposition', which included an aviation section. There he met Chanute, who had submitted the only entry in a competition for 'Gliding Machines':

Mr Chanute informed me that he did not anticipate much success, nor did the machine meet with much.

The operator [a Mr W. Avery] stood on the ground with his arms resting on the lower portion of the glider, which he carefully balanced. Attached to the front of the glider was a long cord connected at the far end to an electric winding engine. On the engine being started the cord was rapidly wound in, the operator running along the ground till the speed was sufficient to raise the glider like a kite. When at sufficient height the cord was loosed by the operator, and the free machine glided to the ground.

I saw a good many attempts, but never saw a really good glide; probably the pace was insufficient for the machine to glide properly. The best I saw was about 90 feet from a height of some 25 feet in the air. The operator at times allowed the machine to go higher, but I did not happen to be present at these times.

Before he left England, Capper had contacted Patrick Alexander, a wealthy patron of aeronautics, who supplied him with letters of introduction to other aeronautical notables in America. Through these, he also secured a meeting with Langley and was enabled to visit the Wrights at Dayton – the latter no doubt being of the greatest potential value. In his report submitted in the November following his return, while many yet doubted – and some even ridiculed – the reports of the Wrights' flights, Capper expressed his belief that the Wrights had:

... at least made far greater strides in the evolution of the flying machine than any of their predecessors.

The work they are doing is of very great importance, as it means that if carried to a successful issue, we may shortly have, as accessories of warfare, scouting machines which will go at great pace, and be independent of obstacles of ground, whilst offering from their elevated position unrivalled opportunities of ascertaining what is occurring in the heart of an enemy's country.

In trying to persuade his masters of the need for greater efforts to ensure that Great

Britain was not left behind by the other powers in the coming revolution in the air, he added:

> England is very backward. There are strong hopes of success in this direction, and such success, with at any rate small machines, may come earlier than is generally anticipated, and America is leading the way, whilst in England practically nothing is being done.

Practically nothing continued to be done.

Within the Balloon Companies, Capper continued to do what he could with the limited resources and the limited technical knowledge available, not to say the limited encouragement from the military establishment. In 1905, in addition to all the other mainstream activities with balloons and kites which occupied the greater part of their time, the military aeronauts also received from him the following instruction, headed 'Gliding Machine':

> Model gliders to be made up and tried under various conditions, usual size 1/6th full. When, if ever, a satisfactory or promising pattern is obtained, a full-sized one to be constructed, and tried close to the ground.
>
> Desiderata : stability, both lateral and vertical, safe descent with a load of 2 lbs per sq. ft of surface.
>
> All experiments and shapes and trials of models to be very carefully recorded, including wind if any in which tried.

The 'if ever' does not suggest the presence of unbounded optimism.

As, during 1904 and 1905, the Wrights made slow but methodical progress, the Old World lagged well behind. The scene in France was the most promising. Alberto Santos-Dumont had turned away from dirigibles and was also exploring the heavier-than-air solution, whilst an army officer, Capitaine Ferdinand Ferber, having first attempted, with little success, to follow the path pioneered by Lilienthal and Pilcher, had, from 1902, turned to experimenting with gliders based on the Wright principle.

However, the most practical contributions were to be made by a young native of the southern city of Lyon, a former architectural student named Gabriel Voisin. Having been experimenting with gliders for some years, assisted intermittently by his brother Charles, he too was now harbouring ambitions of progressing to a powered machine. Earlier events had drawn the Voisins to Paris, where after initial struggles, they had established a workshop in the rue de la Ferme at Billancourt, on the south-western edge of the city and only four or five kilometres from Santos's own airship hangar at Neuilly.

In 1906, Voisin and Santos joined forces to design and construct a large tail-first – or canard – biplane, to be powered by a 24-hp Antoinette engine and which, with vertical panels stretched between the wings to form 'boxes', leaned very much on Hargreaves's box-kites. The long square-sectioned fuselage and another box-kite forming the front stabiliser completed the ungainly, rectangular appearance of the machine. By the end of the summer, on 13 September, the machine was ready for its trials and, accompanied by officials from the Aéro Club de France and a large crowd of sightseers, Santos and the two Voisins took the *14 bis*, as it was called, to the wide open space of the Bois de Boulogne, which lay conveniently nearby on the city's western outskirts. Santos's objective was the Archdeacon Cup, offered for a flight of at least 25 metres – hardly an excessively ambitious target, but one which that day proved to be out of reach. After a first abortive attempt, a second try saw him managing to struggle into the air, but only to fall back again almost immediately, with damage which sent the machine back to the Voisins' workshop for extensive repairs.

On 23 October, he returned to the same spot, ready to try again. Watched by the usual crowd of onlookers, keen to see the famous aeronaut's latest exploit, he made a number of attempts to fly, all of which were rendered unsuccessful by various mishaps. It was four in the afternoon, with the numbers of his faithful following undiminished, when his clumsy-looking machine was made ready for another go. Once more, Santos-Dumont climbed aboard and the engine was started. With the pilot standing erect in its fuselage, looking more like the helmsman of a boat than an aviator, the craft began to roll forward over the grass, slowly gathering speed until the moment arrived when it became apparent to the watchers that its wheels had lost contact with the ground, remaining so for a respectable time before they returned once more to earth. The flight was lengthy neither in time nor in distance, but although in the Gallic excitement of the moment there was some confusion about the exact distance which Santos-Dumont had flown, the generally agreed figure was about 60 metres and the Aéro Club had no hesitation in awarding him the prize, though for an achievement which could scarcely be described as triumphant. Not only had he lacked the means to control his machine directionally, but his flight scarcely compared with that which had taken place nearly three years earlier at Kitty Hawk, on that first day of the new era, when Wilbur Wright had been able to cover ten times the distance; not to mention that of a year later, when he had remained in the air long enough to achieve a flight representing a distance in excess of twenty miles.

Some time was now spent in modifications which were aimed at giving the pilot a degree of lateral control, in the shape of a controllable surface mounted within the outermost wing box on either side, and three weeks passed before, on 12 November, Santos-Dumont returned to the Bois, to see if he could better the small success of his earlier visit. Once more, he kept the audience waiting until the day was well spent.

However, on this occasion, it had a more extended performance to keep it amused, for the latter was divided into two acts, with Santos second, though naturally top of the bill. The first act was in the hands of a new member of the cast, who had turned up with his own machine, with which he hoped to emulate or preferably exceed the Brazilian's earlier achievement. It was also a biplane – although not a canard, it was also powered by an Antoinette and it had also been built in collaboration with Gabriel Voisin. Its owner was a big bluff fellow with a luxuriant if straggly moustache and his name was Louis Blériot. Within two or three years he was destined to achieve great things, but on that day, his time was yet to come. After several runs along the ground without the achievement of anything resembling flight, a last attempt resulted in an encounter with rough ground which left his machine severely damaged. Bearing the

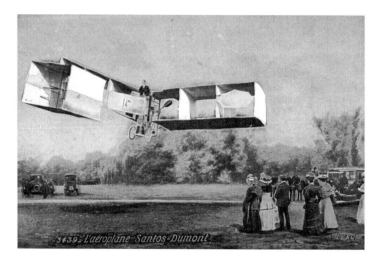

Santos-Dumont on the bridge of his *14 bis*. (Author's collection)

pieces, he retired defeated, leaving the stage empty and awaiting the entry of the man of the hour.

Santos, too, began with several preliminary ground runs, while the crowd watched, uncertain of what to expect. At last, with the pale autumn sun now quite low in the sky, Santos was satisfied and ready for the real thing. Once more, the engine roared and his machine surged forward, gradually gathering speed as it did so. Slowly, the box-like stabiliser at the front began to rise, the wheels lost contact with the grass and the crowd cheered as their hero ascended slowly and majestically upwards. *Le petit Santos* had flown again! This time, he not only managed to remain airborne for a distance of some 220 metres, but he was also able, by means of his new control surfaces, to make cautious changes to the direction of his flight.

As it happened, the onlookers on that occasion included a visitor from England – one Alfred Harmsworth, owner of the *Daily Mail* and lately raised to the peerage with the title of Viscount Northcliffe of the Isle of Thanet. Although the Brazilian aviator's new feat could still scarcely be said to bear comparison with the Wrights' achievements, Northcliffe, already a tireless evangelist for aeronautics, both civil and military, was greatly impressed. So much so that shortly afterwards, it is said, he delivered himself of the assertion that 'England is no longer an island'. Future events, not least those of the summer of 1940, were to show that this was something of a journalistic overstatement and that, provided that the skies could be adequately defended, the presence of the sea still counted for a great deal. However, in 1906 and in the years immediately following, with so much to be learnt and still more to be accomplished, his words seemed to carry an ominous weight.

In Great Britain, progress was even less notable than it was in France. Although there was by no means any lack of men who were convinced of the great importance and the assured future of the aeroplane, among them numerous aspiring designers, toiling away in sheds and workshops up and down the land, there was at that time not a single practical flying machine to be found anywhere in the island. For civilians and soldiers alike, the balloon and – for the latter at least – the kite were still the only means of getting up into the air.

Even across the Atlantic, progress had come to a halt, for in October 1905, the Wrights themselves had voluntarily suspended their flight trials: for the next two and a half years, neither brother once left the ground. Instead, they turned their energies both to improvements to their design and to negotiations with different prospective customers, including both the US and the British governments. These proved to be far from straightforward; those with the latter involved an exchange of correspondence which began in February 1905, continued throughout 1906 and included a visit to Dayton, in the August of that year, by the British Military Attaché in Washington, Lieutenant Colonel Gleichen. On his return to Washington, Colonel Gleichen reported that the Wrights:

> ... will not take a penny less than $100,000 for the Flyer. This includes training a British operator and granting full rights to the manufacturer under patents on the mechanical details. Whether these rights are granted or not makes no difference to the price. I gather these rights are of little or no value unless accompanied by the 'confidential scientific knowledge' for which they demand another $100,000.

The suggestion that the sum of $200,000 (in those days equivalent to about £40,000) be expended on the acquisition of a flying machine about whose performance many still expressed doubts, from an obscure pair of bicycle dealers on the other side of the Atlantic, when the following year's Army Estimates for what was still defined as 'Ballooning' were to be set at a mere £11,500, was scarcely calculated to be greeted warmly by the British Army establishment. Even Capper now shifted his ground. A few weeks after seeing Gleichen's report, he wrote to the Director of Fortifications and Works:

> I cannot advise any further action being taken in this matter. I consider the prices asked by the Wright Bros. are out of all proportion to the benefits to be gained. One has no certainty whatsoever that their claim of having special 'confidential scientific knowledge', for which they demand £20,000, is based on fact.
>
> As regards the Flying Machine itself: I have but little doubt that we shall be able, thanks partially to the scientific attainments and ability of Lieutenant Dunne, to turn out within a reasonable time a Flying Machine on much the same lines as that of the Wright Brothers, but we hope superior to it in several essentials, at an infinite fraction of the cost demanded by them.

It is in the second paragraph that we find the probable explanation for Capper's desertion of the Wrights. Lieutenant John William Dunne was an officer of the Wiltshire Regiment who had been invalided home from the South African War and placed on half-pay, but who had recently joined the staff of the Balloon Factory. He had been nominally engaged in the post of assistant kite designer, but his ambition and his efforts were directed towards a much higher goal. With the connivance and encouragement of Capper, he was by that time working, not on kites, but on the design and construction of an aeroplane. If, as Capper believed, Dunne could produce the goods, it might well turn out to be cheaper – and certainly more agreeable in a patriotic sense – to provide the British Army with British aeroplanes, rather than to have to purchase them from the American cycle dealers. As for the latter, on 20 November 1906, Capper was advised by DFW that Lieutenant Colonel Gleichen was being instructed to 'inform Messrs Wright that the Army Council has decided that it would not be advisable to purchase their machine, especially in view of the great cost.'

So that was that. It was not that the Powers-that-Be were disinterested by the military possibilities of the aeroplane. The protracted negotiations with the Wrights show that they were at least prepared to explore its potential. The difficulty lay more in the fact that there were so very few people in places of influence who, on the one hand, were able to visualise aviation's future potential and, on the other, had much understanding of the technicalities of the subject. An illustration of this latter point can be found in a report compiled in October 1907 by a certain Captain G. S. Olive, who was serving at that time in the War Office and who had been tasked with examining the current situation in the air. He reported that 'considerable attention is being paid by the French military authorities to the development of the aeroplane; and the idea that it is in this direction that the true solution of air navigation will be found, appears to be gaining ground.' He then produced a comparison between heavier-than-air and lighter-than-air aeronautics which he believed favoured the former, since: 'It cannot be denied that a vessel in which the wind is utilised as a means of propulsion must be superior to one for which wind is the principal obstacle to overcome.'

It is difficult to fathom quite what Olive had in mind in coming to this conclusion. Did he have some idea that an aeroplane could harness the wind to propel itself, in the same way as the more familiar sailing vessel? However, he was a little closer to the mark when he sadly concluded that the main drawback of the aeroplane was that 'whilst they can all fly more or less, they invariably damage themselves on alighting.'

Capper, now filling the dual roles of Commandant Balloon School and Superintendent Balloon Factory, was, as a member of the Aeronautical Society, amongst the better educated in the field. He continued to explore all the other avenues he could find which might lead to the discovery of a practical flying machine for the army's use. In April 1907, an exhibition of model aeroplanes was held at the Royal Agricultural

Hall, Islington. Capper requested and was granted permission to attend. He found little to encourage him.

> Taken all round I do not think we have learned very much from the machines exhibited – beyond one or two points. The only machine to my mind that flew with real promise was that shown in No.3, Mr A.V. Roe's back-steering machine.

There thus steps on to the stage another of the very earliest of the early British pioneers: Alliott Verdon Roe. Roe had begun his career as a merchant navy engineer, then, returning to dry land, had joined the ranks of those who believed fervently in the future of the aeroplane. Capper's assessment was confirmed by the judges. Roe's 'back-steering' (i.e., with its engine at the rear) machine was awarded first prize and its designer lost no time in turning his thoughts to the construction of a full-size example.

The other entries, apart from one which also attracted Capper's attention – a glider submitted by the Parisian-born José Weiss, who later worked with another pioneer, Frederick Handley-Page – typified all too well the limited state of progress of aeroplane design in the country as a whole. Amongst them was one which harked back to that tempting blind alley of so many early experimenters – the flapping wing – and which was the brainchild of another sapper, a Major R. F. Moore RE (Retd). For his purposes, Major Moore had opted to copy not any of the birds of the air, but the flying fox. If, by following that path, he appears to fit the popular image of the eccentric and slightly batty inventor, the evidence of the extensive and profound studies which he carried out suggests otherwise. Back in 1897, he had published a long paper on the subject in *The Aeronautical Journal* and had taken out a patent on his idea two years after that. In any event, it was typical of Capper's determination to investigate as many paths as he could that, despite his expressed doubts about the viability of the project, he gave it his support and extracted the modest sum of ten guineas from the War Office budget to purchase a pair of Major Moore's wings. In addition, the latter was granted facilities in the Balloon Factory to continue his experiments for a further two years, at the end of which time it had become evident that, whatever birds and foxes could achieve by their own particular methods, for Man a fixed wing and a rotating propeller were the only means by which he would be able to join them in the skies for at least some time to come. Major Moore and his work fell back into the shadows, to figure no more in the history of aviation.

Greater promise seemed to lie in the ideas of two other aspiring designers, both of whom were employed at the Balloon Factory and whom we have already met, namely Samuel Cody and John Dunne. While it could hardly be said of this pair that they were backed by unlimited resources, they at least had the support of Colonel Capper and the army's aeronautical depot, small though it was. By contrast, a third striver, their contemporary Roe, who was destined to become one of the leading names in the British aeronautical industry, was obliged during those early days to struggle on completely alone, supported by little more than his own determination.

All three had been studying the problem of flight for several years. In Cody's case, it was in 1905 that he had first begun to turn his thoughts away from kites and airships and towards the building of an aeroplane. If the steps he took were slow and deliberate, the reasons lay not only in lack of resources, but probably also in his own nature and – for lack of any formal technical education – his empirical approach. He was, for all that, far from being just a showman, moving solely within the make-believe world of the theatre. From quite early in the century, he was certainly in touch with such influential persons in the military aeronautical establishment as Baden-Powell, Templer and Capper; he was on terms of friendship with that enthusiastic patron of aviation, Patrick Alexander, while his kiting work had earned the recognition of

Above left and middle: The Cody glider kite, on the ground and in the air. (Jean Roberts. J. M. Bruce/G. S. Leslie)

Cody's 'Motor Kite', on the Common outside the balloon shed. (Jean Roberts)

the Aeronautical Society. It is therefore reasonable to assume that, assisted by such contacts, he had been introduced and gained access to some of the experimental results and theoretical data which were already available, which would have greatly assisted his education as a would-be aeroplane designer.

Like the Wrights and unlike Langley, Cody began with a glider, which was constructed at the Crystal Palace, where he had established his workshop the previous year. This 'Glider Kite' was of biplane configuration, its detailed structural design recalling to some degree its kite ancestry, although lacking the box form of the latter. The pilot lay prone on the lower wing, occupying a cradle, by means of which he could exert a rudimentary control over his machine. After initial trials at the Crystal Palace, it was taken to Farnborough, to the area on the southern side of the Basingstoke Canal known as the Long Valley, where its test-flying was continued, manned and unmanned, tethered and finally free, with some success. These flights represented useful if rudimentary piloting experience for Cody, though he did not keep the fun all to himself. His stepson Vivian was one who 'had a go', as were some of the Balloon School's aeronauts.

The next logical step was to fit a kite with an engine. A Cody kite was so equipped, using a puny 12-hp Buchet engine, and then 'flown' suspended along a wire, much as Stringfellow's model had been forty years previously. This was scarcely flying as the Wrights knew it. It was not even trying to fly in the way that other would-be pioneers were trying, gathering bruises and broken timber in the process. But the race is not always to the swiftest.

John Dunne had begun his own experiments on his return from South Africa, in the form of both helicopters and gliders, and was for a while associated with Sir Hiram Maxim. By July 1907, while Cody was preoccupied with the *Nulli Secundus*, Dunne had completed the construction in the Balloon Factory of a biplane glider, designated D.1, which was based on a design philosophy quite different from that of his contemporaries.

Dunne proposed that his machine would embody automatic stability – a characteristic which was highly regarded at a time when it was widely expected that the principal duty of the military aeroplane would be that of reconnaissance, thus continuing to fulfil what had been the function of the army's aeronauts since balloons were first introduced. Blessed with this useful quality, the Dunne machine could, it was hoped, maintain itself in balanced flight by counteracting any destabilising effect

The Maxim-Dunne glider, pictured at the Crystal Palace. The bearded Maxim is at right centre, while John William Dunne stands at the far left. (National Archives)

due to turbulent air without any intervention by its occupant, and thus allow him to concentrate on the essential military business of observation of the enemy's activities. Its designer contended that he could achieve this effect by drawing his inspiration from a plant which grew in tropical latitudes, called the zanonia. The seed pod of this plant is equipped with wing-like extensions on either side, on which, after leaving its parent, it glides to earth, much like the seed of our native sycamore. Copying Nature's aerodynamicist, Dunne gave the wings of his machine a 30-degree sweep-back, with increasing wash-out – i.e., a diminishing angle of incidence – towards the tips. In addition, it had neither a tail nor a front elevator, their functions being replaced by moving surfaces at the wing tips. The D.1 also possessed no undercarriage as such – merely a four-wheeled trolley on which the machine could be moved about and from which it was to be launched.

The project was distinguished by another feature – namely secrecy, in order to prevent what was considered to be its revolutionary design from being copied by undesirable – even foreign – parties. To this end, it was decided to seek some sparsely populated area where it was thought that the machine could be tested, safely hidden from inquisitive eyes.

During the war in South Africa, both Dunne and Capper had made the acquaintance of the eldest son of the Duke of Atholl, John George Stewart-Murray, Marquis of Tullibardine. The Marquis, widely and more familiarly known as 'Bardie', had been commissioned in the Royal Horse Guards (the Blues) in 1892 and had seen action with the cavalry at Omdurman, before volunteering for service the following year when the next imperial war, against the Boers, broke out. With the ending of that conflict, Tullibardine maintained his military associations, expanding the Yeomanry regiment, known as the Scottish Horse, which he had raised and commanded in South Africa during the war. With such a background, Bardie readily ensured that his father's permission was obtained for the flight trials of Dunne's aeroplane to be carried out in the sparsely populated uplands which formed part of the Duke's estate in Perthshire overlooking the family home, Blair Castle, and the associated village of Blair Atholl.

Thus it came about that in July 1907 Dunne, accompanied by the dismantled D.1, his civilian assistant Percy Gurr and a small party of sappers commanded by Lieutenant Francis Westland RE, set forth from Farnborough on the long railway journey north which ended when they alighted at the little station in Blair Atholl village, just outside the gates of Blair Castle itself. From there, they set out to climb up to the site chosen for the trials, which lay about a thousand feet higher up, on the grassy braes which lay between the steep-sided gorge of Glen Tilt and the lesser valley containing the Tilt's tributary, the Fender Burn. There, a wooden shed had been erected by local labour, in which the glider would be housed. For the humans, tents had been deemed to be adequate shelter and these had been pitched about a mile to the southward. The terrain they had chosen was characterised by meandering contours defining the slopes and hilltops from which, with the help of the wind, they hoped to soar into the air and test Dunne's theories in practice.

When all was ready, Colonel Capper came up to act as the test pilot. He had as much experience in this art as anyone else available, that is to say very little, but such was the way of it at that time. Watched by Tullibardine and a sprinkling of the local gentry, a number of glides were attempted, culminating in the almost predictable crash landing – an event which unfortunately took place during a visit by the two officers responsible for controlling Farnborough's aeronautical activities, Major-General Hadden, Master-General of the Ordnance (MGO), and his subordinate, Brigadier General Ruck, Director of Fortifications and Works. The enforced halt for the necessary repairs allowed two lately arrived 12-hp Buchet engines to be fitted, to enable the next phase, flight under power, to be attempted. Given the highly inadequate, not to say unsuccessful, amount of 'flying' which had been achieved with

Glen Tilt in 1907: The Dunne D.1 being brought out of its shed. (J. M. Bruce/G. S. Leslie)

The D.1 is lifted on to its wheeled cradle. (J. M. Bruce/G. S. Leslie)

the machine in the glider configuration, this seems unduly precipitous, to say the least. Unfortunately, time was pressing, for by then the shortening days were reminding them of the approach of winter, with its limited hours of daylight and indifferent flying weather ...

Meanwhile, the intense secrecy was maintained, numbers of the Duke's ghillies being mobilised to hold back inquisitive intruders. Even the local people, it was said in later years, were ordered at certain times to stay within their crofts on the hillsides and keep the curtains drawn! However, despite – or perhaps because of – all the efforts at concealment, rumours began to circulate and the area inevitably attracted the attentions of the press. Persons of a sufficiently enterprising and inquisitive bent were soon probing

With the slopes of Carnliath behind him, Colonel Capper is in his seat and ready to go. (Blair Castle)

The D.1, with Capper aboard, lifts into the air. (J. M. Bruce/G. S. Leslie)

After the crash: D.1 being inspected by onlookers, some knowledgeable, others less so. (J. M. Bruce/G. S. Leslie)

the security screen for holes through which they might crawl undetected, striving to obtain at least a distant peep at the mysteries beyond. By the time the machine was ready to begin its powered trials, the *Daily Express* had its 'Special Correspondent' in the area who, writing from nearby Dunkeld on 26 September, seems to have contrived to approach near enough to get the gist of what was going on:

> The machine, a lightly built, delicately framed structure, was brought out from its shed shortly before midday. In general appearance, as seen through a pair of powerful field glasses, it is like a large butterfly, with wings always extended, and an airiness that would seem unequal to the results it is expected to achieve.

He spoke more wisely than he knew. Going on to describe that day's abortive attempts, he reported that:

> The engineers who are in charge of the station ran the machine for some distance on attached wheels, when the motors responded to the touch of the man on deck who sits immediately behind the whirling screws. But before the aeroplane rose into the air a gust of wind blowing heavily down the valley from the east swept by, and the ropes by which the machine was held were not released.
>
> The machinery was stopped awhile, but a few minutes later the pulsating of the motor again broke upon the stillness of the mountain air. The screws revolved once more at so rapid a pace that in the sunlight they looked like catherine wheels, but the wind rose into a gale that stormed down the gap, and realising the impossibility of further experiments the aeronauts stopped the motor and carried the machine back into its resting place.

Another dispatch the next day from the same source had no more progress to report, but was able to compensate for this with a gripping tale of cloak and dagger:

> Two agents of a foreign Government actually penetrated the mountain fastnesses. They were observed behind a ridge which commands the aeroplane shed, to which they had crept under cover of a Scotch mist. The Marquis of Tullibardine's scouts saw them, and made rapidly up the slope. The foreigners retreated, and left behind them a telescopic lens, field glasses and cameras.

When fairer weather did eventually favour the party's efforts, the limited success achieved with the glider and the even more limited flying experience of the pilot made another crash more or less inevitable. This duly took place, and with the year now well advanced, trials were abandoned for the winter and the party returned to Farnborough with the pieces, for further repairs, reflections and modifications.

Colonel Capper, in his report of the trials, tried to illuminate them with the most favourable light he could devise:

> The result, though to an unskilled eye merely disastrous, in effect showed that Lieutenant Dunne's calculations and experiments were entirely correct, the machine remaining poised during a period of eight seconds.

Meanwhile, Cody, encouraged and assisted by Capper, was engaged in building his first proper aeroplane in the Balloon Factory workshops. With his duties as Chief Kiting Instructor (which included being lent to the Royal Navy – who were at that time showing renewed interest in kites – for ship-borne trials in the Solent) and his involvement with the *Nulli Secundus* claiming much of his attention, it proved to be some considerable time in the building, a period which was not diminished by that all-too-frequent headache of the early pioneers, the need to acquire an engine offering adequate power. This latter finally became available during the summer of 1908, in the shape of a 50-hp Levavasseur Antoinette, and it was September before the complete aeroplane at last emerged for trials. It took the form of a biplane, endowed with the hopefully portentous title of 'British Army Aeroplane No.1' (BAA No.1). It owed much to the Wright Flyers, being equipped with a forward elevator, or foreplane, and a rear-mounted, fixed vertical stabiliser, but departed from Wright principles to the extent of having a wheeled undercarriage, rather than skids, being intended to rise from the ground entirely under its own power, unlike the Flyer, which was launched by a form of catapult. The engine arrangement was similar to that of the Wrights, driving two contra-rotating pusher propellers. The wings, unlike those on the Wrights' machines, were covered on the top surface only. So far as directional – or lateral – control was concerned, a rudder mounted above the top wing seemed to be the only means by which this was to be achieved. Cody had given the question some thought and had originally intended to complement the rudder with ailerons, positioned at the extremities of the wings, but for the time being had decided against them. In those days, the other method used to alter a machine's bank angle was by 'wing warping' – in other words, by differentially distorting the wing profile, to increase the camber of the wing section (and hence the lift generated) on one side, while decreasing it on the other. This was the method the Wrights used, but was not incorporated in the Cody. Or at least, so it has generally been thought; recent research, however, derived from a more sophisticated analysis of the relevant photographs, now allows us tentatively to suggest otherwise.

Whichever control system was used, the pilot's means of operating it comprised a wheel (for directional control), which was mounted at the top of a column (for control in the pitching plane), the latter being pivoted at its base to allow it to be moved in a fore and aft sense, while both the wheel and the column were connected to their respective control surfaces by cables. There were no rudder pedals as later became the standard mode, and Cody's feet, with no duties to perform, were free to be planted firmly and comfortably on the floor of his 'cockpit'. Finally, for experimental purposes, the overall wing camber and its incidence could be altered on the ground. The machine was considerably larger and heavier than the original Wright and could not be said to present an impression of either beauty or grace.

While Cody advanced laboriously towards his goal, Roe, like Dunne, was already attempting to 'collect the breeze'. His own chosen testing ground was at Brooklands, in Surrey, where he might well have expected to find fellow-feeling and a welcome from similarly adventurous and forward-looking young men at the newly opened motor racing track there. While that may have been so, it was certainly not the case with regard to the Brooklands management, which seems to have looked upon him as nothing but an unmitigated nuisance. The first of his designs was a tail-first biplane, powered by a JAP motorcycle engine, which supplied all of nine horsepower to turn a rather primitive pusher propeller. Such exiguous assistance having altogether failed to get him into the air, he managed to arrange for the loan of a 24-hp Antoinette engine. This was not immediately available, so, rather than allow himself to be subordinated to events, he had himself towed up behind a motor car a few times, which at least enabled him to test the airborne behaviour of his craft. That the arrival and installation of the new engine, in May 1908, should then coincide with a notice to quit from the Brooklands management was just one more example of the kind of obstacle course over which the dogged young pioneer was being forced to run in order to reach his still-distant goal. He negotiated a brief stay of execution, during which he at last recorded the solid achievement of making some short airborne 'hops'. Although not true flights – the longest appears to have been no more than sixty yards – Roe was on his way. Unfortunately, by then, he was also on his way out of the gates of Brooklands. This finally took place in mid-July, and although he at once began searching for an alternative site, for a while, his work found itself at a halt.

The British Army Aeroplane No.1 in October 1908. (J. M. Bruce/G. S. Leslie)

A front view of BAA No.1, somewhat askew, with its propellers turning. (J. M. Bruce/G. S. Leslie)

A. V. Roe's first biplane, fitted with its inadequate 9-hp JAP engine. Behind: the celebrated banked racing track at Brooklands. (Author's collection)

Roe working on his biplane, now fitted – temporarily – with a 24-hp Antoinette. (Author's collection)

2

Europe Awakes

While reactionary forces bound young Roe to the earth, progress at Farnborough could scarcely be described as dynamic. Dunne had passed the winter of 1907/8 in building a small second machine – another glider – with the designation D.3, which would be used to explore the general handling characteristics of his designs. At the same time, the D.1 was rebuilt to convert it into the D.4, to be powered by a 30-hp REP engine. But this all took some while and by the time everything was ready for the return to Scotland, the summer, with its better flying weather, had once more nearly run its course.

Samuel Cody, for his part, had even less progress to report. With the *Nulli Secundus* rebuilt and demanding his attention, he had been obliged to abandon his aviation work for a while and concentrate once more on lighter-than-air matters.

Across the Channel, on the other hand, events of a more positive nature were taking place. In 1907, following their collaboration with Santos-Dumont, the Voisin brothers succeeded in designing their own successful aeroplane, another pusher biplane with a front-mounted elevator. Although of somewhat rudimentary design (there were no roll controls, turning being achieved on the rudder alone), the the Voisins' machines were the best thing France had produced so far and several examples had been built and supplied to customers keen to take to the air. Foremost amongst these was the Anglo-Frenchman Henri Farman who, not content with teaching himself to fly, was already pursuing ambitions in the design field, by incorporating in Voisins' machine ideas of his own. By the autumn of 1907, he had made a number of flights of an elementary nature from the military training ground at Issy-les-Moulineaux, a couple of miles away on the other side of the Seine, which he and another would-be pilot, Léon Delagrange, had chosen as their flying field. Starting with short, straight flights, he gradually learned to manoeuvre his machine in the air. On 13 January 1908, Farman took an important step forward, when he yawed his modified Voisin around a circuit of one kilometre, remaining in the air for 1 minute and 28 seconds. It was the first such flight in France, gaining him the Deutsch-Archdeacon *Grand Prix d'Aviation*, worth 50,000 francs. However, *les Frères Voisin* were not the Wright Brothers. Before many months had passed, Farman's feat was to be eclipsed by Wilbur Wright himself, in the course of a series of demonstration flights from French soil which were to be both a revelation and an inspiration.

The Wrights had not wasted their self-imposed grounding, but had built several new and improved versions of their original Flyers, which are now usually referred to as the Wright Type A, and one of these had been lying in its packing case at Le Havre for some months, waiting for Wilbur to arrive. In May 1908, he took passage by transatlantic liner and disembarked at the same port. Renewing contacts he had made on previous visits, he arranged for his machine to be transported to Le Mans, where he planned to reassemble it in the factory of a friend, Léon Bollée, who would in due course build engines for some of the later Wrights. The job proved to be considerably more lengthy than he had expected, for when the case was opened, Wilbur found

84   *L'Aéroplane Voisin. – LL.*

Above left: A Voisin aeroplane in 1908. (Author's collection)

Above right: Henri Farman and Gabriel Voisin, who formed a short-lived partnership. Their collaboration came to an abrupt and acrimonious end when Voisin sold a machine, which he had previously promised to Farman, to another customer. (Author's collection)

22   LES PIONNIERS DE L'AIR
M. Henri FARMAN, sur son Aéroplane, boucle un Circuit fermé
de 1,500 mètres, le 13 Janvier 1908,
et gagne le premier Grand Prix d'Aviation " Deutsch-Archdeacon " (50,000 fr.)

C. M.

Henri Farman, accompanied by much jubilation, winning the *Grand Prix d'Aviation* at Issy-les-Moulineaux on 13 January 1908, for the first flight in Europe around a circular course. (Author's collection) the contents in some disarray, insecure packing having caused the components of the dismantled aeroplane to suffer considerable damage when the case was handled during its journey and storage. Philosophically, after his fashion, he set to work to effect the necessary repairs.

In France, as in Britain, there were many, even in 1908, who chose to believe that the Wrights had not flown as they said they had. In France in particular, the successes of their own pioneers, limited though they were, had served to encourage this disbelief. If the Wrights were liars, then it was Santos-Dumont – almost a Frenchman – who had been the first man to fly, followed by the increasingly impressive feats – as it seemed – of their own pilots. June passed and then July. Farman was flying, Delagrange was in the air, so was Blériot, so was Ferber, yet there seemed to be no sign of the American emerging from his workshop, ready to confront the doubters. The sceptics were reinforced; one newspaper put it bluntly, asserting, '*Le bluff continue.*' The target of their disparagement remained indifferent and got on with his work.

August had begun its course by the time Wilbur had satisfied himself that the machine was finished and ready to show its paces. On the 8th, the Flyer was carried to the nearby racecourse at Hunaudières, where it was prepared for flight. Its launching pylon was erected and the aircraft hoisted on to the take-off rails. A large crowd had assembled to watch, its emotions consisting of a mixture of anticipation and scepticism. However, as soon as Wright was launched into the air, these were rapidly replaced by admiration, as he immediately showed a facility in manoeuvring his craft which confounded his former detractors and amply demonstrated his machine's superiority over any which his hosts had so far managed to devise.

Happily, the latter, far from being deterred, were spurred to greater efforts, so much so that, by that autumn, both Henri Farman and Louis Blériot, who had now joined the former at the front of the stage, had acquired the ability and the confidence to leave their own flying fields and fly across country for the first time. Wright's reply, on the last day of the year, was a flight of over two hours circling his airfield at the Camp d'Auvours, some ten kilometres to the north-east of Le Mans, to which he had shifted his operations. This earned for him the world records for duration and closed circuit distance, as well as the Michelin Cup for the longest flight around a closed circuit that year. On the other side of the Atlantic, Orville was performing a similar and equally impressive series of flights for the benefit of the American army at Fort Myer, Virginia, albeit sadly marred by a crash in which his passenger was killed and Orville seriously injured.

30 October 1908: Farman prepares to take off from his flying field near Châlons-sur-Marne, at the start of the world's first cross-country flight. (Author's collection)

The Wright Type 'A' outside its shed at the Camp d'Auvours, near Le Mans. (Author's collection)

Middle and below: Two more views of the Wright aeroplane at the Camp d'Auvours, showing, in the lower picture, the weight being raised in the launching pylon. (Author's collection)

Colonel S. F. CODY in his Aeroplane.—London to Manchester flight.

Throughout this time, reports of the activities of both the Wright brothers were appearing in the *Daily Mail* almost every day. On 5 October, with such positive evidence that the aeroplane was showing itself to be a practical means of transport, the paper announced that it was offering a prize of £500 for the first pilot to succeed in crossing the English Channel, in either direction. This was the second prize it had put up – and was not to be the last – in Northcliffe's determination to do what he could to advance the cause of aviation. Two years earlier, fired by the revelation in the Bois, he had announced a reward of £10,000 for the first pilot to fly from London to Manchester. The latest initiative, with its implied disturbance of Britain's insular seclusion, created immediate interest – although the wide disparity between the value placed by the *Mail* on a flight across the perilous waters of the Channel and one above the relatively benign countryside of the English Midlands seems surprising!

Wilbur Wright, having already demonstrated his capability with a flight of nearly twice the distance involved, was the clear favourite, but disdained involvement. However, other names soon appeared in the lists, some by then eminently credible, others less so. One of the latter kind was a certain Prince Serge Bolotoff, twenty-one years old and apparently a member of the Russian royal family. The Prince, it was reported, had 'invented' an aeroplane, which was to be constructed for him by the Voisins. It would be a triplane powered with a 100-hp engine and would be 'self-righting'. He hoped, said the *Daily Mail*, to make the attempt in about a fortnight's time.

By the time that the two Wrights were astonishing their respective audiences with their skills, both Cody and Dunne had resumed their own considerably less impressive efforts. With the *Nulli Secundus*'s brief second career over, Cody was free to return to his now-complete aeroplane. For his own flight tests, he disdained the secrecy surrounding the Dunne project, simply choosing for the purpose the adjacent Farnborough Common, the site from where the Balloon School had habitually launched its aerial vehicles.

At that stage in aviation's development, with no proper airfields yet in existence in Great Britain, the use of Farnborough Common as Cody's testing ground seems to have been not so much a considered choice as a natural continuation of the use of a location which lay conveniently just outside the doors of the Balloon Factory and which had been perfectly suitable for all the aerial craft which the Balloon School had operated up to that time. Apart from its convenience, however, for Cody's purpose the Common had little to recommend it. It was far from flat, with Jersey Brow a short distance to the west, while the Swan Inn Plateau arose little more than a hundred yards to the south. Worse, it was dotted with copses and other vegetation, while, as if such fixed hazards as those were not enough, both members of the public and cattle were free to roam and, if not controlled, were liable to add to the obstacles confronting a would-be aeroplane pilot.

On Saturday 19 September 1908, the ungainly-looking machine was wheeled out of the airship shed for the first time, accompanied by its designer and Colonel Capper. The former sat himself between its array of spruce struts and wires, the engine was started and the pilot began a painstaking programme of tests, which were prudently restricted to taxiing the aeroplane about at moderate speeds, to allow Cody to start familiarising himself with the behaviour of his machine and its response to movements of the controls, as well as exploring the behaviour of the engine.

Although secrecy had been laid aside, Capper was by no means anxious for Cody's creation to be plagued by excessive newspaper curiosity. Therefore, two days before the aircraft's first emergence from the privacy of its shed, the factory had taken the step of writing to the editors of certain of the national dailies, enjoining them to, in effect, stay away, ostensibly on safety grounds:

> Dear Sir,
>
> I wish to ask for your kind cooperation to prevent risk of accidents to the public, in the event of trials being made shortly, with an aeroplane designed by Mr Cody.
>
> No attempt will be made to fly in the initial experiments but if the Press should publish information that the experiments are taking place, or are about to take place, the experiments will inevitably be greatly interfered with by the crowd, and there will be constant fear of damage to someone, whilst the policing of the ground entails a great deal of extra work on the police and troops, and is well nigh impossible to carry out properly.
>
> For these reasons I earnestly hope that you will refrain from publishing anything on the subject until after the initial experiments.
>
> Should these experiments result in sufficient success to warrant the Press sending representatives, I will then let you know that attempts will be made to fly, but will ask you not to publish the fact beforehand, otherwise the crowd that would assemble would effectively prevent any attempt to fly.
> Yours faithfully
> A.D. Carden, Captain R.E.
> for Superintendent, Balloon Factory

In these days of unbridled media interference in any activity which catches its eye, it must perhaps be the subject of some surprise that Capper thought it possible to make such a plea – and even greater surprise that it should have received apparently sympathetic responses. The reply from the Standard may be taken as a representative sample:

> Dear Sir,
>
> Many thanks for your letter, and we shall be glad to have the information when the Aeroplane makes the definite trial. Meantime, we will abstain from sending down specially, and are relying on you to give us notice in advance, as you so kindly suggested. We know, of course, that you cannot guarantee that the Aeroplane will go out on any suggested day.
> Yours faithfully
> C. Watney

Such a courteous and cooperative reply induces wistful thoughts of how much more *restrained* journalists were in those far-off days, until we read this plaintive protest which Capper received from the *Daily Express* a few days later:

> Dear Sir:

The other day you wrote to us to ask us not to mention in any way the aeroplane trials which were about to be made.

I naturally gave instructions to everyone concerned that the matter should not be dealt with.

I can only conclude that your letter was a circular one and that it reached the 'Chronicle' office just as safely as it did the 'Express'.

I was, however, I confess, surprised to see the enclosed in the 'Chronicle' and I should really be grateful if you would give your attention to the matter.

It is extremely hard on a newspaper which does its best to act in good faith, to be confronted by this sort of thing which practically places good faith at a premium.
Yours very truly,
W. Holt-White
News Editor

The *Daily Chronicle* article in question was a report describing, in some detail, the machine's outing on the 19th, which makes our hearts go out to Mr Holt-White, that he should thus find himself beaten by a competitor acting in such an underhand way. Or rather it does until we remember that, the year before, it was his man who, by furtive clambering across the Scottish hills, had stolen a march on the other papers at Blair Atholl!

A month passed, with the incorporation of various adjustments and modifications interspersed between further careful exploratory trials, including some airborne hops, sometimes on the Common, occasionally further off on Laffan's Plain, while the journalists seemed to experience no difficulty in contriving to report such activity as took place. During this period, the work suffered further interruption when Cody was once more called away for a while to assist the navy's kiting experiments. This laborious rate of progress was hardly calculated to please the press, which had already found in this flamboyant American, whose achievements seemed to consist of nothing more than running his 'invention' around the Common, a convenient object

Kiting with the Royal Navy: unusually, in this case, the chair or basket normally used has been replaced by a breeches buoy. (Jean Roberts)

of ridicule.

At this point, as we wait for Cody's return, we have perhaps found a suitable moment to digress, in order not to omit a short reference to an item which, while not usually to be found amongst the equipment of an experimental engineer, he seems to have found of great use and which subsequently became a celebrated part of Farnborough folklore – namely, Cody's Tree. According to tradition, it was at some time during those years that the tree in question was chosen by Cody to provide him with a stout if homely anchorage to which he could on occasion tether his aeroplane for the purpose of test-running its engine, possibly even to the extent of measuring the thrust developed. It was, in fact, one of a number which formed the copse lying alongside the Farnborough Road, just south of the factory, through which, later on in 1911, the Lebaudy dragged its mooring ropes in the course of its mad circuit around the Common. Much later than that, the remembrance of its participation in Cody's achievements made it honoured among trees, so that, protected by its humble fame, it was spared while the others around it fell to the woodman's axe, as more and more space was cleared to accommodate an expanding Royal Aircraft Establishment. It was even granted a plaque, nailed to its trunk, which commemorated its role in the great events with which it was associated. Many years later still, it fell a victim of common mortality and died of some arboreal disease; however, though all attempts to save it failed, it remains commemorated, for an aluminium replica was made and installed in its place. This still stands on the Farnborough site, by way of a monument, though it is perhaps a pity that its subject is depicted, not in the proud and useful days of its virility, but with twisted branches, forlornly innocent of all leaves, as it was at the end.

It was 13 October when Cody at last returned from the sea and the aeroplane was once more brought out of its shed. On that day and the next, he made several runs during which he succeeded in rising into the air for a significant distance, though without accomplishing that which could be claimed as a flight. It was two days later that he finally broke free. The key seems to have lain in the facility to adjust the camber of his wing section, which he had now reduced, thus improving the wing's lift/drag ratio, or in other words, reducing the drag tending to restrict the speed of the machine while allowing the wing to contribute nearly as much lift as before. He had also adjusted the pitch of his propeller blades, in an effort to obtain the maximum forward thrust from his engine.

On Friday the 16th, BAA No.1 once more emerged onto the Common. The Union flag, which had hitherto been modestly attached to the base of a wing strut, was now fluttering defiantly from the top, presaging greater things, as in fact it turned out. To begin with, Cody made another short 'hop' of about 50 yards, at the end of which he alighted on the Swan Inn Plateau – having thus flown uphill. There, he turned his machine about and prepared to return.

It happened that Capper was absent that day and it may well be that the designer-pilot, feeling himself freed from the Colonel's restraining influence, allowed himself more scope than he had hitherto. Capper himself, in his official report, records Cody's 'astonishment' that the machine then 'went to a considerable height'; Cody, on the other hand, in his lecture to the Aeronautical Society in the following December, suggested that he had been somewhat fed up with being 'accused of doing nothing but jumping with my machine', so that it would seem as if, goaded in that way, he had gone out deliberately intent on trying for real flight. It is certainly true that Cody the showman had seen to it that several photographers were present that day. At all events, with the cat away, that return journey developed into something more than a 'jump'.

The conditions he had chosen were not ideal. Whether Cody had at that time come to appreciate the simple basic rule which ordains that take-offs should, whenever

No 'hop' this time: BAA No.1 makes the first flight in Britain, on 16 October 1908. (Jean Roberts)

Middle and below: Unhappy ending! Two views of the damaged BAA No.1 after its first flight, from the starboard side (*above*) and from the rear (*below*). (Jean Roberts)

possible, be made into wind is not clear (certainly he did later, since he made the point in his December lecture to the Aeronautical Society). At any rate, when Cody set off from the Swan Inn Plateau on that particular day, he did so with the easterly wind behind him. His other problem was posed by his airfield, if such it can be called. The available landing area upon which Cody now gazed, as he prepared to launch himself on his first serious attempt to fly, would be viewed with disdain, if not alarm, by a modern pilot. Farnborough Common in those days was just that – a common, on which Nature was allowed full rein. Its surface was, appropriately enough, nothing but rough pasture with, in particular, a generous endowment of trees, thick enough in its more western reaches to be described as woodland. Although the part of the Common over which Cody was proposing to fly was relatively open, it was strictly limited in extent and certainly not free from encumbrances, in the shape of several small copses.

With his engine running at full power, he surged forward down the helpful slope and his wheels once more lost contact with the earth. In a shallow dive and with the light tail wind also helping him along, his ground speed became quite impressive and he soon found himself being carried beyond the comfort of the open space he had been used to. He was no more than a few feet off the ground, but it was sweeping past below him in a grassy blur at something approaching forty miles per hour. Samuel Cody, the consummate horseman, was riding a new kind of steed with whose wilful ways he was yet to become familiar, while he was handling controls in the use of which he lacked any practical experience. As he struggled to cope with these difficulties, another part of his brain found itself having to take into account the obstacles towards which his line of flight was swiftly carrying him. A clump of trees was getting alarmingly close, their tops reaching up to his own height and above. Now, whether he wished to or not, Cody was going to have to try to turn his machine in the air for the first time. Manipulating the controls as best he knew and probably hindered by the turbulent air in the vicinity of the trees, he was only partially successful. Banking to the left, he swept over and past them, though not without being pressed downwards by the unruly air, his left wingtip lightly touching the ground. Scarcely recovered from this encounter, he almost immediately found himself confronted with a second copse. With no more than seconds in which to react as he careered onward, he once more turned his control wheel. Slipping inwards as he turned, his left wing once more struck the ground, this time with a finality which pulled him down and round with a rending of wood and fabric as the machine came to a halt, with various pieces of its structure assuming attitudes sadly askew from their designer's original intention.

The pilot himself emerged unharmed and indeed triumphant, for although the flight had ended in an unfortunate manner, he had nevertheless demonstrated sustained flight and in doing so had covered a distance which, when measured, was found to be some 1,400 feet. Capper, turning up later in the day, was greeted, one might surmise, by an atmosphere of excitement and satisfaction, mixed, however, with trepidation, since unfortunately there was now an aeroplane, property of the War Office, lying in the airship shed with a crumpled left wing, buckled wheels and other damage. Repairs and modifications would keep it there for the rest of the year, but that day Cody had made what would come to be recognised as the first proper flight in Great Britain by a British aeroplane.

To Capper fell the delicate task of reporting these mixed fortunes to higher authority, in the best light he could manage. In two of the three reports which he submitted that day to the Director of Fortifications and Works, he stated successively that he did 'not propose to abandon trials with this machine', that he considered the aeroplane to be 'probably better than the Farman Delagrange type' and that 'Mr Cody has constructed an aeroplane which shows considerable promise'. DFW, in passing the reports up to the next level, the Master-General of the Ordnance, gave them his support, approving both of the continuation of the trials and of the retention of Cody to perform them. So far so good; though, since the whole project was Cody's brainchild, it might seem, on the face of it, a matter of surprise that, once the former point was conceded, the latter one needed any confirmation. However, one flight, with a broken aeroplane as a result, scarcely represented the scale of achievement which might be needed to overcome the anti-aviation (and anti-Cody) elements which dwelt among the higher reaches of the War Office.

Meanwhile, some six weeks before this significant event, the other protagonist, John Dunne, had returned to the hills above Blair Atholl to resume his abortive trials of the previous year. On 2 September, he was joined by a team consisting of a twenty-three-year-old militia lieutenant by the name of Lancelot Dwarris Louis Gibbs, Dunne's assistant Percy Gurr and two Royal Engineer corporals, all of them wearing civilian clothes in a continuing effort to avoid attracting the attention of inquisitive but unwelcome eyes.

The weather was not promising. Under lowering clouds and carrying the components of the small glider D.3, they made their way up Glen Tilt and climbed its side to the same operating base they had used the year before, on the undulating moorland below the sloping side of the hill known as Meall Dail Min. Whilst D.3 was bestowed in the shed which had been their hangar the previous year, the little party, in pouring rain, erected the tents which would once more be their own accommodation. D.4 had been left behind in the valley, in the castle's Lower Park, where a second shed had been erected to house it. It was yet to be fitted with its engine, for this had been left behind at Farnborough, where some difficulty was being experienced in bringing it up to a satisfactory condition.

The next fortnight was marked by almost continuous rain, sometimes accompanied by gale-force winds for good measure, as D.3 was slowly erected. By mid-September it was complete and ready for its trials. The Highland weather, however, was not, so to fill the time, perhaps usefully, the glider was slung from the shed roof and the men took it in turns to sit in it and hone their reactions, by learning to operate the controls as the glider was tilted this way and that.

After a few days of this rudimentary Link Trainer practice, the weather turned drier

The Dunne D.4 in the Lower Park at Blair Castle in 1908. (J. M. Bruce/G. S. Leslie)

and they at once seized the chance to venture out with the machine. With the local buzzards already demonstrating what good flying weather it was, as they soared and wheeled above their heads in a stiff westerly breeze, D.3 was placed on its trolley and pushed over the rough grass to some rising ground nearby, from which Dunne himself performed some short glides. Further flights of twenty to thirty yards followed during the next seven days, but by the end of the month, this strenuous activity amid the rigorous conditions of a Highland autumn had taken its toll and Dunne succumbed to the recurrent fever which had driven him from the army. Descending to the gentler conditions in the valley, he dosed himself with quinine, while with the help of Cpl Hughes and Percy Gurr, he concentrated on the erection of D.4. The party which remained in the windy hills to continue with the flying of D.3 had been increased to four by fresh arrivals, amongst whom was Lieutenant Westland, although he took no part in the flying (Dunne confided to Capper his view that 'his nerve is a bit gone') and soon faded completely from the scene. His departure left the field clear for Lancelot Gibbs to become the expedition's sole test pilot, for which task he revealed a considerable relish, treating the inevitable crashes with a blithe joviality.

On 9 October, he had an altercation with the turbulent air which he was learning to ride (on the D.3, the pilot sat in a form of saddle, with his legs dangling in modern hang-glider fashion):

> ... the wind then although both controls were down more or less took charge and lifted me about ten yards to the right. I brought her up to the wind and came down again, she then went up with a rush and lifted me till my feet were more or less powerless and came down again but with the right wing first which got caught in a small mound of grass. The wind then took the left part round ... and firmly deposited me and the glider upside down.
>
> I called out for the men to run like flies but they were not in time and over we went but in going over I had plenty of time to think so knowing that I should be deposited on my head if I did nothing I curled up like a ball (or at least as much of a ball as 6 ft 5 in can do) and came down as happy as plum duff. It must have been very funny to watch.

Surprisingly, only five days were needed to repair the resultant damage before they were out again, trying to find a cooperative wind, blowing up a suitable slope. Gibbs, having achieved only a few short glides from fairly gentle slopes in only moderate breezes, roamed off in search of a richer pasture. He found it on another hill nearby, whose greater elevation and steeper incline promised more ambitious results, and in his report to Dunne, he enthusiastically proposed it as his next launch site:

> ... I think starting well up I should be able to clear the trees, they are only 20 to 25 feet high...from the trees to the top is only about 150 to 200 feet up, so should get off in a stride or two...

Dunne hastened to veto his assistant's bold proposal.

But so far the project was hardly yielding the success for which Dunne and Capper had hoped. On 16 October, Gibbs made a series of glides into a 20-mph wind of which the best measured no more than 150 feet and 12 seconds duration. Later the same day, at around the time that Cody, some 400 miles to the south, was registering his epoch-making flight, Gibbs's efforts ended in a combination of farce and disaster:

> I started running with her to try and make her lift again but after a few paces I caught my foot in a mound of gorse and fell right through the A-piece and pretty well smashed up the whole of the centre.

That was enough for Dunne; he instructed the enthusiastic Gibbs to abandon trials with the small glider and bring his party down to the lower level, where he was anxious to bring D.4 up to flight-readiness, although its engine had still not left Farnborough, as the men of the Balloon Factory sought to make it function adequately. The day before, Dunne had received the following wire from Capper:

> ... the Pelterie engine has been giving a great deal of trouble. We have had to re-construct parts and another lever broke yesterday, so I am having a new set of levers and tappets made. They should be through by Saturday. We were unable to test the thrust owing to this breakage. The engine has been apparently running very well.

On 4 November, the engine, with its chassis, finally arrived, followed the next morning by Captain Alan Carden RE, the Balloon Factory's assistant superintendent. The latter opted to take a room at the local hotel, deeming a tent amid the Scottish moors in autumn unnecessarily Spartan. There he found Dunne, still far from well, also in residence, having forsaken his own tent for the warmth of the hotel no earlier than the previous day. Another fortnight passed, spent on fitting work and adjustments under Carden's direction, at the end of which all was deemed to be ready and D.4 was taken out for its first tests. Compared to the D.1 of the previous year, it now had, by virtue of the 'chassis', a permanent wheeled undercarriage, reminiscent, like the earlier trolley, of a large perambulator. A system of belts and drums carried the engine power to a pair of propellers, while vertical stabilising surfaces had been added between the tips of the upper and lower wings. The total weight of the craft, including pilot, was 1,035 lb and the wing area was 504 sq. ft, resulting in a wing loading of just over 2 lb per sq. ft, compared to about 1½ for the Wright and rather more than 2½ for the Cody. Some taxiing runs were carried out to explore its general behaviour, during which it exhibited no great desire to leave the earth. More days were then lost in further repairs to the engine; Saturday the 21st was a particularly discouraging day. The engine seemed reluctant to deliver its full power and some time was spent in hopeful activities such as spark plug cleaning, checking the timing and stripping the carburettor. With the engine once more assembled, the frustrated sappers were rewarded with a complete refusal to start. Further investigation then revealed that a certain L/Cpl Crossfield had connected up the plugs wrongly, a discovery which, with night approaching, brought a profitless day to its gloomy end. In his diary of events, Captain Carden forbore from recording what words, if any, passed between himself and the guilty man.

More discouragement was to follow in the next week, which was taken up with further engine faults and the necessary repairs, some of which involved train journeys to Pitlochry and back, where the nearest workshop facilities were to be found. Meanwhile, with every day that passed, the days grew shorter and the season moved remorselessly through autumn towards the approaching winter.

At last, on 30 November, all difficulties seemed to have been overcome and D.4 was wheeled out once more, this time hopefully to fly. With Gibbs at the controls, four attempts at flight were made, with different settings of the wing incidence. The machine remained loyally in contact with the ground, except that on the last run, its attendants, desperate to detect some portent of eventual success, noted that it 'lifted once when crossing slight hollow'. Four days later, it left mother earth again – for a distance of 10 yards. On 10 December, this record had been raised to 40 yards but, alas, the Scottish winter was once more signalling that their time was up. The following morning they began packing up in preparation for their return south, with very little to show for their efforts.

Colonel Capper prepared another report for the Director of Fortifications and

Works which cannot have been any easier to compose than earlier ones. In the letter accompanying the report, he tried to make the best of an exercise which, to a critical eye, would seem scarcely to have produced any worthwhile results at all:

> I forward herewith report on trials with Lieut. Dunne's Flying-machine.
>
> These trials, though appearing a failure, have in fact proved of very great value. The gliding trials have established the merits of the machine as regards stability, the running trials have put us right as regards construction in many points, and have proved the ability of the machine to steer.
>
> Though the H.P. is undoubtedly low I am of opinion that on suitable ground and after a comparatively inexpensive lightening of the chassis, and by using a lighter operator, we may yet get this machine to rise with the present engine. It is certainly worth while making the trial and I would advise this to be done before putting a heavier engine in the machine, which would mean the entire re-construction of the whole thing. At the same time I have come to the conclusion that it is almost impracticable for us to carry out these trials and keep them secret.
>
> During this season the papers have been exceptionally kind to us in refusing to publish any details and the Duke of Atholl has also shown the greatest kindness in putting his private park at our disposal. This park, however, is not very suitable as a trial ground as it is not really level and there are a number of trees dotted about it. Nor has the Glen Tilt Camp proved satisfactory as a site from which to practice gliding.
>
> I would recommend, therefore, that we put the machine together again at Aldershot, and carry out the trials here as soon as practicable, merely altering the chassis in view of the experience gained and using a lighter operator.
>
> The gliding experience is doubtless of very great value, but it is so difficult to get that we shall have to manage without it, and there seems but little doubt that rising from the ground for very short flights will be the easiest way to learn.

In fairness to both Capper and Dunne, a serious bugbear had been the use of an engine of faltering performance (Capper reported that, although the REP's nominal horsepower was 30, it rarely delivered more than 24), whose inability to accelerate the machine to flying speed was not helped by the unsuitably rough ground of the unwisely chosen testing ground. However, these technical subtleties are unlikely to have had great impact on the gentlemen in Whitehall, who, from the vantage of their desks, could only discern that no practical benefit had resulted from a not-inconsiderable outlay of time, manpower and money.

While dubiety hindered aviation's advance in this country, in France it continued to bustle forward; Louis Blériot and Henri Farman, building on their successes in the air, had now become aeroplane manufacturers. As the New Year dawned, the small staff in the former's workshops at Neuilly was working on a new project, a small monoplane called the Type XI, which in due course would accomplish great things. At around the same time, frustrated by the poor flying weather which the winter months had now brought to northern France, Wilbur Wright decided to move to the southern town of Pau, in the ancient county of Béarn, where he could hope to find better conditions. The town authorities were quick to welcome him and provided a suitable airfield in the open countryside on the north-western side of the town, at a location called la Lande du Pont-Long, where a hangar was erected. There, the famous American aviator pursued his operations with further demonstration and passenger flights, now extended to include the world's first flying school, Wright having started to give flying instruction to three selected pupils.

His days were warmed by the presence of Orville, recuperating from his injuries, and their sister Katherine, who had landed at Plymouth on 11 January and then crossed to France, in time to join Wilbur in Paris, before all three set off for Pau a day or so later. Once they had established themselves, they could count on a steady flow of visitors, especially from the other side of the Channel, for Pau in those days was a fashionable resort, much frequented by wealthy Englishmen. While King Edward might favour the sea air and the gaming tables of Biarritz, sixty miles to the west, there were others who found the quieter atmosphere of Pau rather more to their taste. Indeed, the town had much to attract a wealthy visitor from the north, particularly in winter, blessed as it was with a climate which was often mild, as well as being the reputed possessor of curative qualities. Its comfortable hotels and other amenities were enhanced by an attractive situation whose outstanding feature was the view of the mountain range forming the southern horizon, which on fine days could best be enjoyed in conjunction with a leisurely amble along the Boulevard des Pyrénées. From this broad promenade, raised above the river valley on a terrace which stretched from the modern Casino at one end to the medieval chateau at the other, the stroller could gaze across a pleasantly undulating landscape which climbed gradually upwards until it blended in the far distance into the sharp-etched rock faces and white peaks of the mountains themselves.

For the visitor from the north who sought pursuits of a more active nature than such gentle saunters, Pau offered a golf course, the first to be laid out in France. Alternatively, if the exercise offered by a tour of the eighteen holes was still not sufficient, another quintessential but more strenuous English sport was available. The Pau Hunt, complete with its stables and kennels, had been established for many years, and any English gentleman who so wished could ride to hounds through the nearby countryside as if he had never left the shires.

And now there was a new diversion. Those who felt inclined could drive out to the flying field and witness the new marvel, about which reports were appearing so frequently in the newspapers. A few of the visitors were driven by more serious intentions than mere curiosity, amongst the earliest of whom being the Hon. Charles Stewart Rolls, the third and youngest son of Baron Llangattock of The Hendre, in Monmouthshire. Already well-known as a racing driver and balloonist, he had met the Wrights previously on several occasions, and in 1908, both he and Baden-Powell had been among the favoured few who were taken up by Wilbur during his demonstration flights at the Camp d'Auvours. Now determined to become a pilot

Wilbur Wright flying above some of his visitors and their carriages at la Lande du Pont-Long. (Author's collection)

himself, Rolls's immediate intentions were focussed on the acquisition of an aeroplane for that purpose and his current visit was part of a tour to that end.

Other arrivals, in early February, included Lord Northcliffe (predictably) and Arthur Balfour, the former Conservative Prime Minister, who drove across from his hotel at Biarritz. They were not immediately rewarded with any flying, since their visit coincided with a period when the region chose to defy its reputation and produce several days of snow. However, when, on the 20th, King Alfonso XIII of Spain, also forsaking Biarritz for a day, motored over to see the marvel, the weather, bowing to this royal patronage, relented sufficiently to allow Wright to oblige his visitors by performing a couple of short flights. The following month, another monarch turned up, when King Edward VII also came across from Biarritz and a second royal command performance saw Wilbur being again catapulted from his launching rail, once alone and then a second time with Katherine on board.

Back in the more commonplace world of the Balloon Factory, Cody had not been idle. On 8 January 1909, he emerged once more with his machine not just repaired, but much modified. The most noticeable differences were twofold. The first concerned the disappearance of the so-called 'fantail', a triangular sheet of canvas which had extended the surface of the upper wing centre-section back to the tail. The second revealed a quite startling dimensional increase: while the wingspan remained the same, something like fifteen feet had been added to the tail booms, making the overall length of the machine nearly 50 per cent greater than before. Amongst other changes, the over-wing rudder had been moved forward to a position between the wings and the front elevator, while the latter had been enlarged and lowered somewhat. Differentially-moving surfaces had been added at the elevator tips to improve lateral control and the radiators had been moved further back and further outboard. Finally, the wing covering was now double – on the lower surface as well as the upper. For experimental purposes, many streamers were attached to points along the trailing edges, in an attempt to study the airflow – and incidentally revealing that, for all his untutored empiricism, Cody had given serious thought to the actions and responses of the medium through which he was attempting to fly.

That same day, Capper penned another long letter to the newspapers:

Dear Sir,

I have the honour to inform you that from now onwards we hope to be making trials with Mr Cody's aeroplane.

I am not at all anxious to attract publicity to these trials, as the ground we have is very cramped and there is danger both to the operator and to the onlookers if these are numerous.

We are, it must be understood, making no effort at present to get the machine off the ground except, it may be, for hops of a few yards. Questions of balance and control have to be studied thoroughly, and we do not want to rise on this cramped ground and have an accident as we had before the machine was reconstructed.

I therefore thought you would like to know that this practising is no serious attempt at flying. When we decide to make a real attempt on more open ground I shall be pleased to give you information confidentially, in order that you may, if you desire, have a representative on the spot. I should, however, be very averse to having the news given out before the trial took place.

When once the thing has been done successfully, of course there will not be the same objection to having some publicity.

I wish you also to understand that I cannot guarantee whether the machine will go out at any particular hour or on any particular date. It must go out just as we find it convenient, and weather conditions or necessities of making slight alterations may delay it from hour to hour, or from day to day.

You will also understand that it is most harassing to be continually asked questions as to when and where the machine is going to be tried, when I do not even know myself from hour to hour what it is going to do.

If I were to put up a notice as soon as we know I should of course attract the crowds that I desire to avoid.

I think it would probably at the present save a great deal of expense and trouble, if the papers desire to get information of these early trials, if they would combine to send one representative down, who could be permitted to stay in the porter's lodge in some sort of shelter and warmth, instead of loafing about, at great inconvenience to himself, in the cold on the Common.

I am,
Yours very truly,
Colonel.
Supt. Balloon Factory.

From the *Express* office, Holt-White sent an emollient reply:

January 9th 1909

Dear Sir:

In reply to your letter of yesterday's date I can only assure you as in the past we shall do our very best to fall in with your wishes. It is not, and never has been our desire to publish any thing that might be detrimental to the interests of the country and I am more than satisfied by your kind intimation that you will do your best to inform us when the serious trial will be made.

Yours very truly
W. Holt-White
News Editor

Meanwhile, Samuel Cody pursued his careful trials. That same day he tried a short 'hop' (an account of which, despite Mr Holt-White's assurance, could be found in the *Express* two days later) and then returned to his shed for a further change, which involved the removal of the differentially moving surfaces from the front elevator and their replacement with 'ailerons' positioned midway between the upper and lower wingtips.

On the morning of the 20th, he flew once more. Having taxied the machine to the top of Farnborough Plateau, he turned the engine off and, in his usual methodical way, walked back to examine the tell-tale tracks, which indicated that he had left the ground in several places. Then, returning to his machine, he turned it round (into wind this time), restarted the engine and opened it up to full power. As he gathered speed down the incline, he eased the nose of the machine upwards: once more his wheels left the ground, as they had done three months earlier. Once more, and for only the second time in his life, he was flying under power. The ensuing flight bore certain similarities to the first one, though with added and even more startling features. Surprised at losing contact with the earth so soon, he sought to check his ascent. Like all tyro pilots, he over-corrected, to find the ground once more rising up to meet him. He reversed his previous action, only to find the ground receding again and with alarming swiftness. Again he lowered the nose. But the land too was descending and his speed once more increasing, contributing more lift, opposing his attempts not to climb too high. To add to his difficulties, his flight path was taking him towards the factory. He was running out of space; he had to land. He moved his control to lower the nose, but in so doing, he caused the forward elevator to generate a higher aerodynamic load than its attachments were capable of bearing. Structural failure ensued. Before the onlookers' startled gaze, the front bamboo members broke, causing the complete elevator to detach itself from the machine and depart rearwards over the top of the

1111. - The British Army Aeroplane - L'Aéroplane militaire anglais, inventé par le Colonel Cody, arrive sur le terrain de Farnborough

Above left and middle: Never any shortage of helpful man- and horse-power from the Balloon School! The much-altered BAA No.1 under tow, on the way to make its second flight. (Jean Roberts / Author's collection)

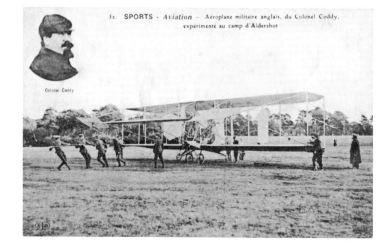

51. SPORTS - *Aviation* — Aéroplane militaire anglais, du Colonel Coddy, expérimenté au camp d'Aldershot

20 January 1909: with streamers attached to the trailing edges of the wings, BAA No.1 takes to the air for the second time. (Jean Roberts)

Another crash! BAA No.1 after its second flight. (Jean Roberts)

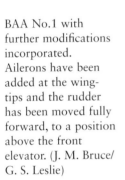

BAA No.1 with further modifications incorporated. Ailerons have been added at the wing-tips and the rudder has been moved fully forward, to a position above the front elevator. (J. M. Bruce/ G. S. Leslie)

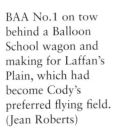

BAA No.1 on tow behind a Balloon School wagon and making for Laffan's Plain, which had become Cody's preferred flying field. (Jean Roberts)

wing. Deprived of its stabilising effect, the craft plunged downwards, to another unhappy meeting with the surface of Farnborough Common and another period of repairs in the factory, Cody himself being, once more, fortunate to escape unharmed. The magazine *Flight* was more than kind about the accident, averring that 'the mishap can hardly be attributed to any fault in the construction', but rather that 'it was primarily due to the absence of sufficient room in which to come to earth', leaving Cody with no option but 'to use the elevator for coming to earth, a proceeding which has probably never been attempted by even the most expert of pilots'. Knowledge of flight and the associated technique of piloting was indeed very patchy in those early days!

Despite the dramatic ending to the flight, only a month had passed before he was ready to try again, having strengthened his forward elevator support structure. He had now also decided to make Laffan's Plain, further away from the factory but less cluttered, his testing ground. On 18 February, BAA No.1 was towed to the new location, where, in the course of a short hop, Cody attempted a turn, but inexperience and trepidation got the better of him, and hastily abandoning the experiment, he came down heavily and burst a tyre in the process. On the following Monday, the 22nd, he tried the manoeuvre again and this time succeeded. From now on, he made steady progress, gradually learning to understand the machine's responses to his control movements and gaining skill and confidence thereby. During that portentous year, he doggedly pursued his trials, improving both his machine and his flying skills, until, by July, he was measuring his flights around Farnborough Common in miles. By that time though, the status of Cody, and of John Dunne too, had utterly changed.

The gentlemen in London who watched over the nation's interests were not blind to the portents for future warfare which were beginning to be exposed by the developing situation in the air. The result was that the Committee of Imperial Defence (CID) was asked to examine what action ought to be taken in that field. In response, on 23 October 1908, a week after Cody's momentous first flight and while Dunne in Scotland was awaiting the arrival of D.4's engine, the CID appointed a body, called the Aerial Navigation Sub-Committee, to which it delegated the task of examining and determining future policy with regard to military aeronautics. Its chairman was Reginald Baliol Brett, the second Viscount Esher, and its members included the War Minister, Richard Haldane; the First Lord of the Admiralty, Reginald McKenna; the Chancellor of the Exchequer, David Lloyd George; the Chief of the Imperial General Staff, General Sir William Nicholson; and the Master-General of the Ordnance, Major-General Sir Charles Hadden, who had witnessed the downfall of D.1 at Blair Atholl the year before. It was in the nature of things at that time that none of them could claim any real understanding of matters in the field of aviation. Indeed, in those early days, one of the major difficulties lay in finding anyone in authority who possessed sufficient relevant experience to be able to make a worthwhile contribution. However, in the course of several sittings during that autumn and winter, amongst the witnesses whom the sub-committee examined, there were four who were credited with being knowledgeable in the subject, though even their knowledge could scarcely be described as extensive. None of them had any experience of actually piloting an aeroplane, for at that time, there was only one Briton who could claim to be a recognised pilot and he had, perforce, learnt his flying in France and, during the time when the sub-committee was sitting, was still living and flying in that country.

Taking the witnesses in order of their appearance before the committee, the first was Charles Rolls who, as has been noted, had for some years been active in that world of balloons and motor cars which served as a nursery for so many of the early aviators. He had acquired the first of his several motor cars in 1896 and had been a keen competitor on the racing track before, in 1901, in company with that other sporting motorist, Frank Hedges Butler, he discovered ballooning. When, that same year, the Aero Club of the United Kingdom (later Royal) was founded, he and Butler were among the founder members. In 1906, he formed his famous motor manufacturing partnership with Henry Royce. At the time that the committee was sitting, he was negotiating with the Wrights to purchase one of their machines, but it would be some time before it became available and, at the time of his appearance before the sub-committee, he was yet to begin to learn to fly. For all that – and the reflection is instructive – although Rolls had no more than one or two short passenger flights to his name, he could claim that this meagre flying experience was greater than that of any of the other witnesses examined.

After Rolls, the second witness was Major B. F. S. Baden-Powell, balloonist, kiting pioneer and immediate past-president of the Aeronautical Society. The third witness, not surprisingly and entirely appropriately, was Colonel Capper himself (who was to enjoy the first flight of his life – with Cody – in the following August). Lastly came the sixty-eight-year-old inventor Sir Hiram Maxim, the designer many years earlier of that steam-driven aeroplane which, although discouraged from flying, had tried to do so and had crashed in the process. Since those days, Sir Hiram had busied himself with other matters and aviation had tended to recede to the periphery of his work.

It was at the committee's second meeting, on 8 December, that Rolls gave his evidence, followed later the same day by Baden-Powell. Both firmly favoured the aeroplane over the dirigible as the military aircraft of the future, in the face of strong scepticism, particularly from General Nicholson. Rolls, in his evidence, pressed the aeroplane's value as a reconnaissance vehicle, a proposition which was met by disbelief from Nicholson, who was inclined to dominate the questioning: 'You are going then at a minimum rate of 30 miles an hour, and a maximum rate of 100 miles an hour, and by that means you are going to see and report what the enemy is doing?' Receiving from Rolls an affirmative reply, Sir William, who was clearly not without some experience of modern life, riposted, 'I can only say that if you travel at that pace in a motor-car you will not see much of what an enemy is doing.'

With his flying experience limited to a couple of circuits in France as Wilbur Wright's passenger, Rolls was left with no choice but to fall back on his much greater experience in balloons, from which 'you can see a great deal'. Unfortunately, since gently sailing balloons were clearly not to be compared with swiftly flying aeroplanes, his response necessarily lacked sufficient authority to correct General Nicholson's confident but erroneous analogy between the view from an earthbound motor car and that from an aeroplane, high above the target of its observations, and the General emerged as master of the field, his belief in the rightness of his views unharmed.

Having completed his evidence, Rolls set off to return to his office in Conduit Street, brooding over the matter as he went. Having been summoned to assist the committee in the role of expert witness, he had had his advice contemptuously crushed by a man exercising the power of his high position but ignorant of the realities of the case. Once arrived and no doubt smarting from the withering dismissal his contribution had earned from Sir William, he immediately sat down and composed a letter to the committee's secretary, Sir Charles Ottley, in which he attempted once more to press his point:

> I did not have an opportunity of answering the objection raised by one of the members of the Committee against the possibility of making observations of any value from an aeroplane when the speed must of necessity be over 30 miles an hour. He mentioned that observations could not be made from a motor-car travelling at

such a speed; but this simile does not in the least apply, for rushing along the surface of the ground on a motor-car is entirely a different thing to travelling at the same speed in an elevated position of 500 or 1,000 feet from the ground. I have travelled at 50 miles an hour in a balloon, and have had no difficulty whatever in taking in all useful particulars of the surrounding country. In the case of an aeroplane, if it cannot take in all the information it requires in one passage it has only to circle round again – say, in the opposite direction.

It is to be hoped that this *esprit d'escalier* by Rolls found a ready ear amongst some of the committee members, if not that of Sir William Nicholson; it is, however, illustrative of the general and widely held misapprehensions about flying in those days that such an explanation needed to be made.

Baden-Powell, following Rolls, also supported the use of the air for reconnaissance purposes, giving an affirmative reply to a proposition put by Lloyd George, who asked:

Would a balloon or aeroplane be of very much use in discovering whether troops, ships and materiel had been accumulated at a given port, say, for the invasion of this country; supposing Germany, for instance, were accumulating ships, materiel and troops?

Lloyd George then took the discussion an important stride further with the question: 'What damage could a continental enemy inflict upon us by these machines?' Baden-Powell's answer revealed that his imagination had advanced beyond most people's at that time – a full seven months before Louis Blériot awakened the country to its first realisation of the possible dangers which the conquest of the air was threatening to present:

I think myself that aeroplanes might be used for invasion in this way : A small machine, such as the Wright type, capable of carrying three or four men, is very easily made and is very cheap comparatively, and a continental nation might easily have several thousand of them made. Then there is no doubt about it they could come over England – these machines can travel several hundred miles – and if each had three or four men on it in that way a good force could be carried.

The examination of the third witness, John Capper, took place a week later. It was lengthy and covered a considerable amount of ground, with most of the early questioning concentrating on balloons, both tethered and dirigible, and on kites. After Capper had revealed himself as an advocate for the use of 'dirigible balloons' as bombers, the questioning turned for a while to aeroplanes. After a rather cursory enquiry about progress at Blair Atholl ('that aeroplane in Scotland') and an even briefer reference to Cody, some time was spent in discussing how high Capper thought an aeroplane could be made to fly, no one, including the Wrights, having yet tried to rise more than a few hundred feet above the ground. Haldane, probably the most scientifically erudite of all the committee, understood that diminishing air density with altitude was a restricting factor, but also acknowledged that height was needed to render an aeroplane safe from ground fire. So – how high was necessary and how high was possible? Capper, clutching at a figure, thought that 2,500 feet might be the answer to both questions.

It was probably with some relief that the committee found itself returning to discussion of the more familiar subject of the lighter-than-air field. Tackled on the possibility of aerial combat and asked how he would propose to attack an enemy airship, Capper responded with an answer which, although it must now seem to us quaint, may appear rather less odd if one considers both the state of technology and the practical experience then at his disposal:

> If it was the ordinary balloon now abroad I should try and cut him in half. You could get above him and let your rope down across him as you go across him. That would be the quickest way to get rid of him, if you could manage it … you should get your anchor into it, or anything like that.

Aeroplanes returned temporarily into consideration when in their case the witness more conventionally suggested 'an ordinary rifle' as the means of attack, thereby correctly anticipating future events during the early weeks of aerial warfare, six years later. After this, the committee reverted to its more favoured field and much of the remainder of the interview concentrated on the use of balloons and dirigibles to assist the artillery.

On 28 January, it was the turn of the last of the expert witnesses, Sir Hiram Maxim. The latter, despite the rather limited practical contribution he had made to Man's conquest of the air, seemed to be in no doubt of his status as the country's leading expert on the science of aviation, beginning by declaring that 'all machines that raise themselves from the earth are made on my lines exactly' and that he 'was the first man in the world ever to make one that would lift its own weight'. He then confirmed his credentials with the even more breath-taking assertion: 'I am familiar with everything that has ever been done on this planet regarding flying-machines.'

At this point, one might imagine the members of the sub-committee starting to exchange uncertain glances with one another. Pushing on with his examination, Lord Esher enquired: 'Do you claim now that you can improve on the Wilbur Wright machine?' Sir Hiram certainly did; he would be 'very sorry' if he 'could not make a better job than that'; he graciously acknowledged that the Wrights 'have got the right thing', but condemned it as 'an extremely rough job'. So 'what is stopping you now from making an aeroplane which is better than the Wilbur Wright aeroplane?' enquired Lord Esher. Well, said Maxim, he was still 'working hard at the drawings' (fourteen years after his last effort!) and he had gone so far as to make a suitable carburettor:

> I found, for instance, there was no such thing as a good carburettor in existence – I mean not good enough to put on a flying machine. No man can tamper with a carburettor whilst he is in the air, the carburettor has got to look after itself then, in all temperatures and with all pressures of liquid. I have made one that will do that.

Well, that's a start anyway. But there were other mountains to climb. Sir Hiram had, he told the committee, already spent £30,000 on his aviation work and his wife, as wives will, had forbidden him to spend any more. Perhaps, then, the cost could be borne by his company, Vickers Sons & Maxim? The trouble there was Albert Vickers, the head of the company, who, although 'one of the cleverest men in existence … has always ridiculed the idea of flying-machines'. After that, although his examination went on for some time longer, the possibility of Maxim actually producing an aeroplane faded away amid less immediate questions such as the height an aeroplane could reach bearing a heavy load (2,000 or 3,000 feet), the interference of cloud with airborne observations and the cost of building an aeroplane (£1,500).

At the end of January 1909, the sub-committee reported to the CID. Its conclusions with regard to aeroplanes were far from conclusive. It was certainly with a large degree of justification that it found that they 'can scarcely yet be considered to have emerged from the experimental stage', but then, moving through phrases such as 'it has yet to be shown' and 'it is not quite certain', it emerged into a fog of indecision with the statement that:

> The Committee have not been able to obtain any trustworthy evidence to show whether great improvements may be expected in the immediate future, or whether the limit of practical utility may have already been nearly attained.

Feeling altogether more comfortable in the lighter-than-air sphere, it recommended that the forthcoming Estimates should include £35,000 for the building of a rigid airship for the navy and £10,000 to the army 'for continuing experiments with navigable balloons of a non-rigid type, and for the purchase of complete air-ships or their component parts'. As for the problematical aeroplane:

> The experiments carried out at the military ballooning establishment with aeroplanes should be discontinued, but advantage should be taken of private enterprise in this form of aviation.

Looked at from the standpoint of the politicians on the committee, this last decision at least had the advantage of transferring all future development costs, whatever they might be, from the public purse to the private sector (the books revealed that the disturbing sum of £2,500 had been expended on the Cody and Dunne trials). Let these and other experimenters struggle on unaided; if they could make something of this tricky question and the results turned out to be useful, the subject could be looked at again, meanwhile, government money could be better directed to supporting the more promising airship. The immediate effect, however, was the recommendation to abandon all trials of both Cody's and Dunne's aeroplanes. This was officially agreed and the pair were duly notified.

On 23 February, Cody had flown again, in the course of which he had again successfully turned his machine in the air and also, for the first time, had landed without any damage. Any elation he may have felt at this evidence that he was now getting somewhere, both with his machine and with his own piloting skills, must have been severely dampened when the very next day the letter arrived from the War Office, informing him that his services were no longer required, although, for contractual reasons, his engagement would not be terminated until the end of September. Dunne was dealt with rather more summarily and he was required to sever his connection with the Balloon Factory by 31 March.

On 5 May, *The Times*, having got wind of these events, published a report 'from a Correspondent' which, while seeking patriotically to show how advanced the nation was in 'aerial navigation', was notable for its inaccuracies. In the previous year's Scottish trials, Captain (*sic*) Dunne had, it seemed, 'not only gained the distinction of being the first Englishman to rise from the ground in an aeroplane on British soil', but had 'achieved several long flights, on one occasion accomplishing a circular flight of over 12 miles in extent'. Seemingly as misinformed of how matters had gone at the Camp d'Auvours as he was of the events at Blair Atholl, the writer was able confidently to assure his readers that '... in efficiency and in ease of control Captain Dunne's aeroplane was superior, as had already been indicated by the earlier experiments, to the Wright machine'.

Both Cody and Dunne were allowed to keep their machines and both continued with their testing and development, on a private basis. John Dunne retained the support of the Marquis of Tullibardine, who had come to share Capper's belief in Dunne's abilities. In association with the Marquis and several other wealthy men, Dunne formed a company called the Blair Atholl Syndicate and continued to produce new designs on the same principle as D.4. Despite the name, however, he did not return to Scotland, but chose the more suitable location of Eastchurch, on the Isle of Sheppey, which was just becoming established as a flying centre, at which to continue his activities.

Cody was also allowed to retain the Antoinette engine until he could purchase another, though only after a certain amount of debate in Whitehall, including a contribution from one unenthusiastic official in the Treasury, the firmness of whose grip on the stage to which aviation had currently advanced may be judged from the following extract:

> Harman feels rather doubtful about Cody at present; in view of the fact that he has been so unsuccessful in the past, it might be thought undesirable to let him use the Government engine and coal for the purpose of further experiments, and the P.A.C. [Public Accounts Committee] might object to the charge for the coal and for any damage to the engine.

However, not all shared these uneducated doubts; thanks to Capper and others less remote from the real world, Cody, as well as retaining the use of the engine, was also able to continue his activities on Laffan's Plain, where he built a shed, near the Basingstoke Canal, not far from the threshold of Runway 07 of today's airfield. Effectively, for the remainder of the summer, since he was still for the time being a War Office employee, his flight trials went on under largely the same conditions as before, whatever the Committee of Imperial Defence may have desired. Working from his new base, he went on incorporating and flight-testing various modifications to his machine, submitting a report on the changes and their results to Capper after each flight. In parallel, he continued to pursue the self-taught flying training course which had begun with his first flight in October. When, in July, he replaced the Antoinette with an ENV of nominally greater power, he was measuring his flights in miles, performing turns and figures-of-eight and navigating his way around the Plain at will. On 16 August, he demonstrated the degree of facility he had attained with his flying when he 'decided to pay a visit to the Balloon Co.'s Camp on Jersey Brow'. After a 'perfect landing' and a sociable meeting with his ballooning friends, he restarted his engine, took off and flew back to his shed by the canal.

In December, he was presented with the Silver Medal of the Aeronautical Society while, early in 1910, he began to build a second machine, with which he achieved a considerable measure of success. The War Office had not heard the last either of him or of John Dunne.

From the mixed fortunes of Cody and Dunne, it is high time for us to return to that other struggling pioneer, A. V. Roe, whom we last saw in July 1908 as he was being expelled by the Brooklands authorities, and find out how he had been faring. After some months of vagabondage, he at last came to rest on Lea Marshes, near Hackney, North London. By that time, he had a new machine ready to try, which embodied fundamental design differences from the model with which he had been struggling at Brooklands. Most obviously, the new craft was a triplane with its engine arranged to drive a tractor propeller, while the canard configuration had been abandoned in favour of a rear-mounted triplane tail unit with twin fins. On the downside, however, the usual financial restraints had obliged him to return the Antoinette engine to the manufacturers and revert for his propulsion needs to the miserable 9-hp of his JAP engine.

By the early summer of 1909, Roe, with a few faithful helpers, was hard at it, driving his new craft up and down his makeshift airfield, straining with the limited power available to rise from mother earth. Sometimes he succeeded in achieving 'flight', never for more than a few yards, never more than a few feet above the

A. V. Roe flying his first triplane – at a rather alarming pitch angle – on Lea Marshes in 1909. (Author's collection)

ground. On not infrequent occasions, these short excursions ended in a broken aeroplane, which had then to be carried back to the workshop, which the Great Eastern Railway had allowed him to set up under the nearby railway arches. To passers-by and others who heard about his activities, which attracted to him the nickname of 'The Hopper', he was just another crank, a young man sitting in a crazy contraption of canvas and wire, with his cap on back-to-front, more likely to kill himself than fly. As for the local authority, this body, having got wind of what he was up to, was busy taking steps to stop him playing with this rather ridiculous but dangerous-looking toy on the public land for which they were responsible. Indefatigably, and refusing to be distracted by the cat-and-mouse game he was obliged to play with his pursuers, he continued to bend himself to his task.

One day that summer, he received a visit from another young man who nursed a similar ambition to design and fly his own aeroplane. He had started a little later than Roe and was at that moment still in the process of constructing his first effort, in a small shed he had rented in Bothwell Street, just off the Fulham Palace Road in London. Financially, however, he was a little better placed than the other, thanks to a thousand pounds which had been advanced by a rich and helpful grandfather. Furthermore, he possessed an engine which would serve him well – one which he had designed himself and whose four cylinders delivered a nominal power some five times greater than Roe's little JAP. Like Roe, Geoffrey de Havilland – for that was the visitor's name – would both achieve his goal and, in later years, taste success as one of the leaders of his country's aircraft industry.

3

The Pilots Assemble

While Cody and the others had been struggling to understand and overcome the mysteries of aerodynamics and thereby design and build a successful flying machine, there were other young men in the country who, though similarly fired by an ambition to fly, looked to others to produce the means by which they could do so. Such aspirant pilots in the England of 1908-9 were, of course, faced with a fundamental obstacle to their desires: there was a distinct lack of aeroplanes available for their purpose. Frustrated in this way, some of them looked across the Channel to France, where they saw that they could find flying machines of a sort, which were at least capable of putting some daylight between their wheels and the ground. One by one, they hastened to Dover and the cross-Channel steamer.

In the lead was a certain John Theodore Cuthbert Moore-Brabazon, who had already spent some time in France, learning, in a somewhat dilettante fashion, to become an automotive engineer. He too had been a member of the ballooning and motor-racing set favoured by a number of well-heeled young men of that period, so his progression to aeroplanes followed a natural sequence. In the summer of 1908, that seminal year for European aviation, he returned to France and was soon caught up in the flying fever generated by the activities of Wilbur Wright, which for the French was enhanced by the recent exploits of their own home-grown pilots.

It was to Gabriel Voisin's workshop in the rue de la Ferme, therefore, that Moore-Brabazon repaired and where he too became the owner of one of Voisin's machines. Although both Blériot and Farman were soon to perceive the profit in passing on their flying skills to others, the first flying school – Wright's at Pau – was yet to open its doors. Lacking such help, Brabazon therefore took his machine to Issy-les-Moulineaux and simply set out to teach himself, assisted perhaps by some rudimentary advice from the vendor. Like everyone else, he advanced by halting steps and hazardous landings. However, by the end of the year he had become what passed in those times for a competent pilot, capable of achieving flights over distances which were being measured in miles.

It was in the early months of 1909, while Cody was starting to fly at Farnborough and Roe was looking for a site on which to pursue his own efforts, that Brabazon returned to Britain with his machine and based himself at Shellbeach, on the Isle of Sheppey, where he continued with his flying, thus performing not, of course, the first flights from British soil, but the first by a native Briton. The next first, a flight by a Briton in a British-made aircraft, still lay in the future.

It was also at Shellbeach and at about the same time, that the brothers Short, who had been making balloons for some years, had established themselves as the first British aeroplane manufacturers, by obtaining a contract from the Wrights to produce a batch of six Type As. Another arrival at Shellbeach was Charles Rolls who, once Shorts had received the Wright contract, lost no time in placing an order. He was allocated the first off the line but, discovering that the machine would not be completed until October, he got Shorts to build him a glider, based on the Wright, on which he could

Les Pionniers de l'air — L'Aéroplane " MOORE-BRABAZON "
Moteur VIVINUS 4 cylindres 40 H. P.

Moore-Brabazon seated in his Voisin (40-hp Vivinus). (Author's collection)

gain some experience while he was waiting for the real thing. This became available in late July, and Rolls now began to divide his time between Hurlingham, where he was always to be found at the summer's ballooning events, and Sheppey, where, following Brabazon's example, he began his own self-taught flying course. His time was destined to be all too short, but within that limit he contrived to be one of those who placed their firm imprints upon the history of aviation's early years.

While Rolls had returned from France, determined to explore the mysteries of flying from his native soil, others took the opposite course and, emulating Brabazon, maintained a steady pilgrimage across the Channel, where wider opportunities seemed to be available. As if to demonstrate the point and encourage such visitors, early on the morning of Sunday 25 July 1909, Louis Blériot flew his Type XI monoplane in the reverse direction across the Straits of Dover, to a triumphant landing on English soil.

By then, the choice of aeroplanes available to the would-be purchaser in France was widening, as other pioneers joined Voisin, Blériot and Farman in the business of aeroplane manufacturing. Having for a while been associated with Voisin, Blériot had chosen Issy-les-Moulineaux for his first flying field, while Farman was using the military camping ground at Mourmelon, near Châlons-sur-Marne in the Champagne region to the east of Paris. At both these centres, would-be aviators with sufficient funds were starting to turn up and place their orders for one of the machines which their designers were now offering. Mourmelon was the centre chosen by one George Bertram Cockburn, whose receding hairline betrayed him to be, at thirty-seven, rather older than most of the other young hopefuls. There, having purchased one of Farman's products, he began his own aerial experiments. These were not without occasional exciting contacts with terra firma, including his first attempt when, as *Flight* put it, he 'pulled the wrong lever or pulled it in the wrong direction', soared upwards and then fell to earth in what was becoming the time-honoured manner. However, after the necessary structural repairs, his advance was to be swifter and surer than many. He progressed from owner to apprentice, from apprentice to pilot and, finally, to competitor, in the space of no more than three months.

Cockburn was followed by other aspirant British aviators, amongst whom was one who followed a somewhat tortuous path to the skies. Robert Loraine was a young actor with an adventurous streak. In 1900, in the midst of an acclaimed portrayal of d'Artagnan, he had temporarily abandoned the stage to serve as a volunteer trooper in the South African War. Returning to England, he resumed his acting career on the London stage and in a few years had found fame and fortune in productions such as *Man and Superman* and *The School for Scandal*. It was 1908 when he was seized

A poster advertising *La Grande Semaine d'Aviation*, which opened at Reims on 22 August 1909. (Author's collection)

by another venturesome enthusiasm. This time it was flying, for which, of course, his first need was an aeroplane. Therefore he too made his way across the Channel and presented himself at Voisin's premises. However, the constructional capacity of Voisin's little workshop was fully taken up with orders from sources more soundly based than that from an unknown young Englishman. Loraine, finding himself at the back of a queue, was obliged for the time being to return home empty-handed, put his aerial ambitions to the back of his mind and concentrate once more on the footlights. Nevertheless, flying had got into his system; the following year he crossed to France again, simply to be at Sangatte amongst the crowd on the shore on that July morning, as they watched Louis Blériot disappear into the Channel mists and write his name in the history books. While Blériot returned to France to prepare for *La Grande Semaine d'Aviation de la Champagne*, the first-ever air show, which was to open at Reims on 22 August, Robert Loraine was once more obliged to travel in the opposite direction, where his professional engagements in London awaited his attention. As soon as he could arrange it, he intended to return.

La Grande Semaine d'Aviation was indeed organised on a grand scale. In the flat countryside to the north of Reims, just outside the village of Bétheny and some thirty kilometres to the north-west of Mourmelon, a great aerial racecourse had been laid out, in confident preparation for the attendance of spectators in their thousands. With the aeroplane become the marvel of the day, it was to be a new, aerial version of 'the Greatest Show on Earth'. A small town of grandstands, hangars, restaurants, shops and gardens sprang up, before which stretched the reason for it all, an aerodrome incorporating a ten thousand-metre racing circuit, its rectangular course marked out by a pylon at each corner. As well as the races, other aerial contests were planned, while it was natural, in that wine-drenched region, that many of the prizes should be provided by the great Champagne houses: Moët et Chandon, La Veuve Clicquot-Ponsardin, Pommery and other renowned names were all represented in the list of trophies.

The event did not enjoy the most favourable of beginnings: a few hours before it

Two views of the grandstand – '*Le Buffet des Tribunes*' – at Reims in 1909, thronged with a
fashionably dressed crowd. (Author's collection)

opened on the morning of Sunday 22 August, heavy overnight rain falling on the chalky soil had reduced the area surrounding the grandstand to a sticky morass, ankle-deep in places, while the prospects of aerial entertainment for the many who braved the mud and the unseasonal weather looked bleak. However, before long, the skies began to clear, and by eleven o'clock, as the ground dried up somewhat in the strong sunshine, the first machine was in the air. From that point on, the success of the meeting was no longer in doubt as the pilots, many by then famous names, one by one coaxed their craft into the air, enthralling the crowds which had flocked to the scene with sights which most were seeing for the first time. In the eight days the show lasted, the total number passing through the gates was estimated to have reached half a million, while the whole affair marked a major milestone in the aeronautical education of the general public – in France at least.

By the time the meeting opened, George Cockburn had become sufficiently proficient and sufficiently bold to enter and be accepted as a competitor – the only Briton in a field of thirty-eight. Not that his compatriots were unaware of the unique event; a number who had the means crossed the sea to join the vast crowds attracted by the new spectacle, including David Lloyd George and the Inspector-General of the Forces, Sir John French. It is noteworthy that the former, in an interview he gave to *The Morning Post* shortly after his return, observed that he 'had not realised how far behind we were until I went to Rheims, our backwardness was the subject of general comment and conversation'. With such admitted ignorance, his contribution as a member of the recent sub-committee could not have been noteworthy.

Charlie Rolls too, suspending his pilot training for a few days, came over to further his education, while of the other Britons who attended, there were at least two whose presence represented a first step in their own ambitions to fly. One was a wealthy motor car dealer named Claude Grahame-White, who was soon to burst upon the scene in his own spectacular manner. He had journeyed to Reims with the express purpose of looking over the aeroplanes on show and of becoming the owner of one of them. However, having entered the flying ground, he was frustrated to find himself barred by obdurate officials from penetrating to the part of the airfield containing the hangars, where the pilots and their associates could be found. But Grahame-White had come to Reims for a purpose and had no intention of departing until he had achieved it. Never lacking in resource, it was not long before he had outwitted the guards and, having once gained entry to the forbidden zone, had sought out Blériot, with whom he was already acquainted. The rest was routine: a contract was duly signed; he had only to wait for the machine to be built. 'Only'? The trouble was, that would take weeks and such inaction was not to be contemplated by one with Grahame-White's energies; the momentum must be maintained. He persuaded Blériot to allow him to be present in the workshops and, indeed, to assist in the construction of his aeroplane.

By 6 November, he knew it to be complete. Very early that morning, therefore, accompanied by a friend, he turned up once more at the Issy-les-Moulineaux hangar, inside which he knew his machine lay, ready to fly. But where was Blériot? Where were Blériot's mechanics? As the minutes passed and the airfield remained deserted, he was prepared to wait no longer. His machine was awaiting him: therefore he would fly it, Blériot or no Blériot. The presentation to the night watchman of a suitable quantity of francs unlocked the hangar and placed his aeroplane at his disposal.

Instead of the Type XI, the model in which Blériot had crossed the Channel, he had chosen to purchase a Type XII, designed for speed and an altogether trickier machine. It was a distinction which was not calculated to deter its impatient and would-be pilot. Climbing aboard, he started the engine and began to experiment with the controls. By the time that the mechanics finally arrived, the Englishman was already flying up and down the field with apparent proficiency. Such success could not go on; in due course, the inevitable happened and the Type XII found itself in the hangar, awaiting repair.

But aviation was gradually becoming more organised; there was now no need to learn to fly in such a hit-and-miss manner. Blériot himself had recently established his first flying school, copying Wilbur Wright by choosing the favourable climate at Pau for its location, and he invited Grahame-White to join him there with his machine, so that the latter could undergo his flying training on a more ordered basis. This he did, but it soon became apparent that the Type XII, to which the Englishman had given the romantic name of *White Eagle*, was too much of a handful to be the ideal craft for a novice pilot (as we shall see, later in its life its uncooperative characteristics led to its acquisition of another, rather less attractive name). Blériot agreed to take it back and generously replaced it with not one but two examples of the more docile Type XI. With these, Grahame-White was now properly launched on his aeronautical career. That winter, beneath the frequently blue skies of the Languedoc, with the snow-capped Pyrénées stretched across his southern horizon, he flew as often as he could, swiftly gaining in skill and confidence, until, just after the start of the New Year, he was awarded his *brevet de pilote* (No.30) by the Aéro Club de France, the first Englishman to be granted any kind of official piloting qualification (others, notably Moore-Brabazon and Cockburn, had, of course, acquired piloting skills earlier than he, but they flew around happily without documentary evidence to that effect until the Royal Aero Club (as it became in February 1910) began to issue its own Aviators' Certificates in the following March).

To return to 1909 and to the meeting at Reims, the other Briton present and anxious to launch his piloting career was a thirty-six-year-old officer in the Royal Horse Artillery, Captain Bertram Dickson. After service in the South African War, he had pursued an active career in various far-flung corners of the world, from Kurdistan to Patagonia. That year, at the end of a spell as a vice-consul in the Middle East, he was returning through France when he decided to turn aside to Reims, to witness for himself the demonstrations of what could now be done with aeroplanes. He was sufficiently impressed with what he saw to decide that, for him too, the future lay in the sky. The following February saw him at Mourmelon, where, on 19 April 1910, he secured his own Aéro Club *brevet* (No.71).

As for Robert Loraine, it was in that same April that he was at last able to escape from his theatrical obligations for a while and become free to pursue his chosen second career. This time he turned his tracks southwards, following Grahame-White to Pau and Blériot's flying school, where he at last found himself seated in an aeroplane, though, as he discovered to his frustration, not yet to fly. With dual-control machines yet to be devised, one method then being used with an inexperienced pupil was to send him off by himself in one of the now-ubiquitous Type XIs, in which he was able to taxi about the field, manipulating its controls and learning by error, but unable to leave the ground. This wise precaution was achieved by the use of a degraded version of the machine, dubbed a *Pingouin*, so-called because it had been rendered, like the penguin, incapable of flying, not only by clipping its wings, but also by tying the elevator control in a forward position. In this way the pupil could be prevented from leaving the ground before he was deemed ready to do so. This was an arrangement which was of no use to the young actor, who was not only impatient to become a real aviator, but who also had little time to spare before he had to return to London, where theatre-goers were expecting his next appearance on the stage. Accordingly, as soon as opportunity allowed, he surreptitiously untied the restraining cord. This time, when he opened the throttle once more, there was no irksome restriction to prevent his hand from pulling the control firmly towards him, in the direction of Up, while the wings, though clipped, were eager to help and still capable of generating sufficient lift to do so. Sadly, their inadequate span would not allow them to sustain their initial promise and the familiar story was once more enacted: after the would-be pilot had been separated from the debris, the latter was carried carefully back to the hangar for some hopeful reconstruction work. For the

Above left: Captain Bertram Dickson at the controls of a Farman. (Author's collection)

Above right: Claude Grahame-White (and friend) in his Blériot XII. (Author's collection)

Grahame-White's Blériot XII, being flown by its owner (inset), before he thought better of it. (Author's collection)

former, however, there was no such tender consideration – only the stern intimation that his welcome on that particular airfield was at an end. Accepting his fate, he lost as little time as possible in making for the opposing camp at Mourmelon, no doubt hoping that no warnings about the mad English actor had filtered through from Pau.

By that time, Bertram Dickson, having acquired his *brevet*, had left and was already establishing a name as an exhibition pilot. In his place, Loraine found another fellow-expatriate, another British army officer – none other, in fact, than Lieutenant Lancelot Gibbs, whom we last saw attempting to fly John Dunne's D.4 beneath the walls of Blair Castle. Gibbs was awarded his *brevet* on 10 July and Loraine, who was probably learning to treat aeroplanes more circumspectly, obtained his own eleven days later.

The number of Britons who had found ways and means of learning the art of piloting an aeroplane had now mounted to over a score. They were for the most part civilians, who were inclined to treat their new activity as either a sport or a commercial enterprise. So far as qualified pilots from the armed services were concerned, there were but two – Gibbs and Dickson, the former not a regular officer, while the latter was on the point of retiring from the army the following month. If one were to visit Farnborough, home of the army's official air service and still known as the Balloon School, in search of military aviation, one might well find the rejected Samuel Cody airborne over Laffan's Plain in his machine, but his would be the only aeroplane in the sky. Of the men of the Balloon School, skilled balloonists, kiters and airship pilots though they were, there was not yet one who could fly a plane. Not that there were enough aspirants anyway. In a letter to the Chief Engineer, Aldershot, in November 1909, Capper had observed:

> As regards finding officers for the School and Companies, I regret to say that I seem to get very few volunteers from the Corps of Royal Engineers.
>
> It is possible that peculiar natural characteristics are required for an officer to be keen on joining a corps which spends so much of its time in the air.
>
> I would, however, point out that a very good and capable class of officer is required, and that if these are not procurable from the Corps of Royal Engineers, it will be a matter of consideration whether we should not endeavour to obtain the proper material from other branches of the service.

Capper had illuminated a theme which, in time, was destined to become both vexatious and tendentious.

There were undoubtedly some members of the Balloon School who were keen to fly – and were encouraged in their aspirations by their air-minded commanding officer. Back in 1908 one of them, Lieutenant Reginald Cammell, last seen up a tree with *Beta*, had been badgering Capper to be allowed to join the little team up at Blair Atholl. In this he was unsuccessful, and for the time being, he had had to be content with being one of the Balloon School officers who in the course of September 1909 were numbered amongst Cody's first passengers. Meanwhile, through the summer of 1910, the Balloon School's time and energies continued to be fully taken up by the operation of its balloons, its kites and its two dirigibles, *Gamma* and *Beta*.

While the latter made its point with two high-profile flights to central London and back, no small part of the school's duties consisted of the holding of training courses, for the purpose of teaching officers from other arms to take charge of balloons in the air, both tethered and on free runs, and other ranks in the handling of balloons on the ground. The courses were controlled by Captain King and Lieutenant Broke-Smith, with the assistance of Lieutenants Waterlow and Cammell. For the last-named, however, all was about to change; at the end of June, the door he had been yearning to open was, at last, unlocked and he passed through it and into a new world.

4

Flying Machines Needed

By the summer of 1909, there was no lack of evidence that the conclusions reached a few months earlier by the CID's Aerial Navigation Sub-Committee had been erroneous. Even before it first assembled, Wilbur Wright had begun to astonish France with his demonstration flights. To these were soon added the subsequent achievements by some of the French pilots themselves, in particular that audacious arrival of one of them on Dover cliff top, over the head of the nation's bulwark, the Royal Navy. Now, the trumpets which had been sounding on the other side were ringing out on the island as well.

Faced with these realities, the government took action. It set up another committee. However, this one, which was given the name of the Advisory Committee for Aeronautics (ACA), was of a composition which gave it a rather better chance of reaching useful conclusions than its predecessor, whose membership had suffered from an inclination which was too political at the expense of technical knowledge. The new body's leaning was much more scientific, its president being the eminent scientist Lord Rayleigh OM FRS, and its chairman Dr R. T. Glazebrook FRS, the current Director of the National Physical Laboratory. Amongst other appointments, the most significant and, one might even say, the most influential was that of a certain F. W. Lanchester. Born in 1868, the year that Stringfellow exhibited his model aeroplane at the young Aeronautical Society's Crystal Palace exhibition, Lanchester, as well as being the designer of a series of popular motor cars, had for some years been interesting himself in the theory of flight. In 1907, he had published his work on wing aerodynamics, which confirmed him as a leading figure in that field.

One decision, stemming from the new committee's deliberations, and far-reaching in its effects, involved a fundamental organisational change at South Farnborough. It was decided that the functions of the Balloon Factory and the Balloon School should be separated, it being recognised that the former was concerned with the non-military activities of design, development and production, while the latter had always constituted the base for the operation of airborne vehicles in the field, as well as the everyday activities of training. Accentuating this distinction, a civilian engineer, Mr Mervyn O'Gorman, was appointed as superintendent of the factory, replacing Colonel Capper, who, however, retained command of the school. Mr T. J. Ridge, who in his spare time was an officer in the London Balloon Company, became assistant superintendent, replacing Captain Carden, who remained on the staff of the Balloon School. The separation of factory and school received further emphasis by a distinction in their chains of command. While the latter remained immediately subordinate to the GOC Aldershot Command, the factory was made directly responsible to the War Office, in the person of the Master-General of the Ordnance.

These arrangements, though eminently rational, were not, however, to take place without the resolution of difficulties which derived not from any technological source but from the clash of individual needs. A deal of correspondence between the two sides, and no little heat, was to be generated before the separation, which had been decided in October 1909, became fully effective in January 1910. The problems derived from agreement as to the division of equipment, premises and staff, which had previously been held in common and shared amicably between school and factory. Amiability now came into short supply: O'Gorman, a somewhat forceful character, lost no time in making sure that he had the pick of both stores and buildings, catching Capper on the hop and leading him to complain to the referee in the War Office, represented by Brig General F. Rainsford-Hannay, the Director of Fortifications and Works, that the only bits and pieces left over by O'Gorman after the latter had taken all that he wanted were of no practical use to the Balloon School. As for the premises which had been left to him, these were sparse and inadequate for his purposes. He even found himself deprived of his secretarial staff, whom O'Gorman either took over or sacked, with no apparent concern for poor Capper's needs. To the latter, it was all the more galling to reflect that the situation which had arisen was the result of having been deprived of one half of his command, which he felt keenly.

These upheavals were all very well and sufficiently minor in nature, provided that they resulted in the acquisition by the British Army of an aeronautical service which could compare with those now starting to take shape in other leading nations, be they potential enemies or possible allies. As things stood, however, there seemed to be no sign of any firm plans to extend the Balloon School's responsibilities to the operation of aeroplanes. One thing was clear: there was to be no return to the days of the British Army Aeroplane or the Blair Atholl Trials. The costs of the design and development of aeroplanes, if any satisfactory ones were to be found, would be borne by the private sector, without any further expenditure of precious government funds. The function of the factory was to act as technical support for the Balloon School, by the maintenance of its airships – and the building of new ones. More fundamentally, perhaps, it was also to become the country's aeronautical research centre, in which the collaboration and resources of the National Physical Laboratory, not far away at Teddington, would be most valuable. So far as aeroplanes went, if indeed there were to be any, the factory was to restrict itself to any necessary repair work; it was not expected to try to produce any more aeroplanes itself. If the latter were eventually to constitute a serious component of military aeronautics, the government, it seemed, was prepared to wait and see what turned up, before committing any more public money to the question. For the moment, in any case, dirigibles were the preferred choice, at least so far as Whitehall was concerned.

In the country as a whole, however, the aeroplane was in the ascendant. For the general public, flight, having become an established fact, was both an object of wonder and an exciting spectacle. Following the lead given in 1909 by the triumphant success of *La Grande Semaine d'Aviation* at Reims, the first flying meetings in this country had taken place shortly afterwards, at Blackpool and Doncaster. The former event had the backing of the Aero Club; the latter did not. Regrettably, this circumstance introduced a strong element of rivalry, resulting in no little bad feeling, while the Doncaster meeting was largely spoiled by the spell of bad weather with which it coincided.

Samuel Cody was among the pilots taking part at the latter venue, and at one point in the proceedings, with the aeroplanes confined to their hangars by wind and rain, he took the opportunity to enliven things in his own inimitable way, by giving the large crowd a little piece of theatre, to compensate them for the lack of the flying thrills of which the elements were depriving them. Having recently applied successfully for naturalisation as a British citizen, he arranged for the formalities to be enacted on the airfield. Incorrigible showman that he was, he added his own flourish to the solemn event: as soon as the papers turning him into a loyal subject of King Edward had been signed, the onlookers who turned their gaze in the direction of the Cody hangar were rewarded with the sight of the Union flag being run up the flagstaff, to replace the Stars and Stripes which had fluttered there before.

Cody taxiing his second machine at the Doncaster meeting in 1909. (J. M. Bruce/G. S. Leslie)

Middle and below: The Bournemouth Aviation Meeting in 1910. *Above:* Grahame-White on a Henri Farman. *Below:* Outside the hangar, Cody prepares his machine, watched by a small multitude. (Jean Roberts)

Aviation had indeed joined the Boat Race, the Cup Final and the Zoo as another source of public entertainment, albeit rather more exciting; it was The Man on the Flying Trapeze with advantages. In the following year, the meetings multiplied, at makeshift airfields up and down the nation. Wolverhampton led the way, followed amongst others by Lanark and Bournemouth. Blackpool saw a second meeting, as did Doncaster, where not a single British pilot or aeroplane took part. The scene in this country was still largely dominated by Voisins, Blériots and Farmans, though some British aeroplanes, produced by Shorts, Bristols and even Avros, were now making their appearance, as were an increasing number of British pilots, bidding to challenge the one-time dominance of the French, with almost their every flight being regularly reported in the papers.

High on the list of thrills offered by the daring young men in the sky was a two-man Anglo-French contest, when Grahame-White and the Frenchman Louis Paulhan competed for the *Daily Mail*'s £10,000 prize for the first flight from London to Manchester, with Paulhan ending the winner in circumstances which combined both high drama and warm sportsmanship. In June, Charles Rolls became the third pilot and the first Englishman to fly across the Channel, accentuating the feat by returning to his take-off point without having landed on the other side, thus turning it into the first double crossing. However, only a month later, the nation's enjoyment of its new and entertaining distraction was tempered by sombre tragedy, when one of its heroes, Rolls himself, became the first British aviator to lose his life in the air, in a fatal crash at the Bournemouth Aviation Meeting.

There was, of course, no question that this event, however saddening, not only to his family, but also to his fellow-pilots, many of whom were on the spot when he was killed, could halt the progress on which they were determined. Two months after Rolls's death, another significant event took place, with the first crossing by aeroplane of the Irish Sea, the pilot being none other than the colourful Robert Loraine. Having taken part in the second Blackpool meeting, he had immediately afterwards flown his Farman along the coast to Anglesey, where he based himself at Holyhead, the nearest point to his planned destination of Phoenix Park, Dublin. For several weeks, mishaps and bad weather frustrated his plans, and it was not until 11 September that Loraine was able to make his attempt. After a short air test, he took off a second time and climbed up into the clear cold sky of a Sunday morning and, with a fresh easterly breeze behind him, set off westward to cover the fifty or so miles of blue-grey water which separated him from his goal.

Flight across the open sea, out of sight of land, demands no little fortitude, or it certainly did in those early days of uncertain engines. When the worst happens, when the propeller stops dead and the engine's comforting roar is replaced by only the soft rush of the airflow, fortitude needs to be joined by a cool head and no small amount of good fortune. Both those last were certainly needed that day, when the worst befell. Loraine had climbed to the great altitude of 4,000 feet and he was grateful for the space he was granted, as he dived towards the sea, hoping that the engine, driven by the windmilling propeller, would fire. It did so, but not before the sea was uncomfortably close below him and, with power fully restored, he hastened to recover the precious altitude he had bartered. In this he was wise, though how wise would be only gradually revealed as, four more times that day, his engine again fell silent. Four more times he dived, restarted his engine, climbed up again and struggled doggedly on, to be rewarded at last by the sight of the promontory known as Howth Head, which guards the northern side of Dublin Bay, looming out of the haze. But Fortune was yet to be satisfied with its day's work. To add to his engine troubles, the rigging wires which held the structure of Loraine's machine in place had for some time been showing themselves unequal to the strain. Already, one by one, several had broken. Although the early aeroplanes incorporated a generous number of such constraints and the loss of a few could usually be tolerated, as more wires continued to snap, the distortion caused by their loss was in the end such as to render his craft uncontrollable. He nearly made it: he was scarcely a stone's throw from the shore when he finally lost control and the Farman plunged into the sea. Extricating himself from the wreckage, he swam the short distance to dry land. Thus, it might have been said that, strictly speaking, his attempt had failed. However, this completion of his journey by water rather than in the air was rightly treated as an irrelevant and petty detail, which was not allowed to prevent Robert Loraine from being acknowledged as the first man to make an aerial crossing of the Irish Sea. Nine days later, with the triumphant pilot once more transformed into the popular actor, Loraine returned to the London stage, to appear in a new play at the Queen's Theatre. Its title? *The Man from the Sea*. Of course.

The following month, Grahame-White, in pursuance of his aim to make the wider public more air-minded, opened the 'London Aerodrome' at Hendon, which, for the next four years, was to draw large crowds, as the scene of regular flying exhibitions and air races. Not far away at Farnborough, the sappers, whatever their personal inclinations, continued to devote their energies exclusively to balloons, airships and kites.

When at Hunaudières in 1908 the French pioneers were first confronted with the evidence of how far the Wrights had advanced, one of their number, Léon Delagrange, is recorded as exclaiming: '*Eh bien, nous sommes battus! Nous n'existons pas!*' Beaten they certainly were not, as Farman and Blériot soon demonstrated, but they did have a bit of catching-up to do. For Britain and the British Army though, the catching-up was of an altogether more serious dimension. By the start of that 1910 summer, despite the excitement now being generated and which was attracting crowds in large numbers to the novel sights on display at the various aviation meetings, the number of home-built machines which had made any proper flights could still have been counted on the fingers of one hand. As the realisation dawned that the aeroplane might, after all, soon be in a position to constitute a significant factor on – or rather over – future battlefields, the question of where the means were to be found which would allow Britain's air arm, currently still known as the Balloon School, to play its part, began to assume more urgent proportions. If the British Army could boast not a single pilot in its ranks, it mattered little, since, with one fruitless exception, no steps had been taken to acquire the necessary aeroplanes.

With the sacking of Cody and Dunne, the light began to fall upon any sources in the private sector, hitherto hardly deserving serious consideration, which might now be showing signs of promise. Cody and Dunne, being themselves now part of that private sector, were in all justice entitled to be numbered amongst such sources, but seemed far from capable of meeting the need in the near future. Cody was well-placed to remind Capper of his existence, as he buzzed around Laffan's Plain, just across the Common from the Balloon School, but there seemed no immediate likelihood of aeroplanes in useful numbers becoming available for the army's use from that quarter. He had certainly shown that he had a practical flying machine and had now completed his second one, in which he had beaten Tom Sopwith, another rising star, to capture the British Michelin Cup, with a flight of 185 miles around a closed circuit above Laffan's Plain on the last day of 1910. However, the output of that gifted but individualistic man, tinkering away in his workshop by the Basingstoke Canal, had so far given no sign that it was ever going to exceed one-offs, as indeed it never did.

John Dunne had also made important advances and in December 1910 was able to demonstrate the automatic stability of his latest design before an audience at Eastchurch which included none other than Orville Wright himself. Nevertheless, his work was still in its experimental stages; he too did not yet seem to be in a position to offer a machine for the army's practical use.

What of other possible suppliers? The Short brothers had already established themselves as manufacturers, with their Wright contract, and were also starting

Cody, in the workmanlike white coat which he often wore. (Author's collection)

to produce their own designs. As 1910 progressed, others joined them, to lay the foundations of what was to become the British aircraft industry. On New Year's Day 1910, the firm of A. V. Roe and Co. (or 'Avros' as it became known) was set up. Roe had now constructed several more triplanes and was flying them with some success. He had even received a couple of orders, but to the army, he probably still looked at that point like an experimenter. The following month, a quite different personality emerged, the Bristol entrepreneur and tram operator Sir George White, to form the British and Colonial Aeroplane Company (later the Bristol Aeroplane Company and usually referred to as 'Bristols' for convenience). At Coventry, meanwhile, the Humber car firm joined the new infant industry by acquiring the British licence to build Blériots. Others were knocking on the door: Frederick Handley-Page had actually formed a company in 1909, but twelve months or more were to pass before he could be remotely classed as a serious supplier of aeroplanes. By then, Grahame-White himself was preparing to enter the ring, to be followed in time by many more, of whom Martin & Handasyde, Robert Blackburn and Tom Sopwith may be offered as leading examples.

However, in 1910, only two of those names – Shorts and Bristols – had got to the point of designing and manufacturing aeroplanes in more than ones or twos. Bristols were the most promising: after a false start with a Voisin biplane known as the Zodiac, for which the company had acquired the British rights, but which failed to fly, it had produced its own design, the Farman-based Boxkite, which not only flew well but was also being turned out in quantity. By the end of the year, a score had been built and were making a significant contribution to the sum of the nation's aerial activities.

In July, a canny move saw the company set up a potentially profitable point of contact with the military establishment by leasing land from the War Office at Larkhill, on Salisbury Plain, in the midst of the army's training grounds. There, it erected hangars and established a flying school, equipped with the successful Boxkite. This ploy eventually paid off, although it was to take some months to do so, while in the meantime the Balloon School expended no small amount of time, manpower and energy in acquiring and attempting to operate a number of other one-off aeroplanes, which, in the end, were to serve little or no useful purpose.

5

A Gift from France

The world was changing, and at some pace: in 1905, horse-drawn omnibuses on London's streets had outnumbered the motor-driven kind by nearly fifteen to one; by 1910, they had become, by a small margin, the minority. Motor cabs, for which in 1905 only nineteen licences had been issued, could in 1910 be counted in their thousands. To men of forty or over, adjustment to this changing world from the one into which they had been born and in which they had grown up did not come as the most natural of reactions. While young men like Claude Grahame-White and Charlie Rolls might, for some years, have been enthusiastically embracing the new and swifter mode of land transport (and were now, with equal enthusiasm, extending their affections to the even newer aeroplane), their fathers and uncles – the very men who held in their hands the powers of decision in the relevant fields – empathised less readily and more warily with these snarling newcomers, which supplanted the familiar and comfortable odour of the stable with the disconcerting reek of burnt oil. As the aeroplane too began to assert itself, it is perhaps understandable that such men should have been slow to envision the promise of aviation and reluctant to disburse public funds in pursuit of a device which, however revolutionary, had certainly in its stuttering advance been slow to demonstrate its practical potential.

Such myopia was not, however, universal; some there were for whom the future was not so obscured by the past. John Capper, now in his fiftieth year, had been positively and doggedly pursuing the goal of military heavier-than-air aeronautics from the moment he was appointed to command the Balloon School. Since that day, he had seen successive hopes in that direction dashed. Firstly, negotiations with the Wrights had come to nothing. Then his two protégés, Dunne and Cody, had been dismissed by remote minds which appeared not to share his faith in the aeroplane's future.

By the spring of 1910, however, with the frustrations of Blair Atholl and the erroneous conclusions of Lord Esher's sub-committee consigned to history, a certain impetus to move forward seemed once more to be accumulating. While much of the Balloon School's energies were still to be expended on the favoured dirigible, 1910 was the year when the British Army began to acquire its first aeroplanes – although the way it did so betrayed a haltingly indeterminate approach and resulted at first in a weirdly ineffectual fleet of machines.

The first of these was none other than the first Wright Type A to be built by Shorts – the one which had been delivered to Charles Rolls in the previous October. Following his appearance before the sub-committee in 1908, Rolls had remained interested in the future of military aviation and, having once joined the ranks of the country's aviators, determined to render what assistance he could to the birth of its new aeroplane corps. This purpose, at once patriotic and hard-nosed, was set in train when Rolls persuaded the War Office to part with the sum of £1,000 in exchange for the Wright, which was delivered to Farnborough by road in April 1910, the ultimate intention being that selected Balloon School officers would learn to fly it, under Rolls's tuition. With the latter's untimely death at Bournemouth, this plan never came to pass and the Wright worked out its destiny lying in a corner of the Farnborough hangar, gradually deteriorating and never, so far as is known, to fly again.

The next acquisition also had its origins some time earlier and took some time to mature, but its contribution, if small, was a positive one. It was in the course of 1909 that the Duke of Westminster and a certain Colonel Joseph Laycock had conceived the notion of acquiring a Blériot XII and presenting it to the War Office as a gift. The precise identity of this machine is not entirely certain, but there is some reason to believe it to have been that same Blériot XII, christened *White Eagle*, which had once belonged to Claude Grahame-White and which he had returned to its maker while he was learning to fly at Pau.

Why the pair chose this particular model rather than the well-tried Type XI to demonstrate their patriotism and philanthropy is not clear. They would certainly not have had the assistance of a very deep well of technical knowledge when making their choice. One reason may well lie in the engine with which the Type XII was equipped. It was a 60-hp product of the ENV company, a firm of British origin, but whose main workshops were situated in Paris. The managing director of ENV was, as it happened, none other than one of the two donors of the aeroplane – Colonel Laycock himself.

In any case, though the months passed, nothing more came of the scheme, as both Laycock and the Duke, with other matters to attend to, allowed it to retire to the backs of their minds. No money had changed hands and the truth seems to have been that Blériot himself, in the absence of any pressure upon him to deliver the goods, simply continued to use the machine for promotional purposes at flying meetings. It was December before Colonel Laycock awoke to the realisation that no bird seemed to be emerging from the egg he thought he had laid. Taking the matter up again, he then extracted from the manufacturer a promise of delivery in one month. In the end, June 1910 had arrived before the machine was finally reported to be available. Arrangements were thereupon made for an officer to be sent across to France, with instructions to inspect it and confirm its airworthiness before acceptance. The man chosen accepted his task with alacrity, for he was none other than Lieutenant Reginald Cammell, who, as we have seen, had long been burning to become a pilot. At last, as he found himself plucked from his work on kites and balloons and embarked on the steamer for France, it looked as if his wish was about to be granted.

Cammell, a burly twenty-four-year-old with a clipped military moustache who had been commissioned into the Royal Engineers four years earlier, was bound for Blériot's

Another picture of the Blériot Type XII – the machine which Reginald Cammell was sent to France to inspect. (Author's collection)

new aerodrome at Etampes, some thirty miles south of Paris, where the Type XII was to be produced for his inspection. Cammell's mission also required him to carry out what he called 'some preliminary assays with the machine, until satisfied that I should be able to fly it on return to England'. At that time, apart from any brief chances he may or may not have been given to control (if that is not too strong a word) the Glider Kite, he had no piloting experience whatsoever.

So far as the financial arrangements were concerned, payment for the machine had still not been made – a situation which was to cause poor Cammell no small concern, since no thought seemed to have been given to this side of the affair and he had received no instructions concerning it, not to mention any means of settling the bill. Although this lack of clarity concerning such an essential feature seems to have been due to administrative failings on the British side, it will have done nothing to dispel the suspicions concerning French perfidy with which Cammell tended to be assailed as time went by.

He arrived at Etampes airfield at nine o'clock on the morning of 29 June and was not immediately impressed by the sight of a rough, unprepared landing ground and the absence both of the machine he had come to inspect and of the great man himself. After lunch, he was somewhat mollified when the aeroplane arrived and, by five o'clock, had been assembled, while Louis Blériot turned up at half-past six. Cammell was to spend the next five frustrating weeks harrying the French and faithfully sending Colonel Capper daily reports of progress (or lack of it), often supplemented by personal letters, in which he expressed his doubts and frustrations in more direct terms than he allowed himself in the reports.

The Type XII was larger, heavier and faster than its stable mate, the Type XI, which had borne Louis Blériot across the Channel the previous year and which was now being turned out in some quantities. Like that machine, the Type XII was a shoulder-wing tractor monoplane, but differed markedly from it in other respects. The two occupants, instead of being able to survey the world from a position above the wing, as in the Type XI, were imprisoned beneath it, the trailing edge of which pressed down upon them, inches above their heads. The claustrophobic effect was increased by the engine, immediately in front, which partially blocked off their view forward, obliging them to peer around or over it. The only compensation of this arrangement was that it allowed a good view downwards. From the engine crankshaft, a chain drive led upwards to the propeller, which was free to revolve on a mounting in the leading edge of the wing.

By 1 July, Cammell's difficulties had begun. The ENV engine was not running very well, but Blériot decided to attempt a flight, with Cammell as passenger. With the engine unable to develop its full power, the 'flight' produced no more than a series of short hops, the aeroplane bounding so heavily over the rough ground as Blériot tried to coax it into the air that, in the end, the undercarriage on one side collapsed completely, demanding repairs which it was estimated would take eight days. To this frustration was added the discovery of the contractual complexities referred to above:

Dear Colonel

I have just returned from Blériot's Paris Office, and have been looking into the financial question. A horrible difficulty has arisen over the payment for the machine. It appears that by the terms of the contract, I am bound to pay for it as soon as it is handed over to me. Blériot refuses to break through the terms by sending in a bill to you, and will not hand the machine over until it is payed for. The only short way out, as far as I can see, is to give him a cheque on Cox, if you will arrange with Capt Laycock to have it honoured. I will try to get Blériot to let me ante-date the cheque, so that you will have a day or two to arrange about it, but I rather doubt if he will let me use the machine under these conditions.

I am very sorry I did not find out about it before, but I really thought the actual purchase of the machine had been arranged for by Capt Laycock. The price is 26,000 francs.

Such was military procurement in 1910! As matters turned out, the necessary repair work would ensure that there was considerably longer than 'a day or two' in which to resolve the matter. While he waited for the repairs, Lieutenant Cammell suggested that he should visit the *Salon de l'Aviation* at Reims – a repeat performance of the previous year's successful show, where no less than forty-six different aeroplanes – all French – were to be displayed. This having been authorised, Cammell, showing enterprise equalling that deployed by Grahame-White the year before, avoided the security cordon placed around the hangars and spent three days marvelling at France's current superiority in aircraft design. He then conscientiously wrote out a long report, describing all he had seen, illustrated here and there by sketches of this or that technical point, covering structural details, engine installations and propeller designs, which he submitted to his superiors in Great Britain.

His admiration for French products did not, however, extend to the aeroplane which was the object of his visit to Etampes and about which he was starting to have doubts, which he confided to Capper in his reports. He had learnt of Blériot's view that it was too difficult for a beginner to fly, while it was becoming increasingly clear that its engine was in need of a thorough overhaul. He had met a Captain Williams, 'who is also apparently something to do with ENVs':

He says the machine was originally designed for a 40 hp ENV, and flew well as such. But Blériot was then madly keen on getting a very fast machine, so put in a 60 hp and also cut down the wings. The result was that it beat all the records for speed (97 miles per hr, which was only beaten yesterday) but was so difficult to handle that they had endless breakages. Grahame White then had it for a long time but Blériot finally took it from him, saying it was too dangerous. He thought that with a beginner it was about 1000 chances to 1 that I should smash it to smithereens at the first attempt. Also he declared the engine must be getting old, and urgently needs an overhaul, as it has been in Blériot mechanics hands for 9 months, and of them he has a very low opinion.

Nor was Cammell's frustration diminished when, on return from Reims, he found that no progress seemed to have been made in the necessary repairs. On the 13th, he reported that the 'new forks' for the undercarriage were 'not even made yet', while Blériot was unreachable, having taken himself off to the aviation meeting at Bournemouth. In another letter to Capper, his patience finally expired:

Dear Colonel

What is to be done with these liars? I am rapidly losing every shred of patience and temper I ever possessed. I have done all I could. I have sworn at them (it says much for the sweetness of temper of my early French governess that I had to look up most of the words beforehand). I have reasoned sweetly with them; I have almost gone on my knees to them.

It is no good; they lie, and smile, and lie again. Blériot is at Bournemouth (he evidently had never any intention of doing anything else) and won't be back till Monday. They have faithfully promised that the machine will be ready by then, but I have no reason to believe any more in that promise than any other past one.

Later in the same letter, Cammell turned to his own prospects. In his ardour to become a pilot, he had been dismayed to learn that another officer was apparently being preferred as the first test pilot of the Blériot when it was delivered to the Balloon School:

> I expect you will think it very foolish of me, but I can't help feeling a bit disappointed in the idea of Boothby having the first trials after all.
>
> If you will allow me, I should like to make a last effort to become eligible for them, and the only way, of course, is by learning to drive the small Blériot myself. I have made the preliminary arrangements with the manager here, and he will let me have one of the 'school' machines for a day or two on fairly easy terms (it will be at my own expense, of course). I have watched 3 people learning this week, and they all could fly by the 4th attempt. I think if I came back able to manage the ordinary type XI, and with the added experience of the two flights with Blériot in our machine, I should be in almost a better position than Boothby to have the first try, don't you?

There were two Boothbys, father and son, both of whom by that time had had some involvement in aeronautics, and it is not clear to which of them Cammell was referring. The elder, Frederick Boothby, was a naval officer who earlier that year had been one of a party of eight which had travelled down to Pau, where they had all been enrolled as Claude Grahame-White's first pupils in the flying school which, taking his example from Wright and Blériot, he had just opened there, so if it was he whom Cammell feared, the latter, yet to begin his own tuition, had perhaps some cause for concern. The son James, a lieutenant in the Royal Scots, had been attached to the Balloon School that summer as a member of a ballooning course, when, it is true, he might have seized the opportunity to importune Capper with his claims. However, such limited aeronautical experience should hardly, one would have thought, have been such as to cause Cammell to express the fears he did.

As for the principal object of his mission, three days later, Cammell paid another visit to the works in Paris where manufacture of the new forks was supposed to be taking place and:

> ... after some bickering, managed to get them to produce the forks from a cupboard, where they have doubtless lain for a week. They are not quite complete, but are now definitely promised for Monday evening.

Blériot turned up again on the 18th and more haggling ensued, this time over the cost of the flying lessons which Cammell was anxious to take. The next day, however, the skies brightened: the new forks turned up and Cammell managed to extract better terms from Blériot for his instructional flying, for which he had in the meantime received Capper's blessing. On the 20th, he was given his first short lesson on a Type XI by Blériot's instructor at Etampes, Ferdinand Collin, before the wind became too strong. Meanwhile, the Blériot XII was being got ready for flight, and during the evening of the 24th, some short flights of sorts at last took place. The engine was still unsatisfactory, but on the 27th, Blériot managed to remain airborne for 16 minutes, though this flight ended with a forced landing in a cornfield, with a damaged tailplane. After repairs, Blériot and Cammell flew again on the 29th, though engine failure resulted in another rough landing which again damaged the tailplane.

Cammell himself, on the other hand, was now fully embarked on his flying course and becoming quite elated with his progress. His initial worry, that he would be quite likely to wreck the Type XII on his first attempt, was now superseded by something like overconfidence, as he reported to Capper that:

> I shall be quite able to manage the machine now; that at least is one good result of the delay. I could get my pilot brevet tomorrow easily, and will do, if I have the time. The

Blériots are ridiculously easy to manage in the air (our own is even easier than the little ones) but the ground steering is very hard until one gets the knack. I am trying to make a speciality of descents in view of the difficulty with our machine, and find I have a fairly good eye for it, so hope to escape smashes with any luck. The flights with Blériot are splendid training, and I have been able to notice lots of details in the slight differences of management from the little machines.

I shall be quite confident of doing well at it, if only the motor behaves when we get it on Salisbury Plain. The lessons will cost me 30 – 40 £ all told, which I can ill afford, but I am glad I have taken them all the same. I was terribly afraid, to tell you the truth, that I would not have the right temperament for flying.

Lieutenant Cammell was not the only foreign would-be aviator at Blériot's school: the Russians, he reported, were there in force:

There are no less than 10 officers here learning or waiting to learn, and some have already passed through. They also seem to have got the very first sold of the latest two-seater Blériots, and two are waiting here now to be tried.

So Russia, too, was forging ahead and forming an air corps, while Britain dallied with one half-trained pilot and one machine – and a gift horse at that! Cammell, however, was able to find some consolation in the quality of the competition:

The Russians have a very bad name with the French mechanics and officials, and certainly the ones here are rather poor specimens. One has been learning for two months, and has succeeded in smashing 3 machines without getting much nearer learning.

Cammell had now been at Etampes for over a month; the aeroplane seemed to fly all right – it was really the engine which was letting it down. Keen to get it home where – hopefully – he could start flying it in earnest, he recommended to his masters that it be accepted as an airframe, but that the engine be sent to the ENV works in Paris for overhaul at Blériot's expense, after which the complete machine would be shipped to England. These proposals were approved by both parties and thus, as it neared the end of a process which had been both long-winded and no more than semi-official, the British Army found itself on the threshold of acquiring its first flyable aeroplane.

As for Reginald Cammell, on 4 August, he returned from his battles in France to his old work at Farnborough, where balloons still held sway and dirigibles seemed to constitute their natural successors. Within days, he found himself involved in the somewhat ridiculous episode with *Beta* in the trees. A short while later, having taken part in the inconclusive experiments involving the dropping of sandbags out of balloons, he was piloting the balloon *Andes*, accompanied by Captain Lefroy, on its voyage to Sittingbourne. As he sailed slowly down the sky, his eyes may well have turned towards the nearby sea and his thoughts have flown across the land to beyond its southern horizon, where the Blériot, with its promise of new excitements, still lay. After all his exertions, he was entitled to hope that when it eventually arrived its test flying would be placed in his hands.

6
Larkhill

Farnborough Common had been all right for launching vertical take-off craft such as balloons and kites, but aeroplanes demanded more manoeuvring space, not least during the ticklish process of landing, than was available on the Common. One area in the British Isles which could supply that in abundance was Salisbury Plain. Not only that, but it was already occupied by the army in force.

It is not clear who was the first to conceive the idea of making use of a part of that sparsely populated area of Wiltshire as an aerodrome, though the distinction may well belong to another of the early pioneer designers, Horatio Barber, who produced a series of machines with the generic name of Valkyrie. They were not ultimately successful and the company which he had formed, called the Aeronautical Syndicate, was destined not to survive beyond 1912. However, several years earlier, when he had first begun his operations, he had rented some War Office land on the Plain, in the area long known as Lark Hill, and it was there that he had a hangar built, a short distance to the south of an ancient track known as the Packway. By mid-1910, two more sheds had been erected alongside it, one belonging to George Cockburn, while the other had been built by the War Office itself, to house the Wright with which Charles Rolls had intended to teach Balloon School officers to fly.

A short while later, the Bristol company also became interested in Larkhill's potential and arranged to lease some of the land from the War Office, where it proposed to set up a flying school, equipped with its successful Boxkites. For this purpose, it would need to extend the line of sheds by adding three more of its own. However, before this plan could be put into effect, the company management discovered that it would first have to resolve a problem of a totally unexpected nature. It became aware that the proposed sheds, if erected in the manner planned, would have a disturbing effect on certain neighbours, albeit ones who did not fit into any conventional category.

A mile or two to the south-west of the emergent airfield lay the antique circle of hewn rocks known to us as Stonehenge, that ring of massive stones which, though its origins are obscured from us by prehistoric darkness, had undoubtedly been erected by human agency and which was thought to have once served as the temple of an ancient and mysterious religion. A central and significant feature of that temple was the stone known as the Altar Table, whose location had apparently been chosen by the circle's builders such that, on every Midsummer's Day, at the moment when the sun first appeared above the eastern horizon, it would be upon that stone that its rays would fall. It was now pointed out that, if the line of hangars at Larkhill were to be extended as intended, the first to be erected would lie directly in the line between the emerging sun and the Altar Table, thus ending this mystical celebration of the solstice which, if no longer holding much significance in the modern world, had taken place without interruption for countless centuries. It is to the credit of the upstart new technology that, giving way to ancient ritual, it paused for once in its headlong advance and obligingly moved the planned location of the new sheds the necessary distance further on. Thus was born the celebrated 'sun gap' in the otherwise evenly spaced line of the Larkhill sheds.

With Stonehenge and Larkhill such near neighbours, it would have been a near-irresistible temptation to produce a composite photograph, as this surely is, depicting the latest wonders circling the sky above the very ancient. (Author's collection)

Once these three sheds had been erected to the satisfaction of all inhabitants, both the living and the ghostly ones of long ago, the War Office followed them with another two of its own. In due time, Larkhill was to become the Balloon School's main operational aerodrome, supplanting the unsuitable ground at Farnborough, although the latter location would remain the home of its depot and headquarters.

Although the great majority of the officers in the two services were, quite properly, pursuing their traditional careers on land or at sea, without discovering any appeal in the possibilities suggested by the aeroplane, there were, like the balloonists before them, a few individualists who were strongly attracted by its magnetic field. If Bertram Dickson was the first, another who followed him soon after was Captain J. D. B. Fulton of the Royal Field Artillery. After toying with the idea of building his own machine, he had decided to sidestep the potential frustrations of that course and had purchased a Blériot instead. Since Fulton was then stationed at nearby Bulford Camp, he had his new toy delivered to Larkhill, where he housed it in Rolls's old shed, which he had been allowed to take over. He spent the months that followed, when his military duties allowed, teaching himself to fly it, benefiting from helpful advice provided by his neighbour Cockburn.

On 30 July, on the other side of the 'sun gap', the Bristol team welcomed the arrival from Filton of its first Boxkite and not long thereafter the Bristol flying school opened for business, increasing still further the aerial activity over the Wiltshire downs. The proximity of considerable numbers of soldiers would ensure that some of its customers would soon be drawn from their ranks.

As summer gave way to autumn, the time arrived for the annual army manoeuvres, which in 1910 were to be held on Salisbury Plain. They took the usual form: large numbers of soldiers were sent out into the countryside, where they formed two teams – or, one should say, the Red and the Blue Forces – with orders to fight a hypothetical battle. For the first time, it was decided that mobile airborne reconnaissance (as opposed to the use of static balloons) should be included in the plan. The Balloon

Dickson in his Boxkite at Larkhill
during the 1910 manoeuvres.
(Museum of Army Flying)

School was able to supply the dirigible *Beta*, but unfortunately, when it came to aeroplanes and the pilots to fly them, it could produce neither the one nor the other.

This discrepancy gave Bristols an opportunity which they lost no time in seizing, by offering the use of two of its Boxkites, and this proposal was duly accepted. That still left the question of who was to fly them. With the army's aeronautical service unable to offer a single pilot, they would clearly have to be found elsewhere. Bertram Dickson the artilleryman was clearly the ideal man for the job, except that he was no longer a soldier, having resigned his commission the previous month. However, he was, as it happened, now in the employ of Sir George White, the very man who was supplying the aeroplanes. So Dickson, so recently a soldier anyway, was nominated to fly one of the Boxkites, on the side of Red Force, while he would be joined by a second aviator – none other than Lancelot Gibbs, who proposed to contribute and fly his own 'racing' Farman, which he had acquired since his Mourmelon days. Gibbs, too, had now forsaken the army, in order to start his own company, which offered both flying demonstrations and instructional flights.

On 10 September, Dickson's mount, No.9 from the production line, was delivered to Larkhill, ready to be test-flown by its pilot when he arrived, three days later. On 18 September, the day before the manoeuvres were due to begin, Gibbs flew in to join him. Both men were ready and impatient to demonstrate the effectiveness of the new means of reconnaissance. Unfortunately, for the next few days, they were to meet nothing but frustration. Although they had been officially invited to the party, they found themselves occupying more the role of outcasts than that of welcome guests, victims of a still widespread prejudice – both within the army and in the nation as a whole – which was marked by a persisting belief that the aeroplane was more an exciting and entertaining marvel than the greatest technical advance mankind had then seen, with a practical potential yet to be fully discovered. Furthermore, as their ballooning forebears had discovered, such prejudice was not diminished when the wrong sort of weather arrived – for the first three days brought strong winds, which ensured that

Lancelot Gibbs seated in the Farman which he brought to the manoeuvres. (Author's collection)

the soldiers pursued their earthbound activities without the remotest sign of either school of aeronautics being able to make an appearance in the air above them. It is easy to imagine the satisfaction which must have reigned in the cavalry messes when the limitations of their upstart would-be rival were found to be so clearly exposed.

However, on 21 September, the weather relented, dawning dry and calm, albeit with a heavy overnight frost clinging to the ground and a seasonal mist lying inert and white in the valleys. At half-past four, Dickson and Gibbs were roused from their beds in nearby Amesbury and driven up to Larkhill through the cold grey gloom of early day, eager to grasp their chance of demonstrating the effectiveness of the new cavalry of the air. Their driver – and the third member of their campaign team – was one of the more dynamic figures in the increasingly dynamic world of aviation – George Holt Thomas, journalist, businessman, friend of Lord Northcliffe and himself the son of a newspaper proprietor. For some time, he had, like Northcliffe, been conducting a campaign to educate the nation regarding the potential importance of aviation. He had attended the recent French army manoeuvres, held a few weeks earlier on the Picardy plain, where he had been highly impressed by the contribution made by aeroplanes, of which as many as fourteen had been present, as well as four dirigibles, all of them being fully and officially integrated in the proceedings. In stark contrast, Dickson was afforded no such consideration. On the previous day, he had managed to persuade someone to give him a general briefing on his duties and had also arranged for a white cross to be displayed at the landing field he had selected near to Red Force's HQ at Codford St Mary, about ten miles to the south and west. At that early hour of the morning, however, he could find no one in authority to give him more detailed and updated instructions. Or even to show an interest.

Gibbs was also meeting with frustration, of a different kind, as his Farman's engine refused to start, leaving him to fume on the ground, while Dickson clambered aboard his own machine and prepared for his mission. Just before half-past five, a puff of black exhaust smoke announced the successful starting of his own Gnôme. With the mass of its seven cylinders spinning satisfactorily behind him, he accelerated slowly away from Larkhill's sheds, his wheels cutting four dark tracks in the frosty grass, and climbed up into the bitter cold 2,000 feet above the Plain, glad of the layers of protective clothing (including the last-minute addition of sheets of newspaper) he had wisely put on. Heading south-west, he made for the valley of the Wylye, beyond which he proposed to carry out his reconnaissance. Turning eastward above the river, he flew first towards Salisbury's tall spire and then south and west again, describing a wide loop in the general direction of Shaftesbury. Nearing the village of Tisbury, his efforts were rewarded by the discovery of units of Blue Force's cavalry clearly visible below him. Armed with this information, he steered north again for Codford St Mary and his chosen landing ground. Needless to say, no white cross had been laid out (too early in the morning?), but he found a suitable landing spot some three miles from Codford, on the top of a local hill known as Wylye Bake, where he touched down after a cold but satisfying 45-minute flight. Once arrived at Codford, he reported his findings, with circumstantial detail, to the staff, who, still at their breakfast, were suitably impressed. It was a triumph which was only slightly blemished when, on a second flight, he made the mistake of landing in 'enemy' territory and was temporarily captured by a mounted patrol. After discussion with the umpires concerning the ethics of his novel position on the field of combat, it was decided that he could be neither 'killed' nor 'captured' and he and his mount were released to continue with their work. That evening, he carried out two more flights, while Gibbs, having overcome his starting problems, also got airborne and made his contribution by confirming Dickson's earlier report.

Their activities were supplemented by the appearance of a third pilot, anxious to play his part in demonstrating the utility of the new scouting facility which was making its tentative arrival. Robert Loraine had been appearing on stage in London but, forsaking the footlights for the flying field, he arrived the next day and took his turn above the manoeuvring soldiers, flying the second Boxkite in which a wireless transmitter had been installed, by means of which he succeeded in sending some messages over a short distance.

As Loraine arrived, Dickson left, booked to fly at a meeting at Milan. There, less than a fortnight later, his short and impressive flying career was to be brought to an abrupt end. An Antoinette flown by the Frenchman René Thomas collided with him from above and, locked together, the two machines fell to earth. Both pilots survived, but Dickson was grievously injured and hovered between life and death for weeks, nursed by his faithful sister Winifred. Although he recovered and returned to aviation, he never flew as a pilot again. Three years later, almost to the day, he died of a stroke, at Lochrosque Castle in Scotland. So passed another who, like Rolls, had promised to be influential in the shaping of aviation – and of military aviation in particular, but whose contribution was brought to an early end by the hazards of the air and the whimsical commands of fate.

As for the 1910 manoeuvres and the part played in them by Dickson and the other two, the short-lived participation of three aircraft, all flown by civilian pilots, although ground-breaking, had scarcely yielded the results and earned the universal acclamation from the army as a whole which had been hoped for by the campaigners. The comparison with the contribution made to the French army's manoeuvres by *its* aviators could not have been greater.

Holt Thomas had not been the only British observer to attend the events in Picardy and to be impressed with the part played by the new means of reconnaissance. On 3 October, *The Times* published a report by its Military Correspondent, Colonel Charles à Court Repington, dealing specifically with that aspect of the manoeuvres. After the first half of his report, describing what he had gleaned from various sources concerning the French High Command's philosophy and future policy with respect to the use of both dirigibles and aeroplanes in war, Colonel Repington then included the descriptions of a couple of reconnaissance flights carried out by two French officers in a Farman. On both occasions, significant bodies of troops had been discovered and reported to the general in command within half an hour of the aeroplane's return, allowing him to make tactical decisions which would not normally have been possible. Summing up an approving, not to say admiring commentary on the current French approach to military aviation, Repington ended his report by expressing his belief that 'the aeroplane, given a trained pilot and a skilled observer, must revolutionize the whole service of reconnaissance, and has already demonstrated its utility to armies'. Such words from one of the country's leading military writers represented welcome support for the advocates of military aviation, although the comfort which they will have derived from them might well have been tempered by Repington's categorical assertion that 'aeroplanes will never supplant cavalry, even for scouting', on account of their inability to operate in poor visibility or strong winds. In his eyes, they were still no more than a 'supplementary arm'.

A fortnight earlier, *The Times* had reported on the manoeuvres at home, with a brief reference to *Beta*'s involvement, as well as an equally short reference to the part played by Dickson and Gibbs. About the latter, it was inclined to be disdainfully dismissive:

> Much fuss is being made about aeroplanes. It may be as well, therefore, to explain that one of these machines has made experimental flights, but can in no way be described as taking part in the manoeuvres.

However, the intervention of Dickson and the others was at least a step in the right direction, towards the aeroplane's acceptance as an essential component of the nation's military establishment, paralleling – and surpassing – the history of the military balloon thirty years before. The aeroplane in general and the Boxkite in particular had gone some way to demonstrate their potential utility in the field. Here at last was an aeroplane, made in Britain, which could do the job and could be supplied in numbers. Bristols might well have expected an order from the War Office without delay. Unaccountably, the latter displayed no such alacrity; although an order was eventually placed, several more months were allowed to elapse while, before this came to pass, a couple of French aeroplanes were purchased on a tentative and experimental basis.

Meanwhile, some twenty miles to the north-east of Larkhill, another scene of aeronautical endeavour was being enacted. It had been during the previous winter that Geoffrey de Havilland had completed the construction of his first aeroplane and had then secured permission to experiment with it on some land near his family home, known as Seven Barrows, a little way south of Newbury, Berkshire. A shed, in which the aeroplane could be housed, was available on the site, having originally been erected for Moore-Brabazon, though the latter had never used it. The land was part of the estate of Lord Carnarvon, whose principal claim to fame, some years later, was due to his participation in the discovery in Egypt of the tomb of Tutankhamun. By the time that event took place, the young would-be aviator had also achieved distinction in his own chosen field, but in 1909, such success remained no more than a distant dream, as the time passed while, despite strenuous efforts, various defects kept his creation firmly confined to the ground.

At last, one December day, all problems seemed to have been solved and the machine stood ready for its supreme test. Determined to put an end to the weeks of frustration, its author clambered aboard and started its engine. Satisfied that all was well in that department, he opened the throttle and began to move forward, gradually gathering speed. At what he hoped was the right moment, he pulled the elevator control towards him and was rewarded by finding his mount lifting into the air. However, its first flight was to be of the very briefest, as the machine's structure showed itself unequal to the stresses it was being called upon to bear and its pilot found himself returned violently to earth, while his non-flying machine subsided around him into one more heap of fractured timber – to the initial anguish of his clergyman father, who was present that day. De Havilland was, however, quite unhurt, and he lost no time in gathering up the broken pieces and returning to the workshop behind the Fulham Palace Road where, undaunted and with the help of his assistant Frank Hearle, he began again.

With little left to salvage from the failure, it was virtually a case of starting again from scratch, so that it was the late summer of 1910 before the pair once more set off for Seven Barrows in a hired lorry, on which they were carrying the fruits of their labours. The new machine bore a strong resemblance to the earlier one, though with an improved and simplified engine and propeller installation, as well as, needless to say, a considerably strengthened structure. Its general lines suggested that its designer had followed the popular fashion begun by Voisin and carried on by Farman and others. In other words, it was a biplane, with twin girders extending behind the trailing edges, carrying at their extremities the fixed tailplane. Between them revolved the single pusher propeller, driven by the engine mounted on the lower wing, behind the pilot. A similar girder structure extended forward of the wings, bearing the moving front elevator to provide control in pitch, in the then classic manner.

The testing ground to which they had returned was a wide expanse of sloping meadowland, bordered on the north by the long grassy mound of Beacon Hill and dropping gently down on its eastern side to the main Winchester to Newbury road. Their shed at the top of the field still awaited them and within its shelter they started to assemble the machine. This work soon accomplished, the object of all their hopes was wheeled outside and de Havilland prepared to discover whether they were true or false. This time, however, he adopted a more systematic approach, beginning with some tentative taxiing around the field to familiarise himself with the machine's responses – for, like Cody and others, he was having to learn his piloting skills at the same time as he was exploring the characteristics of an untested aeroplane. After a week or so of these cautious trials and as experience bred more confidence, he took matters a step further. Increasing power and his forward speed, he lifted his craft into the air, carefully and more gently than the first time, and flew a short distance before letting it sink back onto the ground. Another advance! He had flown and had returned to earth without damage. Unhurriedly, as the days went by, he pursued his careful progress, not without minor incidents and the necessary repairs, but gradually extending the length and height of his hops and learning as he did so to match the movements of his controls with the responses of his machine.

Then, one day, with confidence the spur, a voice in his head told him to take the ultimate step. Taking his courage in both hands and keeping the engine at full power, he allowed his machine to fly on, taking him higher and further until it was clear that he had flown so far down the field that he would be unable to land straight ahead as before. This time, with his bridges burnt, he would for the first time have to fly around and make a complete circuit of his field. As Hearle watched anxiously with upturned face, de Havilland gently banked the aircraft, nursing it into a gentle turn until he was facing the way he had come. Then, flying on past his take-off point, he made another careful turn, to bring him back on to his original heading, ready to return to earth. Partially closing the throttle, he began his descent. Judging his approach with greater accuracy than many another beginner pilot of the future, he completed his triumph by setting his machine back on the ground, quite undamaged. In the following weeks, he continued gradually to improve his expertise, while gaining confidence in his machine. By the time that Bertram Dickson was delivering his reconnaissance reports, de Havilland had proved to his own satisfaction that he had produced an aeroplane which could fly, and fly well.

As all these different happenings confirmed that aviation was now firmly on an ascending path, that autumn, across the Atlantic in Chicago, an event of special poignancy took place, when the falling leaves marked not only the end of summer, but also the passing of that early apostle of aviation, Octave Chanute. Approaching his ninetieth year, he had lived long enough to see the torch, which he had done much to keep aflame, taken up and fanned to an ever-growing fire.

The few trees around Larkhill were also shedding their leaves when the Balloon School at last acquired its first flyable aeroplane. At three o'clock in the afternoon of 6 October, a small party of Royal Engineers alighted at Amesbury railway station and made their way up the hill to the Plain, where they took possession of one of the War Office sheds, setting up their own accommodation under canvas nearby. An aeroplane had also arrived by rail, having been sent over from France, dismantled and packed in its crate. The party was under the command of Lieutenant Reginald Cammell and the aeroplane was, of course, the Blériot XII. Lieutenant Boothby was also with them; although Cammell had not been able to shake him off, the fears he had expressed in his letter to Capper had not been realised. It would be Cammell, as a sapper and therefore in command of the detachment, who would decide who would be doing the flying. However, he would be expected to let Boothby 'have a go' from time to time.

The next day, after parading at half-past eight, the men set about assembling the Blériot. This was accomplished without difficulty and flying was planned to begin on the following day. Eager to get started, Cammell ordered an early turn-out and the machine had been pushed out of its shed and was ready to fly by the time the sun had risen. Unfortunately, the ENV refused to start. It took some time to trace the trouble to a faulty switch and the only event of note that day was a pay parade in the afternoon.

On the third day, with the engine problem cured and the weather deemed flyable, the party was again paraded at an early hour and the machine then towed a short distance north, to the foot of Knighton Down. The undulating nature of the terrain and the persistent mist made for poor flying conditions, but Cammell was able to make five flights, all quite short, before later in the day the weather deteriorated further. His longest flight lasted for 15 minutes, during which he ventured a little further into the mist and lost his way, until Stonehenge loomed up unmistakably in the gloom to show him his position. Thankfully, he landed nearby and, having gathered himself together, took off again and flew quickly back to his shed. During the day, Boothby was allowed to perform some short ground runs.

Further flights followed, with proceedings frequently interrupted by bad weather and repairs due to heavy landings. Cammell was discovering both the limitations of his mount and some of the pitfalls involved in this still-new skill of piloting:

> The Rudder effect is very weak still (it was greatly strengthened after the first flight in France) and in certain conditions it seems very hard indeed to turn to the right. Possibly, however, I did not allow sufficient cant during the turns. One's natural inclination is to remain level at all costs.
>
> At present I am fully occupied with stability and steering, and am not able to observe at all. The very undulating nature of the ground is very disconcerting at first. The hills seem to rise up and hit one. The mist, of course, greatly increases one's difficulties.

On 28 October, a particularly heavy landing put the machine in the hangar for three weeks and brought the following repentance from its pilot:

> I greatly regret the accident which is primarily due, of course, to my own inexperience. The great lesson the Blériot people dinned into me was 'never let the machine lose its "way"', as it drops at once and is quite uncontrollable. However, on this ground it is extremely difficult to know if one is going up or down (I have often felt that I must be falling rapidly, when really I was only coming to a hill). My first idea was

to blame the machine (it always is) and I am afraid I rather gave Broke-Smith that impression, but on further reflection I believe it was almost entirely due to me trying to climb and turn at the same time without accelerating the engine.

Young Cammell was finding out about stalling! It sounds as if a full spin was not allowed to develop only because of his habit, widespread at that time, of flying so close to the ground. Many modern pilots, were they to be called upon to fly the tricky Type XII, while attempting to cope with its capricious 60 hp and lacking the luxury of an airspeed indicator or, at such a low altitude in such misty conditions, much in the way of a visual horizontal reference, might sometimes have found it difficult to maintain a safe flying attitude. It was, one would surmise, during those days of discovery at Larkhill that the machine earned its unenviable soubriquet of 'the Mankiller'!

The Blériot was still undergoing repair when 3 November brought a diversion in the form of John Dunne, who arrived with a new machine, in the devising of which Capper himself had taken a hand, apparently using parts of a monoplane glider which Dunne had built at Farnborough in 1906. Dunne and another pilot made several short flights, which Cammell described as promising.

With Bristols's flying school now fully functioning and Cockburn and Fulton also frequently in the air, the air above Larkhill was becoming almost crowded. On the 15th, another significant event took place. Fulton had by then advanced his flying skills to the point where he felt himself ready to be tested for his Royal Aero Club Aviator's Certificate. As luck would have it, on the day appointed for his test, his own Blériot lay in its shed, unserviceable. Nothing daunted, he went next door, borrowed Cockburn's Farman – a type he had never flown, and a biplane to boot – and passed the test for his certificate (No.27) on that. It would not be long before his new qualification found him fresh employment.

Towards the end of the month, the Blériot XII was ready once more. As his skills developed, Cammell began ranging further afield and staying airborne for longer, though never rising much more than a hundred feet above ground level. By the end of November, he was ready to contemplate the next leap forward: his first cross-country flight. No man for half-measures, his intention was nothing less than a ferry flight from Larkhill to the factory at Farnborough – a distance of some 46 miles. On the morning of the 29th, he went up to try out the conditions, circling over Stonehenge and Knighton Down and for the first time climbing up to the giddy height of 500 feet. The autumnal mists had not diminished and, with the visibility along his intended route looking very poor, he decided, after an uncomfortably cold 40 minutes in the air, to come down and postpone his departure until the afternoon.

The machine was once more prepared for flight and soon after midday he took off to have another look. As the ground slowly fell away and the view opened out, he found that the visibility, though still restricted in the misty atmosphere, had somewhat improved. As he circled above the Avon valley, he could see, to the south-west, the scattered blocks of Stonehenge standing up above the surrounding land, their weathered faces catching the watery sunlight. Looking in the opposite direction, along his intended track, no longer up-sun as in the morning, he was able to see much further. He made his decision, turned his nose eastwards and started out on his adventure, leaving below him the toy figures of his small detachment, faces upturned outside their shed, watching as his machine slowly dwindled and finally disappeared from their view into the mist. With any luck, he could hope to be at Farnborough by two o'clock.

Like the other aeronauts in the Balloon School, he was not without experience of cross-country flying, in both balloons and dirigibles, so contact navigation, by picking out and identifying features on the ground, was no new skill, except that those features were coming into view and passing beneath him rather more quickly than he had been used to. He began by following the railway line south-eastwards from

Amesbury and then on to Stockbridge. He had come down to about 400 feet above the ground, no doubt leaving not a few faces gazing upwards from garden and field, drawn by the unaccustomed sight and sound in the sky above them. At Stockbridge, he made a slight error and, finding himself approaching Winchester, somewhat to the south of his intended track, he landed near the village of Crawley to look at his map. Completing this manoeuvre successfully, he took to the air once more, correcting his flight path and soon striking the helpful railway line from Winchester, which offered to lead him onwards to Basingstoke. But now the wind, playing its malign hand, began to strengthen. At 300 feet over Micheldever, the turbulence induced by the railway cutting there became strong enough to persuade Cammell that he should land and wait for calmer conditions. Struggling on another couple of miles, he found a suitably large field near North Waltham, where he brought his machine successfully to earth.

The rest was anti-climax. At three o'clock, with the wind seeming to have abated, he resolved to set out once more. He began his take-off run, but was obliged to abandon it when he found the machine becoming uncontrollable. The problem was traced to a broken bolt, but, with the necessary repairs proving impossible that day and wind and rain arriving the next, Cammell had no choice but to end his gallant attempt, the Blériot finding itself ignominiously dismantled in a cowshed, before being conveyed by road to Farnborough. Once there, its destiny was to see it becoming a sacrificial assistant to the plotting of O'Gorman in the factory.

7

A Motley Collection

Gradually, the aeroplane was gaining acceptance. During his visit to Wilbur Wright at Pau in February 1909, Lord Northcliffe had written to Lord Esher, the chairman of that CID Sub-Committee which had so dismissively put the aeroplane aside in favour of the airship:

> I have been here some time making a study of the aeroplane. Our national muddle-headedness has rarely been seen to worse disadvantage than in this particular matter, aviation. Here, some seven hundred and fifty miles from London, is a machine which can fly perfectly at forty miles an hour, at any height up to about a mile. It is stated by the German and French officers here to be practically 'unhitable'; provided with wireless telegraphy, the operator can scout an enemy's positions in a way possible by no other means.

The CID had by that date taken its decision to confirm the sub-committee's recommendation to dispense with Cody's services, so we need have no fear that Northcliffe's rather intemperate and disparaging remarks in the same letter about the English aeroplane arrangements being 'in the hands of an American who, on his own statements, knows nothing about aviation' and who 'got the appointment because he knows something about kites' in any way affected that decision. Perhaps, though, his other remarks did constitute the nudge which raised the first uneasiness in Esher's mind: that heavier-than-air aeronautics now deserved more serious consideration than it had received from his committee. By the autumn of the following year, his change of heart was complete, witnessed by the note which he issued on 6 October 1910, when the evidence of the Salisbury Plain manoeuvres and, more importantly, of those in France was to hand:

> The manoeuvres in Picardy have made it quite clear that the experimental stage is over, and that an army would be seriously handicapped in the field if its commander were unable to take advantage in the use of aeroplanes in tactical reconnaissance.

Going on to suggest the desirability of purchasing 'thirty or forty' aeroplanes for the army's use, he concluded his short note by posing a number of questions – which he termed proposals – and by sounding a warning:

1. Whether a corps of aviators should be formed.
2. Whether a school of practical aviation should be established, and if so, where.
3. From what class the personnel should be selected.
4. By what department of State such a school should be organised and controlled.
5. Whether the personnel of officers and men should be handed over in time of peace respectively to the navy and army authorities, and left under their permanent control.

6. Or, whether they should be interchangeable, and should be lent to the navy and army authorities for the purpose of manoeuvres.

7. Under what head of the estimates the cost of the purchase of aeroplanes should be charged.

I am concerned to make these remarks and suggestions, because in view of the German fleet of airships, and of the use of aeroplanes in the recent French manoeuvres, it must be obvious to those interested in forecasting the probabilities of the next great war, that unless some immediate and rapid development takes place in aerostation and aviation by the British naval and military authorities, Great Britain may find herself labouring under grave disadvantages, for which the Committee of Imperial Defence would not unnaturally be blamed.

These words from such an august and relevant pen will have given great comfort to men like Fulton and Dickson and indeed foreshadowed much that would be put in place some eighteen months later. For the time being, however, there still remained a great deal to be learnt and accomplished – and other minds to be convinced – before the ultimate goal was achieved.

Meanwhile, command of the Balloon School had passed into the hands of Major Sir Alexander Bannerman RE, John Capper having been appointed Commandant of the School of Military Engineering at Chatham, on promotion to full colonel. The inflexible nature of the army machine had obliged him, after seven years of striving, to hand over his command just as his efforts to endow the British Army with an aviation service were showing the first real signs of bearing fruit, although some time was yet to pass before the harvest would ripen. By the day of his departure, the Balloon School had succeeded in getting its hands on just two aeroplanes – the Wright and the Blériot – and a short time later, both could have been discovered resting in the Balloon Factory, distinctly unserviceable. In the face of sustained public agitation by George Holt Thomas and Lord Northcliffe, whose sword was never wont to sleep in his hand, the War Office – not yet quite ready nor sufficiently ambitious to embrace Lord Esher's thirty or forty – cautiously decided to add two more machines to its embryonic fleet. As it happened, Holt Thomas had now become the representative in this country of the interests of two of the leading French designers, Louis Paulhan and Henri Farman. It is with interest, therefore, that one notes, not only that the War Office continued to shop in France, but that its choice fell upon machines from those same two constructors. Instead of the Farman, it might just as well have purchased a Boxkite – as indeed it eventually did – since both owed their inspiration to the earlier Voisin, and thus have patronised British industry, an omission which incensed A. V. Roe, provoking him to write:

> ... it is very unlikely that the government will get anything but the standard Farman that we know so well, and had been made successfully by several English manufacturers. In any case, it is far better that our money should help to build up the English industry than our foreign rivals.

As for the Paulhan, that was to prove a very strange concept indeed.

The first to arrive, in December, was the Farman, known as the *Type Militaire*, purchased for £1,008. It differed from the standard Farman by the addition of a third rudder and of extensions to increase the span of its upper wing. With its arrival, we find appearing on the stage another personality who, like Fulton, furnishes an example of an increasing trend whereby more and more of the army's aviators would be found from outside the ranks of the Corps of Royal Engineers. Captain Charles James Burke, of the Royal Irish Regiment, was another of those who had chosen the French path to the skies, having learnt to fly at Farman's school, where he was awarded his Aéro Club de France *brevet* on 4 October 1910. Along with Fulton, the twenty-eight-year-old Burke, whose

Charles Burke's Henri Farman *Type Militaire*, Air Battalion serial no. F.1. (RAF Museum)

ample form had earned for him the unkind nickname of 'Pregnant Percy', had recently joined the Balloon School on attachment. Each had barely two months' experience as qualified pilots and could scarcely be described as old hands, but both had flown solo and both possessed pilot's certificates, which was more than any other member of the Balloon School could boast (including Cammell, for he did not take the test and acquire his own RAeC certificate until the end of the year). Burke it was, therefore, who was chosen to carry out the early test-flying of the Farman.

Farnborough was, of course, still the headquarters of the Balloon School, so it was to that place, rather than Larkhill, that the machine was delivered and it was from Laffan's Plain, on 7 January 1911, that Burke made his first flight in the aeroplane, newly released by the factory, which had checked it over after its arrival. This flight was completed successfully, but unfortunately, a second one later the same day was not, when the machine's far-from-experienced pilot lost flying speed, dropped a wing and crashed, with severe damage both to himself and to the aeroplane. While the former went into hospital, the latter was carried into the Balloon Factory for its own extensive repairs.

Fulton, meanwhile, had been charged with inspecting the other intended purchase and observing its flying capabilities, before recommending its acceptance. Accompanied by the ubiquitous Holt Thomas, he had crossed over to France just before Christmas. Paulhan's machine awaited them at St Cyr, the home of the French army's cadet school, within cannon-shot of the formal gardens and the elegant façades of the Chateau of Versailles, and even nearer to the scene of Clément Ader's disappointment in 1897, the army camp of Satory.

Fulton had not been the original choice, Major Bannerman having proposed that Lieutenant H. R. P. Reynolds RE, a Balloon School officer, should be sent. Reynolds had qualified on balloons and kites the previous summer, but had never flown an aeroplane. Such an omission from the list of his credentials seems not to have constituted, in Bannerman's view, a serious drawback. After all, Cammell, when he was sent to Etampes, had been no less handicapped. However, that was in earlier days, when the army was unable to boast a single qualified pilot. Now it had two. Unfortunately, to Bannerman, they suffered from an even greater shortcoming: not only were they merely 'on attachment' to the Balloon School, worse – they were not even sappers. It would appear that the Balloon School's Commandant, as a sapper himself, was keen to keep control of the army's aerial service in the hands of the Royal Engineers, as it had always been, with a certain inherent resistance to allowing officers from outside the Corps, like Fulton, into the club. It was a stance which was

Two views of the Paulhan machine which was acquired by the Air Battalion. (Author's collection)

becoming ever more difficult to maintain, as Capper, with greater clarity of vision, had already recognised a year earlier. DFW was of the same opinion and, aware of how matters stood, specifically required Bannerman to find an officer for the task who was in possession of a pilot's certificate. Bannerman, as he was bound to do, obeyed his superior's command, but could not refrain from lodging a protest:

> I still adhere to the opinion ... that more benefit would be derived by sending one of my Engineer Aeronauts to be trained in France, insisting that the vendor of the machine should instruct him in flying it as part of the purchase price; but if an officer with a pilot certificate is required, I recommend that Captain J. D. B. Fulton, Royal Field Artillery, should be sent.

So Fulton it was who went to try out the Paulhan 'experimental' biplane. The latter was its creator's first sally into the aeroplane design field, following his triumph over Grahame-White in the London-to-Manchester race, and it embodied a design feature of the more eccentric kind. Disdaining the manifest advantages conferred by the principles of streamlining and drag reduction which his rivals were now embracing with increasing devotion, Paulhan had produced a wing and auxiliary surfaces whose leading edges embodied two spanwise ash strips, one above the other, held apart by spacers disposed in a concertina form, and between which the air could flow freely, though turbulently, before passing over the wing surface proper. Two parallel fore-and-aft beams, constructed in the same manner, carried the forward elevator, the two crew seats just in front of the wing, the Gnôme engine and its pusher propeller and, at the rear, the rudder and a fixed horizontal stabiliser. The method of construction chosen was thought to possess the merit of high strength, albeit at the expense of aerodynamic cleanliness.

At all events, Fulton found himself able to send a positive report concerning the machine's qualities and the purchase was duly approved by DFW. On 19 January, while Burke and the Farman were still recovering from their separate injuries, Fulton reported again to Bannerman, confirming that he had flown the Paulhan and considered that it flew well, though 'very fast'. There then took place the inevitable crash, when the pilot 'landed awkwardly' as he turned at too low an altitude – as ever – to avoid touching down on some plough. The damage, to one wing and the propeller, was made good by Paulhan, at the War Office's expense, while Fulton took the opportunity in his report to make the following plea:

> I suppose it is to be sent to Farnborough but if this is not definitely settled, I hope very much you will consider whether it would not be better, at any rate at first, to keep it at Salisbury Plain, where the good surface and much less hampered flying space are a great deal more suited to such a fast machine : especially for teaching beginners, which I suppose will be done.

The Paulhan was, nevertheless, like the Farman, delivered to Farnborough. On arrival, it was immediately abducted by O'Gorman and taken into the factory's care, where it was to remain for some little while, being subjected to certain improvements.

While he was in France, Fulton had seized the opportunity to visit the French army's camp near Châlons-sur-Marne, some 120 kilometres east of Paris, where a military School of Aviation had been established. Like Colonel Repington, he was impressed by the considerable lead that French military aviation enjoyed over that in his own country. Substantial sums had been allocated to it, resulting in facilities and equipment which were far more extensive and an organisation with objectives which were well in advance of those currently being contemplated in his own country. Already, he reported, twenty permanent hangars had been erected, with more planned, while there were as many as forty pupils learning to fly. A part of Fulton's report which was of especial significance was that which dealt with aviation's status within the French army. As in Great Britain, it had been born a child of the engineers; it was now recognised, however, that to constrain it narrowly within the field represented by that arm was no longer desirable:

> It has been decided, therefore, to constitute a special corps to deal with aviation, and this corps will not be attached or related to any existing arm of the Service. It is this change which is proceeding at present.
>
> The organisation at Chalons Camp is nominally divided into two parts, controlled respectively by the Artillery and Engineers, and it is the custom, probably from habit, to regard the two parts as separate – even to the extent of a certain friendly rivalry. But I learn that, officially, aviation either is or almost immediately will be controlled direct by the War Office, and will be regarded as a separate Arm.

In England, matters were rather less forward. The Balloon School, after its short and very limited flurry of winged activity, had become once more totally reliant on hydrogen for its aerial ascents. The condition of those few aeroplanes which it had contrived to acquire may be summarised as follows:

Machine	Date of arrival	Current state
Wright Type A	April 1910	In store; unflyable.
Blériot XII	October 1910	In the factory being rebuilt.
Henri Farman 'Type Militaire'	December 1910	In the factory under repair, following Burke's crash.
Paulhan 'Experimental'	January 1911	In the factory, being 'improved'.

That was not much of an air force. It is true that there was also Fulton's Blériot XI, while Cammell was soon to invest in a Blériot XXI, with one or two others following suit. In those less formally constrained days, these machines were flown by their owners and, although privately owned, were regarded as being on army business. That business was probably no more at that stage than the ongoing gathering of much-needed flying experience by the pilots involved, but in the current circumstances, a highly valuable activity in itself. However, it was a strange way to run a flying service. The Minister for War, Richard Haldane, reporting to the House of Commons in February, put the best possible gloss on it:

> Now I come to aeroplanes. We have purchased five, which are available for practical instruction. Three are of the latest pattern – the Farman, Paulhan and de Havilland. Besides that we have just completed the purchase of four additional biplanes from Sir George White of Bristol, of the British and Colonial Aeroplane Company. ... That will give us nine aeroplanes altogether.

This was hardly descriptive of the reality as the Balloon School knew it. The 'de Havilland' was that same machine which its designer had successfully flown at Seven Barrows and which had indeed been purchased by the War Office. However, its acquisition had been arranged by the civilian O'Gorman, with no involvement of the military side at Farnborough, and it had gone straight into the factory, where it stayed. No army pilot would ever get his hands on it. As for Sir George's four Boxkites, the truth was that, far from their purchase being completed, the official order was yet to be placed and delivery of the fourth machine would not take place until the summer was well advanced.

Samuel Cody, from his position as neighbour and close acquaintance of both the Balloon School and the factory, knew better than Richard Haldane how things lay. Well aware of the lack of aeroplanes available to the army aviators, he seized the moment and offered to sell them his second machine, with which he had just won the Michelin Cup, at a price of £850. This proposition was forwarded to DFW, but the warm support of Major Bannerman which accompanied it was quickly cooled by DFW's rejection, which advised the latter that 'a "Cody" Aeroplane cannot be ordered this financial year, but the question of purchase in 1911-12 will be considered.'

Further eulogies from Bannerman, in May and again in the following January, met with the same stony dismissal, by which time, the claims of other designers had found more favourable responses.

8

A Matter of Power

The achievement of true flight depends on a number of things, but since the first and most fundamental requirement consists of mastery of the earth's gravitational pull, it goes without saying that an engine which can supply the necessary power while contributing as little as possible to an aeroplane's total weight must feature amongst the more desirable elements in its design. Indeed, it will not have escaped the reader's notice that, among the problems which the early pioneers found themselves having to overcome, not the least was the finding and acquisition of an engine which would provide that necessary power to get their machine off the ground and into the air. The fact was that there were, in those early days, very few suitable engines available. Who can say that, had Roe in 1908 been blessed with more than the miserable nine horsepower of his JAP, or had Dunne been supplied, like Cody, with a 50-hp Antoinette, rather than the lesser and always uncertain power of the REP, it would not be one of those two who would today be recognised as the designer of the first successful British aeroplane?

However, in 1908, with the aeroplane yet to reveal itself as a viable mode of transport, it is not surprising that almost the only internal combustion engines which lay to hand at that time should be those intended for earth-based projects such as motor cars, in which application the weight of the engine was of rather less critical importance. In a field where the market prospects were of such small proportions, engine manufacturers would have sensed little encouragement to design engines specifically for aeronautical applications, where, for example, attention to weight-saving needed to be high in the list of the designer's considerations.

There were, nevertheless, exceptions to this impasse, of which the leading example was the Antoinette, a water-cooled engine with its cylinders arranged in a V-8 configuration. For it was as early as 1902 that its bearded and portly creator, Léon Levavasseur, had started work on his vision of an engine to power the aeroplanes which he was confident would soon be needing them. As a result, when, in 1905, Louis Blériot began to cast around for a suitable engine to install in his first practical, albeit unsuccessful project, the Blériot III, it was a 24-hp Antoinette which he chose, continuing to use the marque in each new model which marked his path to eventual success. When, at the end of October 1908, he flew his Blériot VIII the 28 kilometres from Toury to Artenay to make only the world's second cross-country flight, he was still sitting behind an Antoinette engine. (Farman had made the first, twenty-four hours earlier, also with the help of an Antoinette.)

As the aeroplane designers began to achieve a measure of success, their achievements encouraged other aero engine producers to follow Levavasseur's lead. Robert Esnault Pelterie, whom we have already met, although not associated with particularly happy auspices, built his first aero engine, a 5-cylinder radial, in 1906 and this was followed by a number of others, all air-cooled radials in either five- or seven-cylinder form. They were not particularly successful and by early 1912 Esnault Pelterie had withdrawn from the engine field (although, having turned also to aeroplane manufacture, he retained for a time his place amongst the pioneers).

Greater success was achieved by the water-cooled engines devised by the Renault company, foremost amongst the motor firms which turned to the air, and in the ensuing years they would be found equipping numerous machines, as Europe prepared for war.

Equally successful was an Italian expatriate, Alexandre Anzani, who had become an aero engine constructor by a curious route. In the early years of the century, he had raced bicycles and then, later on, motorcycles, both with considerable success. Then, after a spell of employment with the Buchet company, he started his own small firm, making both motorcycles and the engines which powered them. Ere long, he found that the latter were beginning to interest the aeroplane designers. His big chance came in 1909. Levavasseur had decided to return to an old ambition – that of designing and building his own aeroplane. Perhaps because it seemed undesirable that the latter should continue to supply engines for use in the products of a potential rival, Blériot at this point looked elsewhere for a different motor to install in his new model, the Type XI. To begin with, he tried an REP, but despairing, like Dunne, of its erratic performance, he ended by replacing it with a 24-hp three-cylinder Anzani. Thus it came to pass that, on the day when Blériot emerged from the Channel mists to his landing on the meadow above the Dover cliffs, it was Anzani, rather than Levavasseur, who was able to claim that his was the power source which had carried him across.

In Great Britain, the dearth of home-grown aeroplanes at that time produced the same effect in the aero engine field as had previously been experienced in France. If there were apparently few men capable of producing effective flying machines, such an exiguous market was likely to give small incentive to any who might have produced the appropriate engines to fit to them. Geoffrey de Havilland overcame the problem by designing his own, which was built for him by the Iris Motor Company of Willesden, North London, but he was very much an exception. For the rest, it was a case of finding and buying an engine from whatever source came to hand and which looked likely to do the job.

Searching the domestic scene, they would have found little encouragement. In principle, there was ENV, whose main output consisted of water-cooled V-8 engines (hence '*le moteur en V*'). However, that company, although founded in England with English designs, possessed manufacturing workshops in both London and in Paris and its centre of gravity could be said to have lain in France. Moore-Brabazon, when he returned to England with his Voisin, 'Bird of Passage', in early 1909, replaced its Vivinus engine with an ENV, Cody used an ENV spasmodically in 1909-10 and Bristols toyed with their installation in a couple of Boxkites. However, until 1911, the ENV company found the greater part of its market on the other side of the Channel.

In fact, Britain's only serious engine manufacturer in those years was a self-taught engineer in his forties, Gustavus Green, who, by 1904, was producing a series of water-cooled engines to drive some of the early motor cars, including ones which he built himself. By 1908, his work had attracted the notice of the balloonists at Farnborough and in late 1909, as was described earlier, a Green engine was fitted to the dirigible *Baby* and another to *Gamma* a few months later, although in the latter case, the Green was soon replaced by two more de Havilland-designed Iris engines.

Nevertheless, Green engines, having made their mark in the aerial world, were very much in contention when the aeroplane began belatedly to emerge from its chrysalis. Moore-Brabazon had a 60-hp Green engine installed in the biplane which had been built for him by the Short brothers and on which, in March 1910, he won the British Empire Michelin Trophy with a flight of 19 miles. Cody fitted the same mark of Green to his second machine, with which, at the end of that same year, he also secured a Michelin Trophy. Roe, too, was at that time choosing Greens for several of his early machines. For all that, however, after their short-lived selection for the two dirigibles, they found no favour with the army aeronauts, whether of the lighter-than-air or the heavier-than-air school.

As 1911 advanced and the pioneer British designers began to show that they could produce viable aeroplanes, the progression which had taken place in France was repeated over here. Other engine manufacturers, such as the New Engine Company (NEC) and the motor manufacturers Wolseley and Humber, were encouraged to devise their own aero engines and offer them to the market which was now emerging. The NEC engines, although only two-strokes, were supercharged and, in a 4-cylinder version, claimed to deliver as much as 40 hp. Humber, having decided to manufacture Blériot monoplanes under licence in its Coventry works, complemented this initiative by producing its own 30- and 50-hp air-cooled engines to power them. Like the Green, such engines were installed in certain other home-built aeroplanes but, like the Green, they too saw no service with the British Army.

Wolseley began by supplying engines for certain civilian dirigibles and were hopeful, apparently, of securing an order for engines to be fitted to *The Morning Post*'s Lebaudy – a prospect which expired with the latter's demise on the roof of Woodlands Cottage. Although a Wolseley engine served briefly with the Air Battalion, it was soon found wanting and replaced by an engine from France.

Indeed, the fact of the matter was that, with the War Office continuing to procure its aeroplanes from across the Channel, it was hardly to be expected that such machines would be powered by other than French-built engines. In any case, another aero engine had by now appeared on the scene, which was not only French but which also embodied a quite radical principle, and was to dominate the scene for the next decade. The age of the Rotary had dawned.

Although, as the years went by, other makes were to arise, in 1909, the rotary engine meant the Gnôme, brainchild of Laurent Seguin and his two brothers. It embodied a remarkably different design principle from that of all other engines then available. In the rotary engine, the cylinders were disposed in a ring around a central crankshaft, just as they were in a normal radial engine, and like the latter were air-cooled. However, the rotary differed from the radial in one very radical respect. Whereas, in a radial engine, the propeller is driven, in the classic manner, by the rotation of the crankshaft, in the rotary engine the crankshaft is bolted to the airframe and therefore prevented from rotating, while it is the mass of the cylinders which is free to rotate, thus revolving around the crankshaft and carrying with it the propeller, which is fixed to it. This seemingly perverse arrangement resulted in a very efficient engine, which tended to possess a significantly more favourable power-weight ratio than its competitors – a quality which naturally commended itself to men whose first and ever-present enemy was gravity.

Reference to Appendix III will reveal that, of the first fifteen machines which were, at different times, available for use by the army's pilots until the profound changes resulting from the reorganisation in the spring of 1912 slowly brought in a much larger fleet, no fewer than nine were powered by Gnôme rotaries. Of the others, only the B.E.1 had a British engine – the Wolseley referred to above – and that only for the reason – albeit a rather contrary one – that it had been redeemed from a French-built Voisin which had been donated by the Duke of Westminster. In any case, this untidy aberration was soon rectified; in June 1912, the Wolseley's troublesome history led to its replacement by another French engine, in the shape of a Renault. An engine from the same company was also fitted to the factory's next product, the B.E.2, and to all subsequent versions of that aeroplane for some time to come.

Two years later, when mobilisation came in August 1914, little had changed: of the engines which propelled the RFC's first four squadrons across the Channel to war, most were Renaults or Gnômes; none were British.

The evolution of the propeller:
(a) Henson's model;
(b) A. V. Roe's first triplane;
(c) the Wright Type A;
(d) the Blériot XXI;
(e) the B.E.1. (Author's collection)

If no aeroplane was of much use without an engine, no engine (in those days) could perform its task without a propeller. When all the questions concerning wing lift, structural strength, stability and control had been answered – at least to the best of the designers' ability – and a suitable engine had been found, there still remained the design of a propeller, or propellers, to transform the rotary motion developed by the engine into the linear thrust needed to drive the aeroplane forward.

As in all power transmission systems, there is inevitably a loss to be suffered in the course of this transformation. The trick was of course – and still is – to keep this loss to a minimum, so that the use of a propeller which was as efficient as possible in that respect was of no small importance. Many of the earliest efforts were, for all that, no more than rudimentary, being of a simple, straight-edged form, with a chord which steadily increased towards the tip, unlike the shapes later adopted and still familiar today, with their slender curves and pointed tips. Men such as Henson and Maxim were strong adherents to the former school, with stubby propeller blades whose maximum chords measured as much as a half or a third of their radii. Other choices, Roe's included, were even more primitive, employing what can only be described as a paddle fixed to the end of a stick. The Wrights, we may be sure, did not omit propellers from the serious thought which they gave to all their work, although they too favoured the principle of maximum chord at maximum radius, albeit to a far more restrained degree.

As aviation technology evolved, propeller design also advanced, as designers gave rather more profound thought to the subject than perhaps was feasible when they were fully preoccupied with just getting off the ground. Thus, with the arrival of machines like the B.E.1 and the later Avros, we find the earlier inefficient shapes giving way to forms something like those we know today, making their own contribution to the improved performances which more advanced aerodynamics and more efficient engines were beginning to achieve.

9

The Air Battalion and the Aircraft Factory

As the year 1910 neared its end, the British Army's aeronautical service was scarcely impressive, as we have seen. In the course of the year, it had acquired its first flyable aeroplane – albeit by philanthropy – which had been flown, to a very limited extent, but then taken from it, never, events would reveal, to be returned. It had then obtained a second machine, which was of a more promising design, and was shortly to take delivery of a third, which was not. As for pilots, it had three, two of whom had benefited from tuition given them in France. For the first time, aeroplanes had taken part in the annual army manoeuvres; unfortunately, being at that time unable to furnish either machines or pilots, the Balloon School had been obliged to see its duties usurped by civilians, flying aeroplanes which had been supplied from private sources. All this scarcely represented a history of dynamic advancement.

Nevertheless, in contrast to the frosty winter into which, a year earlier, British military aviation had been plunged by the findings of the CID Sub-Committee on Aerial Navigation, the first months of 1911 were to see the emergence of the first green shoots of spring. After the initial germination induced by Lord Esher's recantation, they were now given further nourishment, thanks to a contribution from another member of that unfortunate sub-committee. The convert this time was no less than the Chief of the General Staff, Field Marshal Sir William Nicholson himself, the same man who, in 1900, had stated his opinion that flying was 'a useless and expensive fad, advocated by a few individuals whose ideas are unworthy of attention' and who, in his confident ignorance, was so dismissive of the aeroplane's possibilities during the sub-committee's sittings. With such a record, Sir William has ever since suffered his share of condemnation as a narrow-minded reactionary where aviation was concerned – criticism which, from today's comfortable standpoint, it is difficult to counter. Nevertheless, remembering the Biblical dictum which, roughly paraphrased, bids us to rejoice over one sinner that repenteth, rather than 'ninety-nine just persons which need no repentance', so perhaps should we extend to him too the justice of our recognition of his change of heart, when, on 17 February 1911, we find him minuting:

It is of importance that we should push on with the practical study of the military use of air-craft in the field and with the training of personnel in observing and conveying information of their observations. I consider that the military personnel employed as observers should also be trained pilots.

The military training of personnel is a matter for which I am responsible, as soon as you can provide the air-craft necessary for the purpose. Even with the present types of dirigibles and aeroplanes other nations have already made considerable progress in this training and in view of the fact that air-craft will undoubtedly be used in the next war, whenever it may come, we cannot afford to delay in the matter.

I am desirous of employing both airships and aeroplanes during divisional and army manoeuvres this year.

So even he came round in the end. With such support from the very summit, however belated, the tide was at last flowing with the aviators, while as for that which in the end counts for the most in support for any cause, the aeronauts found it in the Army Estimates for the coming twelve months. Military aeronautics had been allocated a total sum of £133,300, representing an increase of some £50,000 over the previous year.

This enhancement of the status of military aeronautics was accompanied by a further consideration of the organisational changes needed, to which various minds applied themselves. At the lower end of the scale, they included that of Reginald Cammell, who was tasked to produce proposals for the immediate future.

Cammell began his report by announcing that he did not intend to discuss 'the many contentious problems which follow from the proposed use of the aeroplane in war'. In other words, as a mere lieutenant of engineers, it was not for him to enter into discussions of higher policy decisions concerning any desirable changes to the command structure currently in place. Instead, he contented himself with undefined references to an 'aeroplane branch', with a permanent specialist staff, whose duties would consist of 'Aeroplane Instruction and Experiment'. It would, in effect, be a cadre, to be expanded into an operational 'Air Company' on mobilisation. Disappointingly, he proposed that officers and men should 'pass through' this unit as part of their training in general engineering duties; even Cammell, the enthusiastic aviator, seemed unable to envisage the new arm as more than just another branch of the army's engineering facilities.

His recommendations were thus restricted largely to subjects of an immediately practical nature, most particularly the aeroplanes, flying grounds and equipment needed for the aeroplane branch to carry out its work. With regard to aeroplanes, Cammell's proposals amounted to a modest total of ten, as follows:

> For instructional training:
>   2 Bristol Boxkites
>   2 Blériot Type XIs
> For experimental work:
>   1 Farman
>   1 Blériot Type XI
>   1 Antoinette
>   1 Paulhan
>   1 Dunne
>   1 Valkyrie or Cody

When it came to a flying ground, despite his experience of Larkhill, he seems to have bowed to the inevitable and accepted that it would have to be Farnborough, although he gave preference to Laffan's Plain over the Common, the latter being still cluttered with trees and, naturally enough for common land, the troublesome public.

As for the unit's internal organisation, he proposed a remarkably small permanent establishment of two officers and eighteen other ranks. Of these, he seemed to think that only two – one officer and one senior NCO – would be sufficient to cope with the instructional work, flying and ground respectively. The rest would constitute the 'Experimental Staff' – a group which, despite its name, would clearly also be required to deal with the day-to-day maintenance of all the unit's machines.

All quite sensible so far as it went, if distinctly unambitious, but it did not constitute the fundamental examination of the status of military aeronautics which was needed and which Cammell had neither the experience nor the authority to tackle. Nor was he free from the fetters imposed on his reasoning by virtue of his membership of the Royal Engineers. Whether by inclination or from obedience to policy imposed by his seniors, he accepted the *status quo*. The fundamental question – whether or not the air corps should remain simply one of a number of activities controlled by the army's engineers – lay below his personal horizon. Such a decision was one to be taken in the lofty eminences of the War Office, uninhabited by subalterns. There a conclusion was indeed arrived at, albeit one which in retrospect must be seen as inadequate and which could hardly be described as radical.

The change was disclosed in an Army Order issued at the end of February 1911, which ordained that the Balloon School, as anachronous in its name as it was in its equipment and terms of reference, was to be superseded by a new unit which, it was intended, would better suit the new military situation which the advent of the aeroplane was slowly revealing. The Balloon School would be replaced by a new formation whose title – the Air Battalion of the Corps of Royal Engineers – indicated that responsibility for military aeronautics was to be allowed to remain in the hands of the sappers. The opportunity to grasp the nettle and accord aeronautics the importance which would make it an independent corps of the army was deferred until another day.

The order took effect on the first day of the following April, with Major Bannerman continuing in command. The new formation had an establishment of fourteen officers and 176 other ranks, divided between two companies. No.1 Company, responsible for the operation of airships, balloons and kites (was it merely coincidence, or a sign of lingering prejudice that the lighter-than-air school was given this numerical precedence?), was commanded by Captain E. M. Maitland, seconded from the Essex Regiment. No.2 Company, responsible for the aeroplane side, was commanded by John Fulton. Consideration had also been given to the formation, on the one hand, of an Air Battalion Reserve, for up to 100 officers who had qualified as pilots at civilian flying schools, and, on the other, of a Territorial Force Air Battalion, which would have incorporated the London Balloon Company. In the event, neither of these latter proposals was acted upon, for reasons which will appear in due course.

To return to the regular Air Battalion, the order had stated, amongst its other provisions, that its officers 'will be selected from any regular arm or branch of the Service on the active list' and it is noteworthy that neither of the two Company Commanders was a Royal Engineer – indeed that only two of the officers in No.2 Company were members of that corps; the sappers' grip on military aeronautics was becoming ever less sure.

Major Sir Alexander Bannerman. (Museum of Army Flying)

The full list of the battalion's officers on its formation was as follows:

Commandant	Major Sir A. Bannerman, RE
Adjutant	Captain P. W. L. Broke-Smith, RE
Experimental Officer	Captain A. D. Carden, RE
Quartermaster	Hon. Lieutenant F. H. Kirby, VC, RE
No.1 Company	Captain E. M. Maitland, Essex Regt (Officer Commanding)
	Lieutenant C. M. Waterlow, RE
	Lieutenant A. G. Fox, RE
No.2 Company	Captain J. D. B. Fulton, RHA (Officer Commanding)
	Captain C. J. Burke, Royal Irish Regt
	Lieutenant D. G. Conner, RA
	Lieutenant B. H. Barrington-Kennett, Grenadier Guards
	Lieutenant R. A. Cammell, RE
	Lieutenant G. B. Hynes, RA
	Lieutenant H. R. P. Reynolds, RE

A set of qualifications were defined, which those aspiring to be 'flying officers' were expected to meet – although, in the event, some flexibility in their interpretation seems to have been exercised. The qualifications in question included: possession of an aviator's certificate, previous experience of aeronautics, good eyesight, good map reader and field sketcher, unmarried, under thirty years of age, a good sailor, a taste for mechanics, of light weight (under 11½ stone).

By this time, with regard to the first requirement, all the officers in No.2 Company had gained their aviator's certificates, at one or other of the civilian schools, with the exception of Reynolds, who was nevertheless included and who obtained his in the following June. By contrast, the 'previous experience of aeronautics' possessed by the Battalion Commander Bannerman was limited to past ownership of a balloon, the *Nebula*, and participation in various ballooning contests at Hurlingham, which, with Ranelagh, was the home of civilian sporting ballooning in Britain. He might also have pointed to the knowledge – though both second-hand and obsolete – he would have acquired from some time spent as one of the foreign military observers present during the Russo-Japanese War of 1904-5, when some limited use of an observation balloon was made by the Japanese at the siege of Port Arthur. The aeronautical experience of his adjutant, Broke-Smith, was similarly limited to aerostation, except that in his case he was able to add kiting. Neither of these two officers, however, was an aeroplane pilot, or even, at that time, betrayed any intention of becoming one.

The fact was that British Army officers who wished to embark on the journey to the skies by the aviation route found little encouragement from official circles. Those who, despite this, were determined to purchase a ticket could do so only on their own initiative, in their own free time and by using their own money. It is greatly to the credit of this small band that, despite the absence of either financial or any other kind of support from above, a number of officers could by then have been found learning to fly at the different civilian schools which had now opened their doors in England. For most of them, it was a step which would literally give them a flying start when a proper air corps was eventually formed.

On the day of the Air Battalion's formation, there were, in addition to those in the above list, four other serving army officers who had learnt to fly and who possessed RAeC aviator's certificates, but who for different reasons had not been included on the strength of the battalion. They were: Captain G. W. P. Dawes, Royal Berkshire Regt, Lieutenant H. E. Watkins, Essex Regt, Lieutenant R. T. Snowden-Smith, Army Service Corps, and Captain A. G. Board, South Wales Borderers. All of them had gained their certificates before the end of 1910 (two, those of Dawes and Watkins, even predated

P. W. L. Broke-Smith. A photograph taken in later years, when he had reached the rank of brigadier. (Museum of Army Flying)

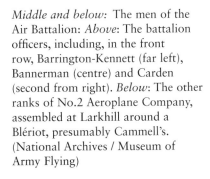

Middle and below: The men of the Air Battalion: *Above*: The battalion officers, including, in the front row, Barrington-Kennett (far left), Bannerman (centre) and Carden (second from right). *Below*: The other ranks of No.2 Aeroplane Company, assembled at Larkhill around a Blériot, presumably Cammell's. (National Archives / Museum of Army Flying)

Fulton's own).

Dawes was presumably ruled out as he was at that time serving – and, in fact, flying – in India. A year later, having returned to this country, he was seconded to the Royal Flying Corps the moment it was formed, was a member of the first aviators' course, which then gathered at Farnborough and, by 1914, was commanding a flight in 2 Squadron.

Andrew Board had been one of the first pupils to enrol at the school which Louis Blériot had opened at Hendon in October 1910. He gained his aviator's certificate on 29 November and immediately took vigorous steps to try to join what was still the Balloon School as an aeroplane pilot. Within days, supported by his certificate and a letter to Major Bannerman from a General Barker, he was at Farnborough, pressing his case to Bannerman in person, but without success:

> Board came up to see me, but I would not hold out any hopes of immediate attachment, as I don't want officers other than R.E. before the 1st April next. I believe two are coming, but I don't know what to do with them during the winter, and I have asked that no more may be sent. We are all cluttered up with work, but it is work for Sappers on the ground, and flying infantry could not help us.

'Flying infantry' indeed! In this episode, it is difficult not to detect further partiality on Bannerman's part in favour of the Royal Engineers, not to mention an apparent priority given to work for 'sappers on the ground'.

At this juncture, Board cannot have been helped by the fact that by the following month he too was out of the country, being posted with his regiment to South Africa. Nevertheless, he continued to fight his case at long range, finding another big gun to fire on his behalf – one of no less a calibre than Field Marshal Lord Roberts himself, who was prevailed upon to write to the Master-General of the Ordnance, Major-General Hadden, in his support. Yet even this gambit proved to be of no avail, eliciting the response that:

> ... there is no chance of any more officers being taken on for the Aerial Corps this financial year. Next year we shall require some but Capt Board's name is not first. There are now 8 officers besides Capt Board who hold pilot's certificates and who are noted for employment all before Capt Board.

This was in January 1911, just prior to the Air Battalion's formation. The indifference shown to Board's efforts to volunteer provides an illuminating glimpse of the aeronautical ambitions in the senior levels of the War Office at that time. If there was an intention to expand the nation's air force a year hence, it seems to have been a highly limited one, readily satisfied by the mere handful of pilots fortuitously available. Board, like Dawes, got in in the end, of course. At the end of 1912, with the need for a proper flying corps now belatedly recognised, he was at last ordered to report to Farnborough, where he became a member of 2 Squadron.

The other two, however, were lost to military aviation. By 1911, Hugh Watkins had resigned from the army, having apparently found a flying job which was more immediately attractive. Dr Douglas Mawson had organised an expedition to the Antarctic, for which, going one better than Scott with his balloons, he had decided an aeroplane might be useful. The machine chosen was an REP monoplane, built by Vickers, with Watkins joining the expedition as its pilot. Both took ship with the rest of the expedition, but all came to naught when, in October 1911, en route in Australia, Watkins crashed while demonstrating the aeroplane at Adelaide. With his machine a write-off, the unfortunate Watkins, now surplus to requirements, was sent home – a fate which, given the misfortunes into which the expedition subsequently fell, was perhaps a blessing in disguise. Not long afterwards, he suffered a second crash whilst flying a Spencer biplane at Brooklands, in which he broke his thigh and was left permanently lame. When the Royal Flying Corps was formed, he was one of the many who applied to join the Special Reserve and was initially included in the list of officers chosen to attend the first aviators' course at the newly formed Central Flying School in August 1912. However, he then failed the necessary medical board due, one might suppose, to the injury incurred at Brooklands, and his military aviation career was brought to an end.

Snowden-Smith, although he made the army his life career, never transferred to its aeronautical service, preferring, it seems, to remain with the corps of transport, and gradually he too dropped out of the flying scene. He was certainly still flying in 1911, for on 8 May of that year, piloting a Farman, he competed in a race from London to Brighton, finishing second to that up-and-coming young aviator, Gustav Hamel, and ahead of two other leading pilots, Graham Gilmour and Howard Pixton.

While the soldiers attempted to turn what few pilots and fewer machines they could muster into an aeronautical unit which could be taken seriously, two other organisations, separate parts of the nation's slowly growing military aeronautical resources, were also striving to establish themselves.

On the one hand, the navy had begun to build its own independent flying service, basing itself at Eastchurch, on the Isle of Sheppey, to where the flying activities started on the less-suitable ground at Shellbeach, a couple of miles to the east, had been transferred. They owed much to the philanthropy of another rich and patriotic aviator, Francis McClean, who not only purchased the land for the aerodrome, but who also placed two Short biplanes at the navy's disposal. Four naval officers – Lieutenants C. R. Samson RN, A. M. Longmore RN, R. Gregory RN, and Lieutenant E. L. Gerrard RMLI – were selected for instruction, which was provided by that other altruistic patriot, G. B. Cockburn, who came over from Larkhill, where he had been similarly occupied on behalf of the soldiers.

Meanwhile, the civilians in what was now called the Army Aircraft Factory were treading their own, not altogether parallel path. As well as the energetic O'Gorman and his assistant Theodore Ridge, a Chief Engineer had been recruited from the Daimler Motor Company in the shape of one Frederick Green (no relation to the engine manufacturer). To these three was shortly to be added a fourth, whose name was in due course destined to resound more loudly than that of any of his current associates.

Geoffrey de Havilland had certainly achieved his ambition to build and fly a practical flying machine; however, he had then found himself beset by a more fundamental difficulty, which he was at a loss to know how to overcome – namely lack of funds, for the months of labour had consumed the whole of his grandfather's gift. Although it had been converted into a successful aeroplane – certainly a worthwhile exchange – the question now was: how could he turn his success into the profitable income which it deserved and of which he was urgently in need, for he had a wife and young child to support? It was a question whose answer the young engineer had almost despaired of finding, but happily, the answer was near at hand, only waiting to be discovered. It was found in the autumn of 1910, through a chance meeting with Fred Green, with whom de Havilland was already acquainted. An interview with O'Gorman resulted, with favourable results. It was really a case of being in the right place at the right time; O'Gorman was keen that the factory should start designing and building its own aeroplanes and the young man who had come to him had shown that he could do just that. He was therefore taken on as the factory's aeroplane designer and part-time test pilot. The deal also included the purchase by the War Office, for £400, of de Havilland's own successful machine, following demonstration flights of its acceptability, which also served as the test for its designer's RAeC aviator's certificate (No.53). As was reported earlier, this aeroplane, far from being handed over to the soldiers for their use, was then retained in the factory, where in de Havilland's hands it served as a vehicle for the flight-testing of various ideas which O'Gorman's small team was now beginning to develop, as its leader began surreptitiously to push back the restrictive boundaries which had been placed around his activities.

Principal among these restrictions was, as has been stated, an embargo on the design and construction of new aeroplanes. To a man of O'Gorman's resource, this was a rule which positively clamoured to be honoured more in the breach than in its observance. Thus, when the Blériot XII was brought in from Micheldever after Cammell's uncompleted ferry flight to Farnborough, the hapless machine, sitting passively on the floor of the balloon shed, appeared in O'Gorman's eyes the ideal means for the further advancement of his plans. From a War Office whose grasp of the technical niceties of the subject was perhaps not equal to the factory superintendent's machinations, he obtained permission to 'reconstruct' the machine. The result was not so much a reconstruction as a total transformation: the Blériot, after disappearing behind the factory's doors as a tractor monoplane with an elevator at the rear, emerged some time later in the quite contrasting form of a pusher biplane with its elevator at the front. How much of the original construction was retained, if any, is in doubt. The ENV engine is believed to have remained the same. This aeroplane was allocated the designation S.E.1 and joined de Havilland's own machine on the flight-line in June 1911.

The latter aircraft was also provided with a new identification, its progenitor finding, to his initial mystification, that he must henceforth refer to it as the F.E.1. On enquiry, he discovered that this novel and cryptic nomenclature complied with a formula which had been devised to define and differentiate what were then considered to be the three possible basic design configurations, namely:

S.E. (Santos-Dumont Experimental) – pusher aeroplanes, with the elevator in front, inspired by the Santos-Dumont machines.

F.E. (Farman Experimental) – pusher aeroplanes, with the elevator at the rear, inspired by the Farman machines.

The S.E.1, purporting to be a 'reconstruction' by the factory of the Balloon School's Blériot XII. (Author's collection, Hants lib.)

B.E. (Blériot Experimental) – tractor aeroplanes, with the elevator at the rear, inspired by the Blériot machines.

The Air Battalion, meanwhile, was able to look forward to a welcome enlargement of its meagre fleet when, in March 1911, an order was at last placed with Bristols for four Boxkites. It was not before time: already rather more than thirty Boxkites had been delivered to or ordered by various other customers – including nine for the Russian government, which was continuing to build up an air corps, whatever the quality of its pilots might have been. At around the same time, 'Pregnant Percy', recovered from his injuries, had been reunited with the repaired Farman and had resumed his training. By the end of the month he was making sustained flights around Laffan's Plain, at what today strike us as extraordinarily low altitudes. For some time, in all his flights, he never rose higher than a hundred feet above the ground.

The Paulhan, too, emerged from the factory's clutches at the beginning of May and was handed back to John Fulton. Not for long, unfortunately: on the 5th, it made one flight, which ended in a crash, whereupon it was returned to the factory, in whose hands it remained for the rest of the summer, undergoing repairs and various modifications. The Paulhan's crash took place on the very day after the Lebaudy dirigible's unfortunate arrival on the roof of Woodlands Cottage and a few days before *Beta*'s own contretemps in the same locality, so it was perhaps as well that Burke had now mastered the Farman. The Air Battalion needed to demonstrate that it could navigate the air successfully in at least one of its machines.

The Paulhan was returned to the Air Battalion in October, but its low popularity index with the pilots meant that it spent most of its time languishing in the hangar. Abandoned and unloved, it was inevitable that it would, in the end, attract interest from another quarter. It was in the following January that it caught the attention of the predatory O'Gorman. Another candidate for 'reconstruction'! An application from the superintendant to DFW was accordingly dispatched:

> I understand that the Paulhan machine is being put out of service. May I be allowed to make a reconstruction of this? The engine and bearers, together with some of the other parts, can be brought into useful service, and I can make a reconstructed machine with the planes and fuselage arrangements as in B.E.1.
>
> I am of opinion, that if I am allowed to proceed with this, a really useful aeroplane

One of the Air Battalion's Boxkites, serial no. F.4, pictured at Larkhill. (J. M. Bruce/G. S. Leslie)

can be made from these parts.

On 3 February 1912, it was therefore returned to the factory, with no regrets, and O'Gorman acquired some more bits and pieces with which to pursue his furtive designs. In this case, however, no record appears so far to have been unearthed concerning their precise fate.

In that same month of May 1911 that saw the brief return of the Paulhan to service, another gift turned up, in the shape of a rather outmoded Voisin biplane, the donor being once more the Duke of Westminster. The Duke had originally purchased it for his own use, being also at that time numbered amongst those who harboured aspirations to become pilots. However, as his Private Secretary, Wilfred Lloyd put it, in a letter to General Smith-Dorrien, then GOC Aldershot Command, 'He has now given up all idea of trying to fly, thank heaven, so has told me that he is quite prepared to give the aeroplane to the army. Would the Flying Brigade [*sic*] care to have it?' The Flying Brigade being so prepared, the Voisin was duly delivered to the Aircraft Factory, dismantled and in crates, as it had been since its arrival in England a year earlier. There it was examined and found wanting. The flying control system was deemed to be obsolete, while the wing structure and canvas covering were so deteriorated that the machine was considered unsafe to fly. The report submitted to DFW and signed by T. J. Ridge ended by requesting:

> I therefore desire to recommend that I may be instructed to fit this machine with certain spare wings and struts which I have in stock and alter the control so that it is similar to the Farman type, and thus enable the machine to be flown by anyone qualified to fly a Farman type machine.
>
> I am in a position to effect these alterations quickly and economically and it would then be equal to a good Farman type machine.

This request being swiftly approved, the factory acquired another airframe which it could 'reconstruct', although prepared to be as little constrained by the design features of the original machine as it had been in the case of the Blériot for, despite the repeated allusions to a 'Farman type', the form in which it would eventually emerge could not have been more different.

In the country as a whole, interest in aviation had now been thoroughly aroused, thanks in no small part to Lord Northcliffe's untiring campaign in the *Daily Mail*. Not the least proportion of his efforts and those of his friends were directed towards pressing the War Office, through public and parliamentary opinion, to adopt a more positive and energetic approach to the army's nascent air service. At Westminster, a number of MPs who were similarly exercised in their minds had formed a Parliamentary Aerial Defence Committee, to focus efforts within the political world. One man whom they had no difficulty in rallying to their cause – indeed, he was there before them – was Claude Grahame-White. On 12 May, he organised at Hendon a Military Flying Display, under the committee's auspices, which aimed to demonstrate to the public, which was invited to attend, the extent to which the aeroplane was now able to play its part in any future war. The crowds which flocked to Hendon were augmented by many public figures, including the Duke and Duchess of Connaught, Prime Minister Herbert Asquith, Home Secretary Winston Churchill and the Leader of the Opposition, Arthur Balfour. The latter and the First Lord of the Admiralty, Reginald McKenna, were amongst those who accepted invitations to joyrides, while the main purpose of the day was fulfilled by demonstrations of bomb-dropping, aerial reconnaissance and the conveyance of dispatches by air. A somewhat discordant diversion was provided by Horatio Barber, the pioneer of Larkhill flying, who was heard to complain loudly because the organisers had not allowed his Valkyrie aeroplane to be included in the display. That apart, the day had undoubtedly been an unqualified success for the aviation campaigners.

The Air Battalion, meanwhile, had progress to report. No.2 Company had now moved to Larkhill, where Burke continued his familiarisation flights on the Farman. On the 18 May, their first Boxkite was delivered, followed by the second only a week later. Three days after that, Reginald Cammell travelled to Hendon, where the Blériot XXI he had purchased was ready for collection. It was a side-by-side two-seater, fitted with a 70-hp Gnôme and based on the successful Type XI, but in comparison to that model's workmanlike lines, it exhibited certain pretensions to elegance. The fuselage began ordinarily enough, with the engine enclosed within the same rectangular cowling as the Type XI, but then aft of the wing trailing edge it tapered markedly into a slim cross-section, finishing at a tail unit whose leading edges were raked backwards, imparting an impression of speediness. It was later described by G. B. Cockburn as 'weird and wonderful', but Cammell probably looked upon it as 'the last word'. Regardless of his complete unfamiliarity with the model, he lost no time in setting off on his return journey, no doubt impatient to show off his new toy to the rest of the battalion, landing first at Farnborough, where he stopped overnight before flying on to Salisbury Plain the following day. With his journey interrupted by an intermediate stop at Basing, due to an overheating engine, it was well after nine o'clock, with the light failing, before he touched down at Larkhill.

The enthusiastic Cammell was soon finding tasks for his new machine. First he tried suspending a compass by chains, to see if he could eliminate vibration. Next, having fitted up the appropriate installation, he tried reeling out in the air a wireless aerial, 100 feet in length – a technique which was to become commonplace in the coming war. Finally, ever venturesome, he tried blind flying through fog, assisted only by a compass and a clinometer – an experiment which he described as 'successful, but rather alarming in gusts'!

Early in June, the battalion acquired yet another one-off. Ernest Maitland, although appointed to the command of No.1 Company, was no lighter-than-air enthusiast to the total exclusion of aviation. The year before, he had purchased his own Howard-Wright biplane, with the intention of joining the small but growing ranks of the soldier-pilots. This ambition was thwarted when, on 1 August, he suffered an accident in his machine in which he broke both legs. This misfortune seems to have decided him to restrict his ambitions to aerostation after all and the Howard-Wright was then flown for a time by his brother officer in the Essex Regiment, Lieutenant Watkins, before being purchased by the War Office for the sum of £625. It was briefly test-flown at Farnborough by de Havilland and then sent on to Larkhill by road. The Aeroplane

A Blériot XXI, pictured at the Military Trials in 1912. (J. M. Bruce/ G. S. Leslie)

Company now had at least the makings of an air fleet, even if it was beginning to resemble more an exhibition of the different schools of current aircraft design philosophy than an air force. It was certainly a considerable advance on Cammell's little detachment of the previous autumn, so much so that it was considered worthy of a serial numbering system, which perhaps took its inspiration from that devised by the factory. Thus, the Farman was allocated the designation F.1, while Cammell's Blériot was B.2. The full list is given in Appendix III.

Of the pilots, only Burke, Fulton and Cammell could remotely be described as experienced, with Hynes, Barrington-Kennett and Connor rather less so, while Lieutenant Reynolds was at that time still taking lessons on a Boxkite at Bristols's flying school next door. Given their minimal flying experience, and with each machine presenting markedly different handling characteristics, pilots tended to be confined to a particular aeroplane, at least until they had become more assured in the air. Thus, Burke continued to fly the Farman, Cammell had his Blériot, while the other officers of the company flew the Boxkites, with occasional outings on the Howard-Wright. Cockburn, returned from Eastchurch, was also on hand to lend his mature experience and advice to the fledgling pilots. The support facilities available to the company, however, were far from adequate and seemed to reflect the disinterest in aviation which was still widespread in the army. Although Bulford Camp lay only a few short miles to the east, no living accommodation was made available for the rank and file, who for some months were obliged to exist under canvas alongside the aeroplane sheds until, with the approach of winter, the Bulford authorities were persuaded to house them in the Royal Artillery lines there.

On 8 June, the Aeroplane Company made its most convincing demonstration so far that it was starting to become an effective flying unit, when no less than four pilots climbed aboard their machines and flew across country from Larkhill to Farnborough, emulating and outdoing Cammell's attempt of the previous autumn. Burke, of course, took the Farman, Cammell flew his Blériot XXI, while Fulton and Barrington-Kennett piloted the two Boxkites. Their route took them via Andover and Basingstoke, at heights between 1,000 and 2,000 feet – quite an altitude for those early days. The next day, they all returned to Larkhill, the whole exercise having been completed without incident.

A week later, Burke set off to fly to Farnborough once more, taking with him as observer one Captain S. D. Massy, of the 29th Punjabis, who had acquired his certificate at the Bristol school the previous month and who had also joined the battalion on attachment. This time they chose a more roundabout route, which took them first to Oxford, where they landed on Port Meadow, a vast expanse near the banks of the Thames on the western outskirts of the city which had seen use in the past by army training camps and which had now been established as an occasional landing field. There, the arrival of strong adverse winds persuaded Burke to defer his departure for Farnborough. Continuing bad weather kept him on the ground for several more days and in the end the plan was abandoned altogether. It was the evening of 23 June before the re-establishment of calm conditions allowed him to take off for the return to Larkhill, accompanied this time by Barrington-Kennett. However, the benign weather did not last; with their journey only half completed, they ran into heavy rain and strong turbulence. Burke decided to come down, but made a heavy landing in which the machine suffered sufficient structural damage to cause further flying to be abandoned, the Farman being dismantled and carried back to Larkhill for more repairs.

Although aviation was undoubtedly a serious business, it also took a leaf out of the motorists' book, in that much of the flying which took place in those days was of a sporting nature, represented by races and other contests. Amongst such contests, one was now announced which was of particular interest to the Larkhill fliers. Mortimer

Singer was a wealthy civilian pilot who had taught himself to fly on a Voisin at Mourmelon in 1909. He now offered two prizes of £500 each to the army and navy pilot respectively who by the end of March 1912 had made the longest flight with a passenger. This was a challenge Cammell could not ignore. He sent in his entry and invited his brother sapper Reynolds to occupy the Blériot's second seat. He designed for his purpose a cross-country circuit which started from Larkhill, passed firstly over Shrewton, led on to Warminster and from there returned to Larkhill. On 15 July, Cammell and Reynolds took off and headed south. They had completed three laps and started on a fourth when the weather intervened: cloud base was no more than 100 feet above the ground and the wind was becoming increasingly gusty. In such conditions, they decided it would be unwise to continue and landed five miles short of Shrewton, having been airborne for fifteen minutes short of three hours and having covered 112 miles. Good work, but the coming months would surely yield time and opportunity enough to improve on that day's achievement.

Meanwhile, the flying at Larkhill gradually extended. A week earlier, a third Boxkite, fitted with a 60-hp Renault engine instead of the usual Gnôme, had been delivered by Bristols's Henri Jullerot, while Massy was beginning under Burke's guidance to familiarise himself with the Farman. As usual, he learnt the hard way. On 17 July, his second flight ended with considerable damage to both wings and the elevator.

Only a week after his attempt on the Mortimer Singer prize, Reginald Cammell was ready once more to enter the lists. The new competition which presented itself was an altogether sterner test – no less than a 1,000-mile race around Britain, sponsored by the *Daily Mail*, with a prize of £10,000 for the winner. The impressive list of thirty contestants contained the names of some of the leading pilots in the world, including the Frenchmen Jules Védrines and 'Beaumont' (a *nom d'air* which concealed the identity of a Lieutenant Conneau of the French navy), Audemars of Switzerland, Weymann from the USA and Gustav Hamel, Samuel Cody and Benny Hucks from Great Britain. The Air Battalion was represented not only by Cammell in his Blériot, but also by Reynolds, the ink on his aviator's certificate just about dry, flying the Air Battalion's Howard-Wright biplane.

The race began on Saturday 22 July in leisurely fashion: when the reduced field of nineteen pilots took off from Brooklands, their task that day was a mere twenty-mile flight to London's other hub of aviation, Grahame-White's Hendon. Seventeen of them having succeeded in this undemanding task, a number made up a party and repaired to the London Hippodrome for an evening's relaxation, secure in the knowledge that, the morrow being the Sabbath, they had until a.m. Monday before the organisers would be calling on them to resume the battle.

On Monday, therefore, at the early hour of four o'clock, Saturday's leaders, Védrines and 'Beaumont', were waved off and sped across the grass of Hendon, climbing skywards and slowly diminishing to specks in the pale northern sky, bound for the first control at Harrogate, with Edinburgh their destination for that day. They were followed at appropriate intervals by the remaining survivors, who included the two Air Battalion men. Cammell was the last away, having been forced down on Hounslow Heath on the Saturday by a broken inlet valve.

By that evening, the race had seen dramatic changes. Only three pilots reached the Scottish capital: the two favourites, Védrines and 'Beaumont', and the Briton James Valentine. Of the others, some were strung out along the course, nursing breakages or faults of one kind or another, while others had retired altogether. Amongst the latter was Cammell, who suffered a burst cylinder head near Wakefield. Reynolds had got to Doncaster, still hanging on, but far behind the leaders.

The next day, the weather broke. In wet, gusty conditions, those who could struggled on, via Stirling and Glasgow, then southwards again to Manchester and Bristol. Reynolds, outclassed, got as far as Harrogate and retired. For the purposes

The third Cody machine, outside his shed by the Basingstoke Canal. (Author's collection)

Cody at the Harrogate stopover during the Round Britain Race in 1911. (J. M. Bruce/G. S. Leslie)

of our history, it suffices to report that 'Beaumont' landed back at Brooklands on the Wednesday, just over an hour ahead of Védrines, to claim the winner's prize. Valentine got back a full two days later to take third place, while the gallant Cody appeared on the fourth day, to become the only other pilot to finish the course.

The Air Battalion would be of little use to an army in the field if it were unable to range back and forth, in order to discharge its duty of reconnaissance, and the hours spent on cross-country flying gradually increased. Such activities naturally added greater relish to what was already an adventurous occupation. Flying away from the comforting vicinity of one's own sheds and setting off across unfamiliar country towards a distant, often hazy horizon, propelled by a not always faithful engine, was an enterprise which, in those days, was not to be undertaken lightly. Once the home airfield was out of sight, an ear would always be cocked for any change, real or imaginary, in the engine's even roar, as alien fields, which might or might not turn out to be suitable for a forced landing, slipped by beneath.

Undeterred by such qualms, Lieutenants Reynolds and Barrington-Kennett were, according to the reminiscences of one of their colleagues, amongst the more enthusiastic exponents of these excursions, for which, incidentally, civilian clothing rather than uniform was always worn. These two young men, having set off on some quite legitimate aerial journey, could then it seemed, sometimes be missing, with their machines, for days at a time. Although these extended absences were ostensibly due to engine or other failures, they did not always earn the approval of their seniors, who were inclined to entertain suspicions concerning the true reasons. For it did not go unnoticed that the pilots concerned sometimes seemed to suffer these misfortunes in the close vicinity of country houses, whose residents naturally offered stranded aviators their hospitality, with comforts and pleasures which they were obliged to endure during their enforced stay.

As the summer months passed, the date of the annual army manoeuvres, which this year were due to be held in Cambridgeshire, began to draw near, presenting the opportunity for a major, long-distance, cross-country flight by the entire Aeroplane Company. Compared to the previous year, the situation was now vastly changed. Not only was the presence of the aeroplane on the battlefield accepted at the highest levels of the army as both relevant and necessary, but the Air Battalion had been formed and – more to the point – possessed the pilots and machines with which to respond. By the time the manoeuvres were scheduled to begin, delivery would have been completed of all the remaining Boxkites ordered – the second Renault-powered machine and two more fitted with Gnômes, making six in all, as well as two spare engine-less airframes.

During the first week of July, therefore, Bannerman travelled to Cambridgeshire, with the object of reconnoitring and finding two suitable landing grounds in the area. Two locations were eventually chosen: Hardwick Farm, a mile or so west of Cambridge on the St Neots road, and Snarehill Farm, to the south-east of Thetford.

In the event, the manoeuvres were cancelled – a decision the reasons for which even now appear to be obscure. However, rather than lose completely the opportunity to gain further valuable and much-needed experience in cross-country flying, the Aeroplane Company was allowed to fly its machines to the manoeuvre area, as it would have done had the manoeuvres taken place as planned. In these circumstances, only the landing ground at Hardwick Farm was used, and that not very extensively. For, in the light of the events which followed, it must be a moot point as to whether the cancellation of the manoeuvres proved to be an unfortunate loss of valuable experience for the Aeroplane Company, or a fortunate accident which limited the exposure to unsympathetic eyes of its unreadiness for serious campaigning.

Charles Burke in the Farman was the first to leave, accompanied by Captain H. R. M. Brooke-Popham, of the Oxfordshire and Buckinghamshire Light Infantry. This officer was currently attending the Staff College, but had been temporarily released on attachment to the Air Battalion to act as an observer. He was, in fact, by then a qualified pilot, albeit without much experience, having gained his aviator's certificate no more than a month earlier, with the Bristol Flying School at Brooklands. The pair took off in the evening of 15 August, intending to reach Oxford, but a headwind which was able to present itself as a serious rival to their own meagre airspeed permitted them to get only as far as Wantage. The next day, they lost no time in continuing their journey and, by early that morning, were landing at Oxford, on the wide open space of Port Meadow. At the same time, Barrington-Kennett, Connor, Massy and Reynolds were making a start from Larkhill, all flying Boxkites. The latter two reached Port Meadow that same day; Connor was delayed at Kintbury, near Newbury, with engine trouble; Barrington-Kennett passed the night at Baulking, near Faringdon, and flew in the next morning. What repairs and servicing that were needed were not greatly facilitated by the fact that all the company's tools had been sent directly to Cambridge, this having been done, Brooke-Popham later asserted, on Lieutenant Cammell's orders 'and caused a great deal of dissatisfaction'.

On the morning of the 19th, with all his chicks except for Connor now gathered round him, Burke resumed the journey eastwards, while the rest of his flock prepared to follow. They were all to meet with differing fortunes, mostly adverse. With Oxford barely out of sight, Burke, still accompanied by Brooke-Popham, suffered engine failure and was forced to put down in a ploughed field, breaking his tail skid in the process. Leaving Burke by the machine, Brooke-Popham toiled back to the city, sought out a coachbuilder and brought him along to effect a repair of sorts. With the day far gone, they set off again, but the approach of night obliged them to land once more, having got no further than Grendon, on the eastern side of Northampton. This was to mark the end of their journey; attempting to leave on the 25th, they suffered a broken propeller during the take-off run and abandoned the exercise, ten days after starting out.

Of the other four, Barrington-Kennett was to be the only one to succeed in reaching his destination and touch down at Hardwick Farm. Massy, landing again soon after leaving Oxford, suffered engine failure during the subsequent take-off and wrecked his machine in the process. Lieutenant Connor went one better: navigating with the help of a map torn out of a *Bradshaw's Railway Guide*, he set off from Kintbury, but found himself in difficulties south of Oxford, as he flew into an ever-narrowing wedge between the cloud base, which was sinking lower, and the ground, which was rising up to meet it. Lucky to be completely unhurt in the subsequent forced landing – unlike his machine – he returned to Larkhill, called for another Boxkite and set off again, but lost no time in wrecking that as well.

Reynolds's effort was the most spectacular of all, in an episode which became legendary. Having left Oxford, he made one intermediate landing (in company with Barrington-Kennett – suspicious combination!) and the two then flew on. By now it was evening and the atmosphere was warm and unstable, with thunder in the offing. Reynolds, having lost touch with his companion in a hazy, cloud-encumbered sky, was nearing Bletchley at 1,700 feet when he started to run into turbulence, which began to increase as he approached a black cumulonimbus cloud towering above him to his right. Deciding to land, he had just switched off the engine to begin his descent when a particularly violent upcurrent seized the tail of the machine and threw it into a vertical dive. Reynolds, lacking safety harness, like all aviators in those days, was pitched out of his seat and found himself deposited on the underside of the upper wing, the aeroplane having become completely inverted. Under these circumstances, with his role of pilot exchanged for the greatly inferior one of helpless observer, he stood up, clung on to a wing strut and waited to see what his machine, left to itself, would decide to do. It began by swinging from side to side, in emulation of a falling leaf. On one swing it became rather too enthusiastic and fell into a vertical sideslip. As Reynolds clung on desperately, his machine then rolled the right way up once more and replaced the sideslip with a dive, though, to add extra zest, this was executed tail-first. It then returned to its old inverted attitude and for the remainder of its return to earth resumed its imitation of a falling leaf, giving Reynolds plenty of time to watch the ground gradually coming up to meet him, for the machine's rate of descent was quite low. This factor – as well, perhaps, as Reynolds's own presence of mind – enabled him to leap clear and save himself just before his mount hit the ground on its last swing, where it subsided in a heap of broken timber.

Meanwhile, Reginald Cammell had been proceeding independently. The Blériot XXI had been undergoing an engine change and was still in its hangar when the others departed. It was the 23rd when he finally set off, landing the next day at Farnborough, from where, after a two-night stop, he completed a successful, if leisurely journey and joined Barrington-Kennett at Hardwick on the 27th, where the latter had, as usual, been passing several pleasant days, entertained this time by the dons of the nearby university.

Thus, of the six pilots who set off on the Aeroplane Company's 'odyssey', as it was dubbed, two only would have been available with their machines to place their mark upon the manoeuvres, had these taken place as originally intended, while five machines, which had suffered damage of differing severity, were carried back to the Army Aircraft Factory at Farnborough for repair where possible. Just to crown this chapter of accidents, Cammell, dropping in at Hendon during his return from Cambridgeshire, placed a blemish on his successful outward flight by attempting to land downwind. With wheel brakes yet to be invented, his landing run became protracted and was only brought to a halt by the doors of one of the hangars. More repairs required, while another of the battalion's dwindling fleet had been added to the list of those temporarily out of service.

They may have been rather short of machines to fly, but at least the battalion's pilots had acquired one more reason to feel wanted: that month the Treasury informed the War Office that it was prepared to sanction the payment of a grant of £75 to each officer who had been 'selected by the military authorities as suitable for Army aviation work and has obtained an aeroplane pilot's certificate at his own expense under civilian instruction'. However, anxious lest it appear unduly benevolent, the Treasury hastened to add that the payment must not be made until the officer in question had satisfactorily completed a six-month probationary period.

As, despite the dubious results of the 'Cambridge Odyssey', aviation slowly took shape as a viable component of a nation's military resources, the aeroplane's ability to penetrate behind an army's defences and discover its commander's dispositions started to emerge as a serious factor in planning for the next war. Even the possibility that they might be used in the invasion of an opposing country, by conveying an attacking force over and beyond the heads of the defenders, as in the vision of men such as Baden-Powell and Fullerton, could not be ruled out. Under these circumstances, the question of how to oppose them naturally began to acquire greater importance. The old, vague vision of aerial fighting between one machine and another was one likelihood, if they could be equipped with the means; if not, or perhaps as well, they might be attacked from the ground by artillery pieces, suitably adapted. In the latter connection, a rather more arcane method, which went under the name of Vortex Rings, also emerged and for a while was accorded serious consideration.

The concept was first brought to official attention in January 1910 by means of a short paper penned by a certain Second Lieutenant Bowle-Evans, of the 15th Battalion, London Regiment. A few months later, this was followed by another, in greater technical detail, which was the product of the lively mind of none other than Reginald Cammell.

In principle, it involved the formation of a vortex in the air, by the firing of an explosive charge inside a conical 'gun' which, if it were pointed upwards, would propel the vortex towards the intended airborne target on which, it was suggested, the violent air movement within the vortex would have a sufficiently destructive effect. Some practical support for the theory was provided firstly by a Dr Pernter of Germany who had some years earlier carried out some experimental firings which were said to have torn apart birds and other objects, and secondly by the farmers of a large region ranging from Hungary to northern Italy, who appeared to use such guns routinely in the belief that they could disperse hailstorms.

Presumably on the principle of not leaving any stones unturned, the idea was taken seriously and was still being officially considered a year later, by which time it had attracted the attention of no less a person than Sir Oliver Lodge, the eminent physicist and Principal of Birmingham University. Writing to the War Minister, Richard Haldane, he supported the idea of carrying out some exploratory experiments, remarking that 'I really think the thing is worth a trial' and promising to try to acquire an example from Piedmont, in Italy, where such devices were on sale.

About the project's subsequent fate, one can only speculate. Since there is no record of its ever going into service, it must be assumed either that there was a lack of official enthusiasm for such an outlandish scheme or, equally likely, if any practical tests were performed, that these failed to suggest any profitable outcome.

The end of summer, with its relatively good flying weather, was now approaching and the question of the future planning of the Air Battalion's activities – and their location – needed to be addressed. No.1 Company, with its balloons and airships, was comfortable at the long-established Farnborough base. No.2 Company, however, although it had been born at Farnborough, had soon found it expedient to remove to Larkhill's wide open spaces and away from the restricted and potentially dangerous ground of its early days which, although partly cleared, was still encumbered by trees and members of the public. In addition, Larkhill was blessed with its line of hangars, providing essential protection against the weather for the vulnerable airframes, while at Farnborough what hangarage there was would have to be shared with No.1 Company and the factory. The major operational disadvantage of the Wiltshire base lay in the need for personnel to make the eight-mile return journey twice daily to and from Bulford Camp by horse-drawn transport, to use the messing and accommodation there, involving an irksome loss of effectiveness. At Farnborough, on the other hand, barracks were readily available in the military lines of Aldershot Camp, while technical support, in the shape of the Aircraft Factory, was equally handy when the inevitable repairs were needed.

Fulton the pilot favoured Larkhill:

> The balance of advantages and disadvantages points strongly to the selection of Salisbury Plain as the winter training ground. In my opinion the Farnborough ground is dangerous and unsuitable, especially for training with machines to which the pilots are unaccustomed. The Salisbury ground is on the other hand an ideal ground for practice with new and fast machines.

Bannerman the administrator leaned towards Farnborough, disapproving of the slackening of discipline which he saw as tending to infect the men in the more free and easy atmosphere of an out-station such as Larkhill, far from the spit-and-polish of Aldershot:

> I think it advisable to recall the whole of No.2 Company for a time in order that the men may live in barracks, do a little drill, and be generally smartened up.

In the event, the company was split; while a cadre stayed on the Plain, the remainder, under the command of Charles Burke, returned to Farnborough. There, the problem of the storage of their aeroplanes – the Farman and two of the Boxkites – was solved in March 1912 by the erection of two portable canvas hangars, although they were welcomed with less than unbridled enthusiasm by longer-established users of the site, such as a certain Major Dixon, who told the newcomers:

> Provided that the turf is not cut more than is absolutely necessary for the foundation frame, there does not appear to be any objection, it will, however, be necessary for the sheds to be removed and the turf replaced by the end of May, as the ground is required by the Cambridge University OTC early in June.

It is to be hoped that, by the time that latter date arrived, matters at the headquarters of the nation's flying service had become the subject of an amended sense of priorities.

During all these events, the men of the factory had not been idle. The S.E.1 (late Blériot XII, the 'Mankiller') had been airborne on a number of occasions in the hands of a now-experienced Geoffrey de Havilland, as had his own creation, the F.E.1. In addition, two more craft were being built: one was a tractor machine and hence known as the B.E.1, the other was a pusher, designated the F.E.2. The B.E.1 was the aeroplane which was being 'reconstructed' from the Duke of Westminster's Voisin. Repeating the ploy used with the Blériot XII, it used the Voisin's 60-hp Wolseley engine, but little else. The F.E.2 betrayed a close resemblance to the F.E.1, the major differences being the installation of a 50-hp Gnôme rotary engine instead of the de Havilland and the total absence of the forward elevator (which by then had also been removed from the F.E.1).

So far, all the factory's test-flying had been carried out by de Havilland, but two others had now emerged within the organisation with ambitions to join in the increasing amount of flying which was becoming necessary, although neither could lay claim to very much flying experience. One was E. W. Copland Perry, who had joined the factory in February 1911, but did not acquire his aviator's certificate until the following September. The other was the factory's assistant superintendent, Theodore Ridge, who had been commissioned as a second lieutenant in the Territorial Force and filled his spare time as one of the officers of the London Balloon Company. He also had not yet gained his pilot's certificate, but had recently been introduced to the F.E.1, under de Havilland's supervision, and had made his first solo flight in that machine on 2 August. Such was the sum total of his piloting experience at that time. On the 15th, flying solo, he crash-landed the F.E.1 on Laffan's Plain, severely damaging the engine and the undercarriage. Two days later, this misfortune notwithstanding, he travelled down to Larkhill to take the tests for his certificate, which he passed successfully that evening on a Boxkite of the Bristol school.

On the following day, the F.E.2 was pushed out of the hangar at Farnborough, complete and ready for its first flight. In the early morning calm, de Havilland took off and performed two circuits around Laffan's Plain. Although the engine was not running entirely smoothly, this was a good beginning for a type which, when fully developed, was destined to give a good account of itself in RFC squadron service.

But a day which had begun so well was fated to end in black tragedy. Ridge, back from Salisbury Plain, grasping his day-old 'ticket' and with two weeks' solo experience to his credit, evidently felt himself to be equal to any challenge which the skies could present. That evening, to de Havilland's dismay, he announced his intention of flying the S.E.1 and nothing the former could say would divert him from that purpose. No doubt his position as assistant superintendent lent him a certain authority over a mere designer-pilot.

His flight was brief. Mishandling the controls in attempting a turn, he lost flying speed, spun into the ground from a low altitude and was killed almost instantly. This time, the former 'Mankiller' was not rebuilt, while another pilot had, perhaps

The New Army Biplane

Above: An early picture of the first F.E.2, with the nacelle yet to be covered with canvas. *Below*: Things to come: when the first F.E.2 visited the Military Trials at Larkhill in August 1912, it was carrying a Maxim machine-gun. (Author's collection)

692

needlessly, joined the ranks of those sacrificed to the advancement of the art and science of aviation.

Ridge's death meant that a total of six British pilots had now lost their lives in the air, but worse was shortly to befall. Horatio Barber had decided to donate four of his Valkyrie aeroplanes to the British government, shared equally between the army and the navy. Lieutenant Cammell was the Air Battalion officer who was ordered to proceed to Hendon to take delivery of the first of the army's pair, which had been offered as an airframe only. Accompanied by a party of mechanics and a 50-hp Gnôme engine, he travelled to Hendon on the morning of Sunday 17 September, where installation of the engine was put in hand. Once this work was complete, Cammell took off for a short familiarisation flight before setting off to ferry the machine to Farnborough.

In the very few years during which the aeroplane had existed in practical form, the solutions to the problem of flight chosen by different designers had taken many forms. The Valkyrie aeroplanes of Horatio Barber were among the more unusual. Its monoplane wing was mounted above a wide twin-girder structure, which extended forward to carry the canard stabiliser and separate elevators. At the tail, these two girders were prolonged aft of the wing trailing edge a short distance of only some three feet, ending in twin rudders. Suspended on the centre-line between the two girders were the pilot and, just behind him, the engine, driving a pusher propeller. The Valkyries were noted both for their inherent instability and for their unconventional flying control system.

Cammell had now accumulated some twelve months of experience in the air, a long time in those early days, but he had still much to learn, as his recent misfortune at Hendon had shown. Now, overconfidence and lack of awareness of undiscovered perils combined to bring about his downfall. He began to fly the Valkyrie around Hendon with the same confident freedom which he had become accustomed to enjoy in the Blériot. Meanwhile, the well-known pilot Gustav Hamel, flying on behalf of a newly introduced airmail service between Windsor and Hendon, had joined the circuit. Possibly to avoid the latter, Cammell began to turn away, banking the Valkyrie at an angle which was steeper than wise, given his unfamiliarity with the aircraft. The turn developed into a side-slip which he found himself unable to correct (not helped, perhaps, by inadequate rudder power). He was by then less than a hundred feet up and, with insufficient height in which he might recover, he and his machine plunged to the ground. Many times, in those early years, when a crash took place, the pilot

A Valkyrie aeroplane, similar to that in which Reginald Cammell met his death. (Author's collection)

escaped unharmed or with light injuries, due in large part to the low speeds involved, whilst Fortune smiled indulgently. Sometimes, however, there were other days when she would turn her head away and withhold the help she might have rendered. This was one of those. As the Valkyrie hit the ground, Cammell, without benefit of any restraining harness and also lacking a protective helmet, was thrown out and landed head-first. He was borne off to hospital, but pronounced dead on arrival.

Thus passed the young man who could claim to be the very first in the British Army to perform his duty as an aeroplane pilot in an official capacity. He had now claimed the melancholy distinction of becoming the first to be killed in the course of those duties. He died as he had lived: always ready to explore whatever aviation had to offer, his eagerness to be in the air prevailing over all dangers, known and unknown. In this keenness to fly, he resembled that other, even earlier aviator, Lancelot Gibbs. Both were in their early twenties, lively, bold and motivated by their sheer enthusiasm for flying. Both, it may be suggested, represent the earliest archetypes of the legions of young men who would come after them, in the cockpits of the Camels and SE5as of the first conflict and later on in the Hurricanes and Spitfires of the second.

Four days after his death, Cammell was laid to rest in Aldershot Military Cemetery, while the surviving three Valkyries remained unclaimed in the hands of their designer. The Air Battalion had in any case been formulating its own ideas about the aeroplanes with which it wished to be equipped in 1912. It had had enough of the rather dubious gifts and one-offs which had served to start it out in life. Nine days before Cammell's ill-fated visit to Hendon, Bannerman, in a letter largely inspired by Fulton, had written to DFW, setting out his recommendations.

The basis of these was that one example each of four types, namely Breguet, Nieuport, Deperdussin and Sommer – all French, be it noted – should be purchased and then evaluated by the Air Battalion. From this evaluation, it was proposed that the choice then be narrowed down to two types, of which four of each should then be ordered.

While we must assume that Fulton had surveyed all possible sources of supply, both in this country and abroad, we have to conclude that he was unimpressed by the possibilities suggested by the scene in his own country, though there were by then a number of names worthy at least of consideration. Firstly, of course, there was Cody, still being promoted by Bannerman, but still working from one small shed by the canal and unsupported by anything resembling a proper manufacturing organisation.

Secondly, there was John Dunne, who had at least formed a company, led by the Marquis of Tullibardine, and in which Capper had a hand. This had both a monoplane and a biplane to offer, still based on Dunne's principle of automatic stability, and the Marquis had recently been diligently pressing their virtues on Bannerman. Reginald Cammell had in fact visited Eastchurch to inspect and try out the monoplane in the air.

Humber, on the other hand, was no longer in the field, having, after less than two years operation, closed down its 'Aero Department' and returned to concentrate on motor cars. So far as real aeroplane manufacturing companies were concerned, there were three at the most. One was Shorts, now well-established and starting to build their own designs, but their small output had been collared by the Admiralty, which was firmly embarked on the establishment of its own independent air service.

Another was Avros which, although it had now made a number of successful aeroplanes, had still not advanced far enough to suggest an ability to supply aeroplanes in the numbers needed.

Finally, there was Bristols. Here, certainly, was a company, headed not by an enthusiastic optimist, but by a hard-headed businessman, and possessing what it could claim was a production line, from which it had now produced some fifty Boxkites, of which six had gone to the Air Battalion, as well as the two spare airframes. However,

The three French aeroplanes which were acquired by the Air Battalion in the autumn of 1911.
Top: the Breguet L1, serial no. B.3, in front of the Larkhill sheds. (RAF Museum)
Centre: the Nieuport, serial no. B.4. (RAF Museum)
Bottom: the Deperdussin, serial no. B.5, with John Fulton in the cockpit. (RAF Museum)

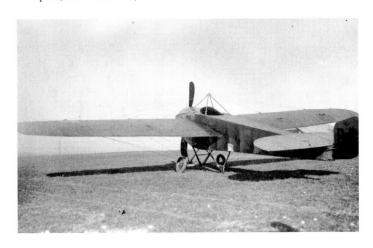

useful as this aeroplane had been while the battalion's pilots were spreading their wings, they now felt, with a summer's flying experience behind them, that they needed something with a higher performance, more worthy of their enhanced skills. The Boxkite, scarcely more than a year after its birth, had become obsolescent. As it happened, the Filton workshops had lately produced a new machine boasting a significantly superior performance to that of the Boxkite. This was a monoplane designed by Pierre Prier, a Frenchman whom Sir George White had taken on as designer. Unfortunately, early in September, Fulton had witnessed a flight at Larkhill by one of these machines which left him with impressions of its flying qualities which were far from favourable:

> Mr Prier started his machine in a direction due west. The machine rose after a run of about 90 yards. Immediately on leaving the ground the machine took a decided list down on the left. Prier steered to the right, thus taking a North Westerly direction, and at the same time apparently corrected the list, for the machine then took an alarming list to the opposite side, namely down to the right: the wings being at a slope of 40 degrees approximately laterally.
>
> The spectators thought a disaster was inevitable, but M. Prier was able to save himself and the machine by his great skill. He switched off the ignition and dived a short distance, eventually righting and flying round several circuits of the aerodrome. The machine continued to fly very unsteadily, eventually making a forced landing some distance away, and the machine had to be towed home.
>
> I consider that the machine in its present state of development is completely unsuitable.

Thus, following this unfortunate and highly unimpressive demonstration, Bristols too were eliminated, at least for the moment, leaving all the domestic possibilities inspected and found wanting. That left Fulton to turn his gaze to the other side of the Channel, where there were several companies already supplying the French air service with machines in some quantities. As it happened, of the four makes suggested in Bannerman's letter, the acquisition of single examples of three of them seems already to have been decided. A Deperdussin monoplane (60-hp Anzani) and a Breguet L1 biplane (60-hp Renault) were delivered to Farnborough on 6 and 10 October respectively, while a Nieuport monoplane (50-hp Gnôme) also arrived at around the same time. After being test-flown a few times by the factory pilots, they were handed over to the Air Battalion. As for the Sommer, an example of this make, happening to come onto the British market, was offered to the War Office at the end of December, but was turned down and in the end no Sommers went into service with the British Army.

Thus, for the time being, French aeroplanes continued to be the British Army's choice. Maybe – but just at hand there lurked another group of people with rather different ideas. After all, sharing the same plot of land was an organisation which actually went under the name of the Army Aircraft Factory. So far as Mervyn O'Gorman was concerned, that meant it was in the business of producing at least one or two aeroplanes for the army's use. Its first effort, the S.E.1, had been removed from the prospectus by Ridge's fatal crash, but the 'reconstructed' Voisin, the B.E.1, was nearing completion. In the afternoon of 4 December, it was wheeled out onto Farnborough Common, from where it made its first flight in the hands of its designer, Geoffrey de Havilland. During the following weeks, its flight test programme continued, as various modifications were progressively incorporated. On some of these flights, the opportunity was taken to carry passengers, including members of the Air Battalion, who may well have been impressed by the machine's maximum speed of 55 mph. Amongst them was Charles Burke, who was taken up in the new machine on

27 December. In January 1912, the airborne wireless pioneer, Captain Lefroy, fitted a set in the machine and, piloted by de Havilland, pursued his experiments as they flew over Salisbury Plain.

The B.E.1 represented a significant advance on the Voisin-inspired biplanes with which the Air Battalion had until recently been struggling. Its performance in all departments – maximum speed, rate of climb and range – placed it in a class of its own. In addition, although owing nothing to John Dunne's design philosophies, it had a degree of natural stability which, in those days, was seen as an admirable quality in a military aeroplane, whose perceived function was that of a mobile aerial platform from which an observer could spy upon a hostile army. It had another attribute: the engine was fitted with long exhaust pipes and noise attenuators which made it seem much quieter than its contemporaries and led to it acquiring the soubriquet of 'The Silent Army Aeroplane', embodying the attractive implication that it could creep up on an unsuspecting enemy and take him by surprise ... Burke certainly found it attractive and had his eyes on it as his new mount, to replace the now-outdated and worn-out Farman *Type Militaire*. On 8 January, he had once more crashed the long-suffering machine; by the 26th, it had been repaired in the factory and was test-flown that day. But Burke's attention had now also been seized by the Mortimer Singer competition, whose closing date was still some two months away; although his own repairs were taking a little longer, he forwarded the following plea to Bannerman from his hospital bed:

> My doctor expects me to be off the sick list in three weeks time so might I request that an application be made to the Factory for a new machine for me....
>
> Up to the present machine being out of date and all the other officers getting new machines, it was useless for me to apply to go in for the Mortimer Singer prize.
>
> With a new machine I will have a chance and am anxious to start practicing as soon as my doctor lets me.

The factory's B.E.1 – dubbed 'The Silent Army Aeroplane' – serially numbered B.7 by the Air Battalion. (Author's collection)

Burke, however, had competition. Barrington-Kennett, who had been allocated the Nieuport monoplane, also had his eyes on the trophy. On the 29th, with his rival *hors de combat*, he covered a distance of 111 miles in the Nieuport, just a mile short of Cammell's effort of six months before. A fortnight later, on 14 February, he tried again, accompanied by one of the battalion's NCOs, Cpl Frank Ridd. This time, after remaining in the air for four and a half hours, they had managed to cover a distance of 249 miles. Burke's chances were looking somewhat thin.

By the beginning of February, a second machine to the B.E. specification had been built by the factory and flown, 'reconstructed' of course – this time from a Breguet, provenance unknown. In natural sequence, it was given the designation B.E.2 – meaning the second machine of the 'Blériot' configuration to be built by the factory. Although the next machine to follow it would be designated – naturally again – B.E.3, a little later on this policy of using the numeral as a serial number was abandoned, to be used instead to indicate a design standard. In the end, this meant that that first B.E.2 would turn out to be the prototype of the great number of aeroplanes which were built in its likeness and which were destined to become a mainstay of the RFC in its early years.

Meanwhile, on 11 March, the B.E.1 was finally handed over officially to the Air Battalion, accompanied by the Factory's Certificate, attesting to its airworthiness and performance:

> This is to certify that the aeroplane B.E.1 has been thoroughly tested by me, and the mean speed of a ¾ mile course with a live load of 25 stone and sufficient petrol for one hour's flight is 58-59 m.p.h.
>
> The rate of rising loaded as above has been tested up to 600 feet and found to be at the rate of 155 feet per minute.
>
> The machine has been inverted and suspended from the centre and the wings loaded to three times the normal loading. On examination after this test the machine showed no signs of defect.
>
> (signed) S. Heckstall-Smith
> for Superintendent, Army Aircraft Factory

The progenitor: the first B.E.2. (Author's collection)

The last paragraph refers to the elementary method, sometimes referred to as 'sand-testing', which was used in those days for checking the strength of a machine's wings, at a time when any theoretical calculation of the strength of aircraft structures was still the exception rather than the rule. With the aeroplane inverted, the downward loading applied by the weight of the necessary amount of sand, appropriately distributed along the wings from tip to tip, conveniently represented the maximum predicted *upward* aerodynamic lift loading, increased by a 'manoeuvring factor', or so-called 'g force', to which they would be subjected in flight. If the wings 'showed no signs of defect' in that condition, the test was deemed successful, in that the structure was considered to be strong enough to withstand the stresses which would be imparted to it in flight.

On 14 March, Burke, fit once more, flew the B.E.1 for the first time and became thereafter its regular pilot, as he had wished. However, with only a fortnight in which to become sufficiently skilled in handling the new machine before the closure of the Mortimer Singer competition at the end of the month, he was obliged to forgo his ambition in that direction and Barrington-Kennett emerged as the unchallenged victor.

Flying of the Breguet largely fell to Lieutenant Hynes, who seems to have drawn the short straw. Following the example set by Cammell and Fulton, Hynes had been sent across the Channel, to Douai in this case, to inspect and learn to fly the machine which, on arrival in the UK, became 'his'. It turned out to be another example of a designer's idiosyncratic ideas. Its wings were constructed around a single tubular spar, to which the ribs were attached with a certain amount of rotational freedom, while the single spar allowed for only a single row of interplane struts, instead of the usual two. The result was that the wings proved to be markedly flexible in flight, while the tail unit, both rudder and tailplane, moved as one, being mounted on a universal joint. Such features must have been as worrying to the eye as they were hard work for the pilot's arms, for the effort required to move the controls was reputed to be high. Cockburn viewed this machine, too, with a jaundiced eye, describing it as 'a most unwholesome beast'. For all that Hynes, at first at least, seemed very pleased with his mount – driven perhaps by pride of ownership, describing it in a letter to his friend Board as 'a fine outfit'.

As for the Deperdussin, the flying of that machine seems to have been in the hands of the company commander, Captain Fulton.

There remained one more aeroplane to be taken on strength by the Air Battalion before the latter passed into history. Despite Fulton's adverse report of the previous September, in January 1912, an order was placed with Bristols for one of Pierre Prier's monoplanes. It arrived at Larkhill on 17 February, whereupon Lieutenant Reynolds was nominated as the lucky man, although for one reason or another he did not make his first flight in it until 17 March. It was destined to be another machine whose contribution turned out to be small. Its second flight was not until 26 April and ended in a crash, due to engine failure. After repairs, it flew again on 20 June – and crashed again – also caused by engine failure. By the time extensive modification work had been incorporated to improve its handling qualities, it returned to service just in time to enjoy only a brief extension to its career, before being grounded by the ban on all monoplanes imposed in September 1912 and probably never flew again.

The question of the choice and supply of aeroplanes was thus being progressively addressed, albeit in insufficient numbers and with mixed results. It was, of course, of central importance, as well as being both urgent and overdue, but it was also a matter which was now to be drawn into and become a part of the wider question of what form the army's air service, which was required to operate those aeroplanes, should take. There was a dawning appreciation that for it to remain simply a lowly battalion of the Royal Engineers, jostling for attention among that corps's many other units, as they engaged in the engineers' more traditional and more familiar activities, would not do. Indeed, there were those who were prepared to go much further, believing that an activity with such a potentially important influence on the outcome of future conflicts should now be withdrawn completely from the sappers' grasp. A further reorganisation of the country's military aeronautics had become inevitable – action which increasing international tension was rendering all the more urgent.

10

The Looming Clouds

For some time, the whiff of future conflict had been hovering in the air of Europe. To the inhabitants of the British islands – and, of course, the French – the greatest menace seemed to come from Germany – at once both powerful and ambitious. Firstly, that nation's moves to create its own colonial empire constituted a potential challenge to the existing British and French empires. Secondly, since, as the British well knew, an empire across the seas demanded a navy to control the routes linking it to the motherland, there had arisen a further and greater challenge, represented by German naval pretensions. For some time now, there had been rising alarm in Whitehall at Germany's accelerating programme for the building of new battleships, which, if unchallenged, would ultimately threaten the Royal Navy's position as the possessor of the world's most powerful fleet.

Then, on 3 July 1911, the nation had awoken to find that these two fears seemed to have combined to develop into a genuine crisis. Seizing on a fragile situation in Morocco, where the French and Spanish were already jostling for hegemony, Germany had taken everyone by surprise by joining in the game. Two days previously, one of its gunboats, the *Panther*, had suddenly appeared off the Moroccan port of Agadir, 'to safeguard German subjects and *protégés*'. Unfortunately, in the eyes of the other nations of Europe it seemed an unduly provocative move which time might reveal as cloaking more sinister motives, although a *Times* leader on the subject, whilst recognising the gravity of the situation, recommended a cautious reaction:

> The step which Germany has taken so suddenly does not, and need not, create 'a grave situation' if the explanations of it given by Baron von Schoen and in the North-German Gazette can be accepted as full and correct. It must, however, add to the anxieties of Europe until sufficient time has gone by for us to feel assured that the German official account of it is not only the truth, but the whole truth. Most people, we imagine, will be surprised to learn that Germany possesses extensive interests in South Morocco.

At a less exalted level, the *Daily Mail* reported, under the headline 'GERMAN COUP IN MOROCCO':

> Germany has sprung a surprise upon Europe. Without a word of warning the German Government has sent a warship to Agadir, on the west coast of Morocco, and has informed the Moorish Minister of Foreign Affairs of the intention of Germany to occupy this port on the Atlantic.

Echoing *The Times*'s restrained scepticism, it went on to assert not only that there are no Europeans at Agadir, but that 'Germany has neither interests nor commerce to protect in that part of Morocco', reflecting the widely held suspicion that Germany's action was a sinister ploy in furtherance of its colonial ambitions. The Prussian, the bellicose and arrogant Hun, was rattling his sabre. Although the little *Panther*, now sitting belligerently inside the Moroccan harbour, was no Dreadnought, it was in the current climate a symbol of the much greater threat posed by Germany's growing strength on the high seas. A new European war, the shadow of which had darkened many minds for some while, seemed that summer to be very close.

As it happened, on the very day the crisis emerged, coincidence had arranged for an event to take place which, though of a quite different nature, seemed to add an ominous codicil to the international furore. On 18 June, the great Circuit of Europe air race had started from Paris, and by the first weekend of July, the surviving competitors were lying at Calais, ready to depart on the next stage, which would take them across the water to Dover. Thus it came to pass that, in the early morning of 3 July, even while the population of Great Britain was unfolding its newspapers to read of the first startling news from Morocco, with its threat of conflict between the European powers, a new and much-reinforced reminder of Blériot's warning flight two years earlier was delivered, as, one by one, an unheard-of total of ten aeroplanes flew without great effort across the island's defensive ditch and landed on the national soil. Some may also have been reminded of Baden-Powell's responses to the Aerial Navigation Sub-Committee, when Mr Lloyd George had asked 'what damage could a continental enemy inflict upon us by these machines'.

As matters turned out, by the end of the year, the crisis had been resolved by diplomacy, with the appropriate treaty being signed on 4 November. Nevertheless, the tocsin which had almost been sounded continued to echo off-stage, and the sense that the day would come when it would ring out in earnest had been strengthened. Would we be ready and able to pull our weight alongside our likely allies, the French? On the oceans, the Royal Navy still ruled the waves, provided our warship building programme continued to ensure its superiority in numbers over the putative foe. On land, the army, though small, had been greatly improved by the Haldane reforms – and in any case, the much larger French army was thought to be more than a match for its German counterpart. It was in the new medium of the air that some people found particular cause for concern.

The French now possessed a military aviation service which could muster, it was said, 174 aeroplanes. In Germany, although that nation had also been backward in developing the aeroplane, this omission had seemingly been amply compensated by its concentration on the airship, in which it had met with considerable success. The German government, like the French, was spending large sums on military aeronautics, while Count Zeppelin's great rigid airships were now regularly flying the world's first commercial air service. If war were to come, there would be no great difficulty in sending them in a different direction, loaded with bombs instead of passengers. Such a scenario had even already been imagined and presented to the British public. Three years earlier, in 1908, *The War in the Air*, by the futuristic novelist H. G. Wells, had appeared. This was a typical Wellsian tale of a war which began with the dispatch by Germany (who else?) of a great fleet of airships, loaded with bombs, to the other side of the Atlantic, where it laid waste to New York, having destroyed an American naval force on the way. When China and Japan appeared on the scene, with equally formidable air fleets, featuring both airships and aeroplanes, the conflict became global, with cataclysmic results of a typically Wellsian nature.

If Wells, with his vivid imagination, took his prophesies to an exaggerated length, his visions were not wholly unmatched to the evolving situation. Man's conquest of the air had undoubtedly brought a new threat, which would demand new means of defence. Yet Britain's flying service was represented by a junior formation of the army's general engineering corps, which could usually manage to put no more than four machines into the air on any given day – machines which, in any case, were by then of an inferior standard to those which our probable ally had at his disposal.

In that same month of November, therefore, the Prime Minister, Herbert Asquith, requested that the Standing Sub-Committee of the Committee of Imperial Defence should at its next meeting examine the country's aerial defences and, having done so, submit its recommendations.

The sub-committee began its work on 18 December. At the same time, presumably fortuitously, one contribution to the debate landed on the desk of the Under-Secretary of State at the War Office, Colonel J. E. B. Seely, which had originated from a highly relevant, albeit somewhat junior source. It consisted of a note compiled by none other than Captain Fulton, revealing, if he was to be believed, a state of some unrest amongst the officers of the Air Battalion, or, at any rate, those of No.2 (Aeroplane) Company.

Fulton's note gave voice to a problem which had been waiting to emerge for some time: the continuing control by the Royal Engineers of a flying service which Fulton contended should be an independent corps, of which officers and men from all branches and regiments would be happy – indeed proud – to be a part. Instead, Fulton asserted, officers posted to the Air Battalion from other parts of the army are merely 'attached' and, worse (particularly, one suspects, to someone like the Guardsman Barrington-Kennett), described as 'Acting Engineers'. Although such points might be dismissed as semantics, they were no more than the undertones of a problem of much more serious dimensions. Fulton and his colleagues in the Aeroplane Company were justifiably proud of their status as qualified pilots – members of a still-select company in the nation – and particularly resented the fact that they were placed under the control of officers who were not:

> The Commandant of the Air Battalion is a Royal Engineer. The 'instructor' of the Air Battalion is a Royal Engineer, but although instructor to the pilots, he does not even possess an aeroplane pilot's certificate, and has never flown an aeroplane. Neither has the Commandant. The 'Experimental officer' is a Royal Engineer, but he does not possess an aeroplane pilot's certificate, and has never flown an aeroplane. In fact, this extraordinary position exists: the whole of the staff in direct control of the aeroplane pilots are Royal Engineers, do not possess aeroplane pilot's certificates, and cannot fly! It is only due to the great tact displayed on both sides that this remarkable situation has not come to a head.

The degree of concern which Fulton felt about the question may be judged from the fact that he took the rather risky step for a career officer of going to the very top, by writing to the political chief of the army himself, passing over not just the head of his commanding officer, but also omitting all the other levels in between.

Moving from the general to the particular, Fulton then described the case of an unnamed young RE officer who had been posted to the Air Battalion 'direct from the School of Engineering at Chatham, in spite of the fact that he does not possess an aeroplane pilot's certificate'. Noting that he was expected to teach this young man to fly, Fulton pointed out that this contravened the Army Order which required that only officers in possession of certificates should be appointed to the Air Battalion and, furthermore, that it was War Office policy that all army pilots should be taught to fly at civilian schools. Not only that but, as he did not fail to emphasise, how could any instruction be given, when the battalion's only official instructor was not himself a pilot? Faced with these events, Fulton feared a plot:

> A careful consideration of the above two points will show that it is open to the Commandant of the Air Battalion to first admit officers of his own regiment to the Air Battalion, and then having got them there, to have them taught to fly. The next step will clearly be to post the newly-taught officers to the Aeroplane Section: and in this simple

way the Aeroplane Section will be easily and quickly converted into an all-Sapper unit, to the exclusion of officers of other Regiments. I have naturally no objection to Royal Engineer officers being represented in a fair proportion in the Aeroplane Section: but having regard to the reluctance which R.E. officers have shewn in taking any initiative in aviation, it would be impossible to convince me that it would be of benefit to the Service if that unit consisted entirely of Royal Engineer officers.

Fulton's frustration about what was perceived as scheming by the RE to keep aeronautics 'in the family' was, as he had implied, shared by the other officers attached to the Air Battalion, as can be seen in an extract from a breezily worded letter which Hynes wrote to Andrew Board during the latter's exile:

The latest scandal is that a 2nd Lieut straight from the S.M.E. at Chatham, whose only qualifications, as far as we know, are he has just over 2 yrs service and is unmarried !!!! has been appointed to the Air Batt presumably to fill poor Cammell's vacancy and is being sent to the gas bag dept and one of the gas baggers has been sent down here to learn flying to fill Cammell's place as an aeroplanist. This is all balls when there are crowds of fellows with certificates howling to come in, and we hope to raise hell over it, but Sapper methods take some getting round.

It was a situation which was all too annoying to officers who found themselves serving as lodgers in a unit, run by the sappers, but in which they, the non-engineers, nevertheless formed the great majority. If they knew of it, they might well have found irony in Capper's observation, over two years earlier, previously quoted, that 'as regards finding officers for the School and Companies, I regret to say that I seem to get very few volunteers from the Corps of Royal Engineers'. The nub of the matter, as Fulton saw it, was that military aviation had now become so potentially important to the fortunes of the British army in any future field of conflict that it urgently needed to be raised in status. It was vital that it should not remain merely a subordinate (and perhaps not greatly loved) unit within the Corps of Royal Engineers, obliged to take its turn among all the other preoccupations of that service.
Seely lost no time in passing Fulton's note on to Winston Churchill, now First Lord of the Admiralty and a member of the CID Sub-Committee, adding his own views:

The whole business of flying in the Army is in a hopeless muddle, and if you can cut the Gordian knot I shall be more than grateful.
    The first thing to do is to separate the aeroplane service from balloons and kites, both for Army and Navy; the two things have little in common, and are, in practice, antagonistic.

Churchill was amongst those who had always believed in the future of military aviation (typically, it would not be long before he gave practical form to his belief by taking a course of flying instruction). His response to Fulton's appeal was both incisive and uncompromising:

Whatever happens the R.E. must have nothing to do with H.M.'s Corps of Airmen, which should be a new and separate organisation drawing from civilian, as well as military and naval sources ...

Fulton could hardly have wished for a more positive concurrence with his views, from such a powerful and influential position (even though one might suspect that there lurked behind it the prejudice of a former cavalry officer with respect to the less glamorous engineering corps!).

There were two more inputs of significance which were available to help the CID Sub-Committee in its deliberations. One came in the form of a memorandum by that other champion of military aviation, Bertram Dickson. In developing Fullerton's earlier predictions about the shape of future wars, no longer to be waged beneath an empty sky, it revealed the clarity with which its author was able to visualise the future:

> In the case of a European war between two countries, both sides would be equipped with large corps of aeroplanes, each trying to obtain information of the other, and to hide its own movements. The efforts which each would exert in order to hinder or prevent the enemy from obtaining information, and the inefficiency of fire from the ground to prevent reconnaissance by aeroplanes, would lead to the inevitable result of a war in the air, for the supremacy of the air, by armed aeroplanes against each other.
>
> This fight for the supremacy of the air in future wars will be of the first and greatest importance, and when it has been won the land and sea forces of the loser will be at such a disadvantage that the war will certainly have to terminate at a much smaller loss in men and money to both sides. In a word, this adoption of aeroplanes in war for the supremacy of the air, with the advantage of the information which the conqueror obtains will insure rather the victory of mental organisation and perfect equipment, than the exercise of brute force.

The other was a comprehensive report by an officer who, although not a pilot, had joined the Air Battalion on temporary attachment and then in August had been sent to the military aviation centre at Châlons, following up Fulton's earlier visit, specifically to report on how the French army had set about tackling the question of military aeronautics. He was Lieutenant Ralph Glyn, who, having served for several years in the Rifle Brigade, was now on the Reserve, having resigned his regular commission in order to pursue a political career.

After a visit during which he benefited from discussions with a number of the instructors and student pilots serving at Châlons, as well as a flight in a Nieuport monoplane, Glyn produced a wide-ranging report, which appeared that October. This covered not only the relative merits of different aircraft types, their construction and repair, the training of pilots and the choice of airfields, but also the principles governing the use of aeroplanes in war and different features of their application in relation to other arms and under varying circumstances. As usual, the Englishman took it as axiomatic that only France possessed a 'Corps of Airmen' which was in an effective condition and that, therefore, it was only in France that one could learn the right steps to be taken to set up an effective Air Corps in one's own country. Glyn's conclusions began by accepting that aeroplanes had now reached the stage where they were a 'necessary service for recognised employment with the army', that 'possession of an adequate number of machines, and a sufficient number of skilled military aviators, would have the effect of increasing the fighting efficiency of the British Army' and that naval and military aeronautics should be 'merged into a joint corps for all purposes of construction and training'. Developing his theme, he recommended that 'every encouragement should be given to officers of both Services to come forward, and that the establishment of the existing Air Battalion may be so altered as to be capable of great expansion'. Clearly greatly impressed by what he had seen in France, he then described at some length the path adopted in that country, in particular the decision that the new service 'should no longer form but a part of the *Génie*' (i.e., the engineers), being careful to add that 'by this no reflection was cast upon the engineers who had so admirably inaugurated the new science as a potent factor in modern war training' – an observation which, in all fairness, could equally be applied to their confreres in the British Corps of Royal Engineers.

Once in receipt of these various contributions, the CID Standing Sub-Committee wisely brought into being another body, known as the Technical Sub-Committee, to which it delegated the work. This met four times in the course of January and February 1912 under the chairmanship of Colonel Seely, the other members being Brigadier General G. K. Scott-Moncrieff, the current Director of Fortifications and Works; Major-General A. J. Murray, the Director of Military Training; Brigadier General David Henderson who, at the relatively advanced age of forty-nine, had lately also learnt to fly at Brooklands and who would first replace Murray in the above post in the following August, and then on the outbreak of war would become the RFC's first commander in France; two sailors – Commander C. R. Samson RN and Lieutenant R. Gregory RN, both of whom had learned to fly with the naval contingent at Eastchurch; and finally Mervyn O'Gorman. This was a committee with a membership whose knowledge and experience in aeronautical matters (for the day) gave it some chance of coming to sensible and informed conclusions. Even so, much of the spadework was done outside that committee, passed down yet another step to a quasi-informal group of three, consisting of Brigadier Henderson himself, a member of his staff, Major Duncan MacInnes RE, and Capt Frederick Sykes, who was currently serving on the General Staff. This latter officer we met some years earlier, during his stay with the balloonists in their summer camp at Rhayader in 1904. Since then, he had been a long-term and consistent member of that small club of junior officers who, from George Grover onwards, had, in defiance of their seniors' disinterest, been adherents to the cause of military aeronautics. He had already given practical form to his beliefs by taking flying lessons on a Boxkite of Bristol's other school, at Brooklands, even interrupting his course to travel across the Channel on leave, in order to widen his experience by flying in some of the French machines. Returning to England, he obtained his aviator's certificate on 20 June 1911, just a month earlier than Brooke-Popham.

The detailed work of this *ad hoc* working party was added to the material from other sources available to the Technical Sub-Committee and, after due consideration, the latter reported to its parent committee on 27 February 1912. It began this report with a preamble which made no bones about the unsatisfactory condition into which it considered British military aeronautics had been allowed to fall:

> The Sub-Committee have been impressed by the evidence which has been placed before them regarding the backward state of Aerial Navigation in this country, when contrasted with the progress made by other great naval and military Powers. To illustrate this, it is sufficient to mention that France already possesses about 250 efficient military aeroplanes, and 150 qualified military and 80 civilian flying men, in addition to several airships; Germany possesses 20 or 30 military aeroplanes, and there are in addition from 100 to 120 aeroplanes belonging to civilians in that country; there are besides some 20 airships in Germany; Italy possesses about 22 military aeroplanes; and these and other countries are engaged in considerable developments of their aeronautical services. In contrast to this, Great Britain possesses less than a dozen efficient aeroplanes, and only two small airships, to meet the combined requirements of the naval and military services in time of war.

The end result of the committees' work was a recommendation that the Air Battalion of the Corps of Royal Engineers should be replaced by a new and higher formation, which it called the Flying Corps – soon to be awarded the prefix 'Royal'. The new Corps was duly constituted by Royal Warrant on 13 April 1912; it was to be divided into four parts: a Military Wing, a Naval Wing (for it had been decided, as Glyn had proposed, that naval flying must also be gathered up in the new arrangements), a Central Flying School and a Reserve. The new Corps was to be subordinate to the

By 1912, the Royal Aircraft Factory had begun its own expansion. To the original balloon shed and airship hangar (centre of the picture) had been added another airship hangar and other buildings. (West is at the top of the picture). (Author's collection)

Director of Military Training. O'Gorman's Aircraft Factory was left undisturbed, other than being granted the accolade of 'Royal' before its name.

The Military Wing was naturally born out of the old Air Battalion, although to be much expanded, for it was established with a total of eight squadrons, borrowing the term for its basic tactical formation both from the navy and from the cavalrymen whose reconnaissance role it was bidding to usurp. Achievement of such a target was well beyond immediate reach and at the outset ambition went no further than the formation of three aeroplane squadrons. A fourth – No.1 Squadron – was effectively the Air Battalion's No.1 Company. This would continue to be responsible for operating the latter's dirigibles and balloons, as well as maintaining two flights of kites, and would remain under the command of Captain Maitland. Overall command of the Military Wing was assumed by Captain Sykes, on promotion to major, while Lieutenant Barrington-Kennett became its first adjutant.

Just as naturally, the Naval Wing set up its home at Eastchurch, on the Isle of Sheppey, where naval flying had begun and evolved, and was placed under the orders of Commander Samson.

The Central Flying School was to be based on Salisbury Plain, where the Air Battalion had found a flying ground which was much more congenial than that on Farnborough Common. On that account, initial thoughts naturally enough leaned towards Larkhill as the obvious location, but further reflection suggested that that site, too, had its drawbacks. Whilst some saw it as conveniently near to the army's training ground, allowing useful cooperation to take place between traditional soldiers on the ground and their new comrades in the sky, a more influential body of opinion was inclined to rule it out on account of the engines' disturbing effect on the horses (the aviators, on the other hand, thought that this would rank as a favourable point, since it would enable the horses to become accustomed to a noise which henceforth would inevitably and increasingly be present). A second, very serious objection concerned the effect on the neighbours – or rather neighbour. It had been noted that, on take-off, the aircraft were obliged to fly over the land to the east owned by Sir Edmond Antrobus. Here, too, the noise which they created was disturbing to the animals below – in this case, the grouse and hares. Sir Edmond's complaint about this adverse effect on his rough shooting was sympathetically received by the like-minded sportsmen in the War Office and, placed alongside the other objection, resulted in a decision to seek another location, not too far away, on which the school might be founded.

After some reconnoitring work in the district, a candidate was found, some seven miles further north, on high ground known as Upavon Down, immediately east of the village of Upavon. Sir David Henderson and Lieutenant Gregory were dispatched to make a more thorough inspection and returned with a favourable report. The land concerned, some 2,400 acres in extent, while considered to be 'better than any British aviation ground with which the members of the Committee are acquainted', had other attributes to recommend it. It not only had a road running through it to facilitate transport, but it was also within handy distance of a railway station; conversely, it was, unlike Farnborough, sufficiently remote as to be unlikely to suffer from intrusion by members of the public; large bodies of troops could be found nearby, to facilitate training in aerial reconnaissance; finally, the owner of the land was willing to sell. Negotiations were quickly and satisfactorily effected and with similar dispatch work was started on erection of the buildings which the school was going to need.

In the original concept, the school's function was that of advanced training; it was there to teach its students how to be military aviators, not how to be pilots – that was still to be left to the civilian schools. Only after an officer had obtained his RAeC certificate by that means (followed, eventually, by his reimbursement of £75) would he be accepted as a pupil on a CFS course. As matters turned out, this idea did not survive without amendment: when the first course assembled at the new location in August, it included a few members without aviator's certificates, while the course syllabus had been expanded somewhat to allow for them to undergo initial pilot training before embarking on the course proper. The pupils would, of course, be drawn from both the services, although administration of the school would come under the War Office. To balance things up, the first commandant was supplied by the navy, in the person of Captain Godfrey Paine RN.

This attempt to persuade army and navy to work together represented, perhaps, something of a triumph of hope over realism and was not to last. It would not be long before the Admiralty, placing its telescope to its blind eye and ignoring the official arrangements, declared its independence, extracted the Naval Wing from the Royal Flying Corps and transformed it into its own Royal Naval Air Service (RNAS). It was an action which was to be the first but not the last oscillation in a seesaw struggle for ownership of naval aviation which, even today, has perhaps not yet seen its final resolution.

As for the Reserve, since something approaching 200 aviator's certificates had now been granted by the Royal Aero Club, there was clearly a sizeable and growing pool of civilian pilots in the country who, if conflict came, could be called upon to assist in bringing the squadrons up from their peacetime size to their war establishment. It was proposed that the Reserve should be divided into two levels: pilots who volunteered to join the so-called First Reserve would receive a retaining fee and would be expected to keep themselves in flying practice. To this end, they were to produce proof of having flown for nine hours, including one cross-country flight, each quarter, all expenses incurred in doing so being reimbursed. Those who joined the Second Reserve would receive no fee, would not be expected to keep up their flying, but would be liable for call-up in time of war.

When the formation of the Special Reserve, as it was finally called, was announced, there was a gratifyingly large response, as letters arrived from up and down the country. The applicants, truly a mixed lot, could be divided into three categories. The first and most valuable group, though relatively few in number, comprised those already in possession of an aviator's certificate. Amongst these were names which by then were notable on the flying scene, led by that of Francis McClean, the philanthropic donor of the navy's base at Sheerness, and James Valentine, along with those of others which would become so, such as Robert Smith-Barry and Geoffrey de Havilland.

The second and very much the largest group was made up of men who, at that point, had had no previous connection with the still limited world of aviation, not a few of whom, it might well be imagined, were impelled by a perception of the romantic image which flying presented, the writers being seized by the vision of a career which combined the life of a soldier (or sailor) with that of the glamorous gods of the air whose exploits were now being reported so frequently in the papers. Although offering keenness and enthusiasm, they were quite unable to supplement these with any kind of piloting experience – indeed, under the conditions then obtaining, it must be extremely doubtful whether many of them, if any, had even flown. These candidates were sent a standard War Office letter of acknowledgement which advised them that, to be eligible for consideration, they too must first be in possession of an aviator's certificate. For many, it must have marked the end of their aspirations. There will, nevertheless, have been some for whom this first rebuff would have been the spur which sent them to enrol, if they possessed the means, at one of the flying schools, unlocking the door to a new world. In a very few cases, four or five at the most, it would have meant the first step on a path which, two years later, was to lead to membership of that special club of RFC pilots who were the first to fly their machines across the water to war.

The third group, the smallest of the three, was made up of the no-hopers, whom it was possible to eliminate at once. One of these, though not exactly typical, was a certain Mrs W. Buller, writing from the Hotel du Grand Cerf in Douai, whose application was inevitably declined by the Army Council, with the apologetic reply that they 'very much regret that the conditions of service in the Royal Flying Corps prevent them availing themselves of your services.'

As a side-effect of the major reorganisation of military aeronautics which was taking place, an earlier proposal to form an Air Battalion Reserve became automatically redundant, as did that for an Air Battalion for the Territorial Force, both being overtaken and replaced by the RFC Special Reserve. The new order also meant the end for the London Balloon Company, though not the end of the aeronautical careers of some of its members, several of whom had already set out to become pilots. Apart from the late Theodore Ridge, they included Victor Barrington-Kennett, a younger brother of the RFC's adjutant, and Thomas O'Brien Hubbard, both of whom, by 1916, were commanding squadrons in France. Barrington-Kennett's career was ended when he achieved the melancholy distinction of becoming one of the sixteen victims of the German ace, Max Immelmann.

As for aeroplanes, in order to equip both the CFS and the squadrons, clearly very many more were going to be needed than had hitherto been planned. Each squadron was to be composed of three flights, with each flight to possess four machines plus two in reserve, making a total of eighteen machines per squadron. The sub-committee had recommended an initial procurement of twenty machines, but with many more to follow. Although twelve of these were to be French, some domestic constructors, among them Samuel Cody, at last found themselves being taken seriously and were also on the list.

Another twenty-five aeroplanes – also a mix of French and British – were to go to the CFS. The list of acquisitions to join the Air Battalion's five surviving Boxkites included Shorts, Roes, Avros, Deperdussins, Breguets, Nieuports and Blériots. Time and events were to modify these initial arrangements, in which that future workhorse of the RFC's flying training schools, the ubiquitous Maurice Farman, did not even figure, but a start had been made.

Another name which was not included in the above lists was that of John Dunne, although it was not for lack of effort on the part of the Marquis of Tullibardine. The latter had written a long and rambling letter to Colonel Seely, extolling the virtues of the latest Dunne aeroplane, which Seely felt obliged to read out to the sub-committee. It could fly at 63 miles an hour, make a complete circle in 9 seconds and rise at 300 feet a minute – indeed, it could 'show a clean pair of heels to any other machine', Bardie asserted, while complaining that he had:

> ... put in a lot more money than I could afford, and so have several other officers, simply to save the invention for the War Office, who were stupid enough to throw it away when they had it for nothing, after having spent a lot of money over it.

Seely was not too keen: 'What are we going to do about a letter of that kind written to me quite unofficially? Do you know anything about Dunne's machine?' he asked. O'Gorman, while thinking it 'well worth looking into', dismissed it as belonging to the realm of experimental research – not what they wanted at that moment. Commander Samson had seen it flying and, though 'it tilts at the most horrible-looking angles', also thought that it was 'well worth investigating'. So it was left at that.

There would be much work for the CFS to do. In order to man the seven aeroplane squadrons envisaged by Seely's sub-committee, the latter had calculated that a total of 182 aviators would be required. Then, taking the gloomiest of views, it had doubled this figure, to cover casualties and other wastage. Military aviation had come alive with a vengeance. It was as well that there were usually a few soldiers among the steady flow of pupils who were being taught to fly at the civilian schools at Larkhill, Hendon and Brooklands. For the time being though, there were insufficient aeronauts to man the four squadrons which had so far been formed.

Of the four, No.1 experienced the least change. Operating the same aerial vehicles that it had always used, it simply carried on in the same vein, although, since nearly all the erstwhile balloonists and airship pilots had absconded to aeroplane flying, it found itself rather under-officered.

No.2 Squadron was formed from Captain Burke's detachment at Farnborough and for the time being remained there, under that officer's command.

In a similar manner, No.3 Squadron grew out of the men and machines at Larkhill and also remained in place. Fulton, however, had gone to CFS as an instructor, where he took command of 'A' Flight, and command of the squadron was assumed by Captain Brooke-Popham, the officer who had been Burke's companion on his unsuccessful attempt to fly to Cambridge the previous year.

As for No.4 Squadron, at that point, it was little more than a name at the top of a blank sheet of paper.

Meanwhile, the two men whom Fulton had invoked as examples of the irrational instructional set-up in the Air Battalion had taken themselves belatedly to Brooklands to learn to fly, in order to make themselves eligible for collaboration in what they now realised had become the senior partner in military aeronautics. Broke-Smith gained his RAeC certificate on 16 April and Sir Alexander Bannerman was awarded his a fortnight later. For the latter, it made no difference; as commander of the Military Wing he had already been passed over in favour of Sykes. On 28 August 1912, in his fortieth year, he retired from the army after twenty-one years service. Broke-Smith, perhaps surprisingly, was appointed to the CFS as a flight commander and instructor, although it was an appointment which lasted only until 11 November of the same year.

With the site at Upavon taking a little while to prepare, a preliminary CFS course, consisting of ten officers, which assembled on 10 April, was obliged to do so at Farnborough. None of the ten, listed below, was a Royal Engineer, but all had obtained their RAeC Aviator's Certificates:

Lieutenant Colonel	H. R. Cook (RGA)
Captains	E. B. Loraine (Grenadier Guards)
	C. R. W. Allen (Welsh Regiment)
	G. W. P. Dawes (Royal Berkshire Regt)
	G. H. Raleigh (Essex Regt)
Lieutenants	G. T. Porter (RGA)
	T. G. Hetherington (18th Hussars)
	C. T. Carfrae (RFA)
	C. A. H. Longcroft (Welsh Regiment)
	B. R. W. Beor (RFA)

The syllabus of the month-long course, which was in two parts and had been prepared by Captains Burke and Brooke-Popham, was not of a nature to commend itself to any of the new arrivals who might have imagined himself being immediately converted into an intrepid birdman. One half of the course consisted of classroom work, including lectures on such highly relevant subjects as theory of flight, aeroplane design, the objects of aerial reconnaissance, meteorology and navigation. The other half took them outside the classroom, where they were at least able to rise into their chosen element. However, far from soaring amidst the clouds on eagles' wings, they found themselves turned back in time, to an era they thought was over, by being taken for rides in balloons, both captive and on free runs, and in airships. The purpose of these activities was based on the prevalent idea that it would be difficult to control an aeroplane whilst at the same time attempting to learn the skills of aerial observation. They were probably also dictated by the fact that, at that time, there were no spare machines available for their use. One of the pupils, Lieutenant Charles Longcroft, had learnt to fly with the Bristol school at Brooklands the previous month and was, as he later recalled, distinctly unimpressed with this reversion to nineteenth century aeronautics:

> Our instruction started by a series of ascents in captive spherical balloons, of which several were available. I have never discovered a better test for finding out whether a prospective pilot is likely to be airsick or not than the test of a captive spherical balloon. Hour after hour was spent in sitting in the basket of the balloon sketching the various parts of Farnborough, describing what could be seen from the balloon, counting the number of cows on the Common, etc. The basket of a spherical balloon never gives one the chance of looking at the same spot for any length of time, as on most days there is a violent combined swinging and rotating motion of the basket. This sketching and report writing instruction from balloons went on for about a fortnight, and was then relieved by an ascent in H.M.A. Gamma, which gave the pilots their first free trip in a Service type of aircraft. This form of instruction, varied with occasional trips in free balloons, continued for about 6 weeks, by which time we were all heartily sick of it.

Upavon became operational in the following August and the first course of nineteen pupils assembled, marking the beginning of an illustrious history, albeit one which took a little time to reach its full potential. For, with the supply of aeroplanes yet to answer the belated orders which had been placed and so match the demands of the expansive schemes which had been conceived, the pupils found on their arrival at Upavon a grand total of four machines available for instructional purposes. Their efforts and those of their instructors soon reduced this number to nil and, despite energetic demands from the commandant for replacements, none were immediately forthcoming. In these circumstances, Captain Paine did as he had threatened to do, declaring the school closed and sending all the pupils off on leave, to await the arrival of replacement aircraft.

11

They Also Served

So far, the business of flying the army's aeroplanes had been the exclusive preserve of officers – which is scarcely surprising given the rule that all budding military pilots had first to learn to fly at their own expense. In 1911, £75 was no mean sum to most people, including many subalterns; to a non-commissioned soldier whose pay, dependent on his rank, lay between six and two shillings (30p to 10p) per day, it was in normal circumstances quite out of reach.

There was also the question of the command of an aeroplane in the air. In those days in particular, with wireless communications effectively non-existent, once an aircraft, be it balloon, airship or aeroplane, had been launched and all links with higher authority severed for the duration of its aerial journey, responsibility for its efficient operation and the safety of its occupants during that time fell entirely on the senior aeronaut on board. In ballooning days, that duty had most frequently – though not exclusively – been performed by a commissioned officer.

Thus, when, in the course of its sittings, the Technical Sub-Committee came to examine the matter of recruiting the many additional pilots who would be required to man the new squadrons, opportunity and established practice had so far conspired together to make the pilot's seat the exclusive preserve of officers. Moreover, this circumstance was soon given further reinforcement by the money factor in another form – namely the pay which would have to be offered to the new recruits, a majority of whom would have to come from outside the army. Clearly, a skilled pilot, regularly risking his life in the air, was entitled to expect a reasonable reward for his bravery. The committee soon found itself facing a complex situation, in which the practical need for the efficient operation of the new arm could not be disassociated from the more personal considerations of rank and class. For, since pay is a direct function of rank, it began to appear that the level of pay necessary would automatically mean that all pilots would have to be officers. Yet, as aviation evolved, as it was even then doing, and its effects permeated downwards through that society's layers, some of the pilots who came forward would be from backgrounds which, given the rather rigid class divisions which governed peoples' lives in those days, would normally place them in the ranks of the non-commissioned.

In performing its duty of trying to advise on how the new corps might best be shaped to accomplish its purpose, the committee found that, in this particular area, it had strayed into something of a minefield as, while considering straightforward organisational considerations, it also found itself obliged to wrestle with the more delicate concerns occasioned by this interplay of money, rank and class, and it devoted quite a significant part of its time to testing this heady cocktail. The Chairman, Colonel Seely, put it plainly when he observed:

> You know the difficulty in this curious society of ours; that we are divided into classes, officers, non-commissioned officers, and men, or people who are called gentlemen and people who are not called gentlemen. We are up against a real

difficulty here. How are you going to classify these gentlemen who join, because some are what we call the officer class, and some are not what we call the officer class. It is a hateful thing to take a sort of snobbish line and say, where all men are running the same risks, you should put one man above and one man below; but still you see the difficulty we shall be in, as there will be an officers' mess, and that kind of thing.

In making this statement, Seely was doing no more than acknowledging the facts of life at that time, facts which were taken as read by all parties, including the witnesses whom the committee called to help as it groped its way to a solution. During the examination of one of them, Bertram Dickson, Mervyn O'Gorman tried to view the problem from a different angle, by asking him whether his idea was that 'the flying man does not need to be an officer because there would be an officer on board his machine'. In other words, would he be just a driver, like the chauffeurs now being employed by wealthy men, in which case, could he perhaps be non-commissioned, with an officer-passenger in command? This seemed to carry them a little closer to a conclusion, although Dickson was prepared to allow no more than a limited concession of the point:

> On certain occasions some men will have to be officers, and on others some men will not necessarily have to be officers, but you certainly will get more value out of an officer as a pilot than you will out of a common man, because all the best pilots so far have not been the man who has got no nerves and is the stolid sort of mechanical person; they have been far more the excitable, nervous-temperamented, generally artistic men. That sort of instinct and character is far more found amongst officers than amongst men.

For Dickson, echoing the attitudes of society as a whole, 'officer', was of course synonymous with 'gentleman'. He would probably have agreed with another witness, the leading aviator James Valentine, who, feeling his way a little further along the rocky road, thought they 'might get a class of mechanic-flyers'. Such men, he thought, 'should pass a course of instruction as mechanics so that they would not only be moderate fliers, but first class aviation mechanics, and so could be employed if there were not enough officers to fly all the machines'.

Valentine had hit upon a concept which, later on, was in fact adopted. For the moment, the Technical Sub-Committee included the following statement of intent in its Report: 'Up to the present time we have only attempted to train officers as fliers. It is now proposed to train non-commissioned officers and men as well.' The lucky men concerned were all found by selection from the ranks of existing trained mechanics and were taught to fly by the instructors at Upavon, as the anomalous requirement for pilots to finance their own tuition edged towards its deserved abandonment. In a further categorisation, presumably based on their perceived skill in the air, the non-commissioned pilots were graded as either 1st or 2nd Class Fliers, where the latter would seem to have been the embodiment of the 'mechanic-flyers' envisaged by Valentine.

The first four to benefit from the new policy were, in order of their arrival in the air, 2/Cpl Frank Ridd, Staff Sergeant R. H. V. Wilson, Air Mech William Strugnell and Air Mech William McCudden (whose younger brother James, following in his footsteps, would win fame and the Victoria Cross as one of the war's leading combat pilots). Ridd gained his certificate on 4 June, followed by Wilson on the 18th, Strugnell on 24 July and McCudden on 13 August.

Ridd probably fell into the 2nd Class Flier category, since later on, when war began, he was serving as a flight sergeant ground mechanic in 3 Squadron. Strugnell and McCudden, by contrast, became properly recognised pilots: the former won the

MC and Bar – and a commission – as a scout pilot in France, while McCudden flew in France with 3 Squadron, before being posted to England as a sergeant instructor, only to lose his life in a flying accident in May 1915. Wilson, on the other hand, never had the chance to reveal his potential, for his flying career was of the very briefest: seventeen days after he had gained his certificate, the RFC suffered its first fatal accident, when a Nieuport monoplane being flown by Captain Eustace Loraine crashed near Shrewton, 4 miles west of Larkhill, after losing flying speed in a turn at low altitude. Wilson had the misfortune to be accompanying him and was killed alongside his pilot.

In the end, the whole question of pilots' ranks tended to be resolved by natural evolution. When war came, accelerating the social changes which had already been brewing and bringing profound modifications to Seely's 'curious society', the problem which had perplexed his committee was largely swept away. The best of the non-commissioned pilots were, like Strugnell, promoted to officer rank, thus rising to a level appropriate to their abilities, as it should be. The others who remained in the ranks were the first examples of the many non-commissioned aircrew who were to follow, in both wars, as the services found it possible, without sacrificing the necessary military mechanism of the rank system, to accommodate the partial breakdown of the hitherto rigid class boundaries which was beginning to take place in the new society.

Of course, amongst the non-commissioned ranks as a whole, pilots represented a small minority. The great majority found their duties lying firmly on the ground, to wit, the repair and servicing of the machines and their preparation for flight, and this account would be sadly incomplete were it not to include consideration of that supporting cast, without whose work the successful pursuit of any flying activity would be, at best, problematical and, at worst, disastrous. This was as true in those days as it is now and indeed has been through all the years between. Scratch the surface of the early pilots' histories and in many cases the existence of a ground-based assistant is revealed who was as indispensable as he was talented. The Wrights, practical engineers *par excellence*, were their own mechanics, but even they found it expedient to enlist the help of a skilled craftsman named Charlie Taylor, who did most of the work of building the engine which first propelled them across the Kitty Hawk sand dunes. Robert Loraine, to keep his fragile Farman airworthy, had the mercurial Jules Védrines, until the latter himself joined the elite company of the leading pilots; Tommy Sopwith's right-hand man was Fred Sigrist, while Geoffrey de Havilland's faithful associate from the start was Frank Hearle.

In the Air Battalion, it was naturally a little different. In that case, the supporting actors were all supplied from the other ranks of the Royal Engineers – sappers who had been trained in the various skills which the army's engineers had traditionally performed, such as telephonic communications, bridge-building and the construction and operation of railways. With the arrival of aeronautics, a minority had acquired the newer and more specialised skills called for by the operation and maintenance of balloons, kites and dirigibles. Through no fault of their own, however, opportunities for the expansion of their expertise in the more demanding techniques specific to aeroplanes had not been particularly great, while, needless to say, there were no training courses within the army itself where it might have been improved. If the pilots were yet to learn some of the finer points of the art of flying, it must undoubtedly have been the case that the mechanics, too, lacked experience in the maintenance of the machines in which the former were being called upon to risk their lives. A few, with sufficient length of service, would have acquired skills as riggers on Cody's War Kites, which would have given them a good start when they came to maintain the similar, if more complex, structures of the early aeroplanes. Others, like Edwin Palmer, who logged a number of hours as flight engineer of the dirigible *Beta*, would have brought to the battalion valuable experience of the vagaries of the early engines. Nevertheless, such men would not have been very numerous, while the perverseness of the military system will quite often have ensured that, having gained experience with the Air Battalion, they would then be posted away to other engineering duties such as those listed above, taking their aeronautical skills with them. Under these conditions, the Air Battalion may well have suffered from a lack of experienced air mechanics, which could have been the source of at least some of the difficulties and disappointments encountered in the Round Britain Race and the Cambridge 'Odyssey'. It was a situation which made for a less than adequate starting base as the RFC contemplated the great expansion represented by the plan for eight squadrons. While this required the recruitment of a large number of pilots, that demand was naturally matched by a corresponding need for an even larger increase in the numbers of ground staff. There were some seventy immediately available to transfer from the Air Battalion to the new corps, including Edwin Palmer, referred to above, and John Ramsey, the saviour of the *Nulli Secundus* in 1907 and by then a Sergeant-Major.

Henry Brooke-Popham and Charles Burke, in a note entitled 'Memorandum on the Training of Aeroplane Personnel', issued around that time, did not fail to identify the need facing the new corps for sufficient suitably trained ground staff, as well as the dichotomy which tended to impede further progress:

> At the outset one is met with this difficulty, that to give the ground staff training there must be flying, and to enable flying to be carried out there must be an efficient ground staff.
>
> To commence training by inexperienced pilots flying with an untrained ground staff will mean, possibly loss of life, probably serious accidents and certainly loss of time and money.
>
> The new personnel, both pilots and ground staff, should commence their training under such conditions, that the pilot can have the advantage of competent mechanics to look after his machine and that the ground staff can be given expert supervision.

In the early months of the Royal Flying Corps's life, although the pioneers from the Air Battalion were augmented by a number of soldiers who chose to transfer from other regiments of the army, numbers were still inadequate. The obvious answer was recruitment from civilian life, but that was by no means assured of success, for the corps was to find itself in competition with the burgeoning aircraft industry, as the new manufacturing companies expanded and themselves sought to recruit the men they needed to build the aeroplanes now being ordered by the War Office in increasing numbers. It was a problem which was much more acute for British military aviation than for the French, who were able to draw from a deep well of highly-skilled mechanics, thanks to that Continental notion which this country refused at that time to countenance – compulsory military service. A particular example of this advantage, quoted by Fulton in his report on French military aviation, was provided by the son of Laurent Seguin, designer of the highly successful Gnôme rotary engine, whom he found at Châlons, performing his *service militaire* and contributing his knowledge for the benefit of the aviators there.

However, there are always, thank goodness, a certain number of young men who are attracted to a military life, and by July 1912, quite a few had come forward to take the plunge and enlist as Air Mechanics Second Class in His Majesty's Royal Flying Corps. Examples of two such recruits were Albert Bell and George Dunville, whose careers illustrated the divergent paths along which men could be led by the demands of the service and by their own inclinations. Bell pursued a career on the ground, by 1918 he was a Disciplinary Sergeant-Major, and when he finally retired after the end of the Second World War, he was the most senior warrant officer in the Royal Air Force. Dunville's career was, by contrast, more exciting but very much shorter. After crossing to France in August 1914 as an Air Mechanic 1st Class, he spent several years in that role before his ambitions turned skywards and he became one of those who were selected for pilot training. In August 1917, he passed out as a sergeant pilot, but after being posted to France, he was killed in action on 5 September, just one more of the many young pilots who were being sent out to fight at that time with inadequate hours in their log books.

However, it was Bell rather than Dunville whom most of these direct entries from civilian life chose to emulate and, as 1912 advanced and more signed on, the gaps in the ranks were gradually filled. With pilot numbers similarly coming up to establishment, these new recruits enabled the first three aeroplane squadrons to reach and maintain their full degree of effectiveness.

THE ENDING – AND THE BEGINNING

On the day that Frederick Sykes assumed command of the Military Wing of the RFC in April 1912, just fifty years had gone by since the time when young George Grover was attempting to persuade his elders in the Royal Engineers that mankind had developed an aerial vehicle, in the shape of the hydrogen balloon, which could and ought to be used to give significant assistance to a general in his conduct of a battle. Although, as we have seen, his ideas were slow to receive the recognition he sought, the point was conceded in the end, and for the space of thirty-four years, British military aeronautics had lain within the fief of the Corps of Royal Engineers, the body from which the impetus for its use in war had arisen.

But now the scene had changed abundantly. The silent balloon, so long the army's sole aerial vehicle, whether twisting restlessly at the end of its detaining cable or drawn obediently by the wind across the listening countryside, had been ousted by the brash and noisy aeroplane. The latter, after a hesitant start, was now demonstrating its ability to range at will above the heads of those who had hitherto thought themselves hidden from such unwelcome curiosity. With the formation of the RFC, this new freeman of the air had in its own turn overcome obstacles of disbelief and had defeated the doubters, to a greater extent than the balloon had ever achieved, and the nation had at last acquired a proper aeronautical service.

With little more than two years to spare before it would be called upon to play its part in the Great War, which many had long feared and foreseen, it had been born none too soon and was none too large. Of the eight squadrons originally recommended by the CID Sub-Committee, when that fateful August Bank Holiday of 1914 arrived, only half that number were at a strength and in an operational state which allowed them, some ten days later, to fly across the Channel to war. As for their function, this was still centred on the ideas which had been prevalent as aviation was being born. Although bombing from the air had long been envisaged by the theorists and aerial combat for possession of the sky was vaguely expected to occur, by some means yet to be defined, aeroplanes were first and foremost seen as the cavalry of the air and their first duty was reconnaissance. The aeroplanes in service reflected this and had not advanced very far since the last days of the Air Battalion, less than three years earlier. When, one by one, the machines of the four squadrons landed on the field outside Amiens which had been chosen as their first base in France, predominant amongst them were Blériot monoplanes, Henri Farman biplanes and, most of all, B.E.2s.

Their arrival could be said to be the culminating flourish of a long fifty-year parade of soldiers, sailors and civilians who had made their contributions during the course of those years. In the case of the earliest of these pioneers, death or retirement had for the most part removed them from the stage. Grover and Beaumont, those first sowers of the seed, were both gone, as were their successors Elsdale, Lee and Trollope, who had tended the plant as it took root and grew. Others, such as Charles Watson and Bernard Ward, survived long enough to see the arrival of the first war in the air, as did Mackenzie, the first battlefield aeronaut, who, having returned to the more habitual sapper pursuits, took part in no more aerial exploits before retiring as a major in 1906. Their immediate successors, those active service aeronauts Jones, Blakeney, Grubb and Heath, having also been diverted to more traditional sapper work in the later stages of the South African War, completed their remaining years with the colours, including those of the Great War, on the ground.

In addition to the foregoing, there are, of course, two other names which should figure in the list of those who should be remembered for their pioneering contributions to the establishment of British military aeronautics. One of them, at least, must stand at the very head of the list. For, although no history of Britain's Flying Service is ever likely to be found which did not honour the memory of Hugh Trenchard, probably associated with a reference to his repute as Father of the Royal Air Force, it is no disparagement of his renown to renew the assertion that the RAF can boast an ancestry which reaches back to well before his arrival on the scene. For, if Trenchard was its father, that robust character James Templer can surely lay claim to the role of grandfather. While Grover and Beaumont laid the foundation stones, Templer was the architect and overseer for most of the building work which raised the first edifice. His was the tenacity which ensured the survival and continuation of the line, enabling a healthy – if always impoverished – air service to be handed on to his successor and the next keeper of the flame, in the person of John Capper.

Templer was, of course, too early to be anything but a lighter-than-air man. Capper, too, had his roots in the ballooning age, but this did not prevent him from being amongst those with a firm belief in the future of the aeroplane from the very start. His duties, and the events of the period during which he discharged them, obliged him to keep a foot in both camps, while fulfilling the role of military aviation's caretaker, as it awaited the aeroplane's tardy maturing. In the end, he found himself precluded from sharing in the consummation when, like so many enthusiasts for military aeronautics before him, he was sent back to mainstream army employment, never to return to the aerial world, eventually retiring with a knighthood and the rank of major-general.

Although all these pioneers had left the stage, their devotion to the cause down the years had left its legacy, in the form of a military unit which, however archaic, however small, at least ensured the existence, dedicated to the air, of not just an organisational foundation but also an air-minded cadre, around which the new corps could be built.

As for the later pioneers – the early aeroplane men – it would not be long before their paths began to diverge. A few, as was to be expected in the perilous medium which they had elected to explore, where death was ever hovering near, were, like Rolls and Cammell, carried off before their work was complete. Of the rest, some remained in the cockpit; a surprising number did not.

Capper's replacement, Bannerman, having after his brief twelve months in command of the Air Battalion been removed from the aeronautical scene by premature retirement, returned to the army when war arrived, like so many, and served in France in command of a battalion of the North Staffordshire Regiment.

Broke-Smith, having relinquished his flying post, found more appropriate work as a staff officer. In March 1915, at the age of thirty-three, he was appointed Deputy Assistant Director of Aviation in Mesopotamia, to where an expeditionary force had been sent from India with the object of ejecting the Turks. After the war, he remained in the East, in a series of engineering staff appointments in India, but no longer in the aeronautical field.

Samuel Cody, though never a soldier, supplied his own homespun talents to the creation of his adopted country's air corps. Remaining a straightforward craftsman to the end, he never progressed from his humble shed on the banks of the Basingstoke Canal and never founded a proper aircraft manufacturing company, as did his contemporaries, Roe and de Havilland. However, in 1912, nearly four years after the rejection of British Army Aeroplane No.1, he achieved vindication of a sort, when the War Office was finally obliged to take one of his aeroplanes on charge.

In August of that year, a competition, known as the Military Trials, was held at Larkhill, with the hopeful object of discovering the best aeroplane with which the RFC should be equipped. Among the entrants which assembled for examination were machines from four established French manufacturers, several from the Bristol and Avro companies and one from Cody's enterprise, as well as some others of more dubious provenance and qualities. After nearly three weeks of wide-ranging tests, which covered not only performance but also such ancillary matters as speed of assembly and ability to take off from plough, the judges awarded Cody first prize, a decision which many, at the time and ever since, have regarded as capricious. At any rate, logic – and the rules of the competition – demanded that his aeroplane be taken over by the RFC and it was duly purchased, while the doubtful utility of the whole exercise was exposed when, at the same time, steps were taken to purchase some additional examples of the B.E.2. This machine, as a government aeroplane, had been forbidden to compete in the trials, but had nevertheless been present and had performed some of the tests *hors concours*, incidentally returning results which demonstrated its clear superiority. As for the Cody, the RFC, faced with a veritable cuckoo in its nest, were not displeased when its creator asked if he might hang on to the machine for a while, in order to compete for another Michelin Trophy, and found no great difficulty in summoning the generosity to comply with his request. The machine was eventually delivered to 4 Squadron at the end of November. Five months later, it suffered catastrophic structural failure in flight over Farnborough and the pilot, Lieutenant Rogers-Harrison, was killed.

We shall never know what contribution Cody might have made in the great conflict which was soon to begin and which, for the first time, was to see the aeroplane playing a significant part, for, twelve months before its outbreak, Fate spoke an earlier and decisive word. In 1913, the *Daily Mail* put up another of its prizes, with a value of £5,000, for a new Round Britain race, this time to be restricted to seaplanes. Naturally, Cody determined to enter and immediately set about constructing a new machine for the purpose. Temporarily fitted with a land undercarriage, it made a number of test flights around Laffan's Plain, preparatory to its conversion to floats. Visitors were many and frequent, some of whom, keen to sample the still-novel experience, were able to persuade the amiable Cody to take them with him. On the morning of 7 August, two more turned up: Lieutenant Charles Keyser, a retired officer of the 20th Hussars, and his friend, a well-known former county cricketer, W. H. B. Evans of Hampshire. After the first flight, with Keyser on board, had passed off without incident, Cody took off for a second time, accompanied by Evans. All seemed to be proceeding as before when, as the machine flew over Ball Hill to the north, the little knot of onlookers gathered outside Cody's shed suddenly realised that it was behaving in an unusual and erratic manner. Scarcely had they taken this in when, to their dismay, they saw it break up and plunge earthwards, falling into a copse of trees on the summit of the hill. The horror of the event was made worse by the sight of the two occupants, who were not strapped in, being thrown out by the violent movement of the stricken machine and tumbling to earth, both being killed instantly.

Cody's funeral took place four days later and was marked by extraordinary manifestations of the high regard which the great-hearted aviator and gifted engineer had attracted from his adopted countrymen. On the official side, although a civilian, he was granted a military funeral, with every mark of respect. Preceded by the band of the Black Watch, the coffin, draped with the Union flag, was carried on the traditional gun carriage and followed by four generals on foot. In the procession were represented every unit in the Aldershot Command, headed, of course, by the Royal Flying Corps. The unofficial reaction was just as impressive: in a spontaneous demonstration of

Cody's Waterplane, designed particularly to compete in the *Daily Mail*'s 1913 Circuit of Britain Race. (Jean Roberts)

The wreckage of Cody's Waterplane, strewn amongst the trees on the summit of Ball Hill. (Jean Roberts)

Cody's funeral: the procession following the hearse stretches far into the distance, with many more lining the route. (Jean Roberts)

affection, vast crowds from the civilian population turned out to line the route of the long procession as it made its way from Cody's home to the burial ground. Estimates varied, but the number seems to have been not less than 50,000. As a final mark of respect, he was allotted a resting place in Aldershot Military Cemetery, where his tombstone may today be seen, lying in company with that of Reginald Cammell.

As for John Dunne, Cody's contemporary in those early days at Farnborough – when he found himself rejected by the War Office, he certainly formed a company for the design and manufacture of aircraft, as has been related. However, although in 1913 the RFC ordered two Dunne D.8s (of which only one was delivered) that transaction represented the limit of the marque's contribution to military aviation.

The Dunne machines were an interesting and successful manifestation of their designer's theory of automatic stability, the efficacy of which was confirmed on more than one occasion. In one case, a French pilot, a Commandant Felix, gave a somewhat startling demonstration of his confidence in the machine's qualities by climbing out of the cockpit and standing on the lower wing, leaving it to the aeroplane to maintain level flight on its own. In another example of its capabilities, it was on a Dunne biplane, on 18 June 1912, that Captain Alan Carden, whom we saw wrestling with D.4's uncooperative REP engine at Blair Atholl, gained his aviator's certificate – an event which would by that time have been sufficiently unremarkable, had not Carden been the possessor of only one arm. Perhaps the certificate ought to have been awarded to the aeroplane, rather than the 'pilot' …

Unfortunately, Dunne's concept of the operational requirements for military aeroplanes did not match the reality which was later to be revealed. He understood, of course, that the aeroplane's great utility lay in its capacity for reconnaissance, extending as it did the range of observation of the balloons and kites which it replaced to far behind the enemy's front line. It seemed, therefore, logical to design an aeroplane which could 'look after itself', while the pilot concentrated on his task of observing the enemy's activities, just as he would have been able to do from his balloon. In his preoccupation with that need for stability, he might perhaps be forgiven, in those very early, faltering years, for failing to take into account, as had Fullerton and Dickson, the likelihood – indeed, certainty – that the reconnaissance aeroplane's ability to range at will over a battlefield would in time inevitably induce measures to try to put a stop to such unwonted snooping, with the result that the sky itself would become a battlefield. Faced with the faster and more nimble fighting aeroplanes which were destined to appear, in a more aggressive sky than the balloonists ever knew, passively

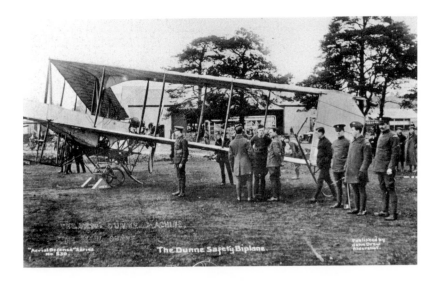

The Dunne D.8 (50-hp Gnôme) which was sold to the RFC. (J. M. Bruce/G. S. Leslie)

stable machines such as the Dunne could not have survived. The B.E.2 series, although based on very different design principles, also boasted a degree of inherent stability, and presented the German fighters of 1915 and onwards with a host of easy victims. Had Dunne also supplied the RFC with machines in quantity, as he had hoped, the added carnage which would have been seen in the skies over Flanders can only be left to the imagination. For automatic stability, whilst academically sound as a theory, was the least desirable quality in warplanes which, when it came to fighting in the air, needed above all things its antithesis – manoeuvrability – in order to survive.

However, Dunne's career had by that time been taking a fundamentally different course: abandoning aviation altogether, he turned to philosophy and it was in this latter field, rather than aviation, that he left his principal legacy. This took the form of a book, to which he gave the title *An Experiment with Time* and which described theories which he had developed concerning the functioning of the human mind. After describing various experiences involving dreams and subsequent events which apparently derived from those dreams, he devoted the rest of the book to developing his ideas whereby the consideration of events gives equal prominence to the fourth dimension, Time, alongside the three spatial dimensions. Although in its presentation the theory demonstrates impressive intellectual activity, the book ends without providing the reader with anything much in the way of a useful conclusion – a circumstance which, it might be thought, interestingly matches the outcome of his aeronautical work.

Dunne's principal companion during those frustrating and fruitless days at Blair Atholl, Lancelot Gibbs, having once learned to fly properly at Mourmelon, was, like many others, seized with the ambition of making flying his profession, by appearing at the aviation meetings which were being organised in increasing numbers across Europe. In April 1910, he travelled to northern Spain, where he had undertaken to perform some exhibition flights at Durango, near Bilbao in the Basque country. Unfortunately, his aeroplane, dispatched separately by rail, was late arriving and was nowhere near ready for flight by the time a massive crowd had assembled, impatient to see the novel spectacle. As Gibbs and his mechanic struggled to prepare their machine, while the other aviators present also revealed themselves, for one reason or another, unable to fly, the crowd became restive and its mood turned from anticipation to one of resentment. The lack of action was apparently confirming their scepticism about Man's ability to fly at all. In any case, even if he could, flying was not proper in a decent God-fearing society, such as Catholic Spain. Smash the unholy machines! The once-festive crowd became an ugly mob, deaf to reason, as stones began to fly and knives were brandished. Gibbs, with his own life under threat, maintained his composure and managed to pacify his immediate antagonists, but with the crowd now out of control, the authorities deemed it advisable to escort him and his fellow-aviators away to safety, their withdrawal hurried by stones and other missiles as the vengeful mob pursued them. The wisdom of this precautionary move was soon confirmed when the hangar, with Gibbs's Farman inside, was burnt to the ground by the angry multitude.

Returning to this country and acquiring a replacement for the lost machine (he was by now keeping solvent only with help from kindly relatives), he appeared before rather more placid spectators at further flying meetings at Wolverhampton and Lanark, as well as taking part in the manoeuvres on Salisbury Plain, as has already been recorded. But for the twenty-five-year-old Gibbs, aviation was not to yield the financial returns which would be enjoyed by some of his contemporaries. At the Wolverhampton meeting, he had suffered an accident which damaged his spine and which in time obliged him to retire from flying. Unable to use his skills as a pilot, Gibbs found work as an aviation salesman, but the call for services of this nature would in those days have been highly limited, and after four months, this employment came to an end.

By June 1911, he was appearing in the Bankruptcy Court, a mischance which clearly indicated that his chosen path had not proved to be viable. The sum involved was not excessive, but for Lancelot Gibbs, enthusiasm and courage had not been sufficient and the world of aviation saw him no more.

What of the little band of pioneer pilots of the Air Battalion's No.2 Company who spent that memorable summer of 1911, struggling with their machines, the elements and their own inexperience, to create the country's first aeroplane squadron? Their fortunes were as varied as might be expected when the chances of war and the hazards of the air intervene.

As foreshadowed above, not all of them continued to fly and carry their early enthusiasm for the air on into the darker skies of war. John Fulton, after a spell at CFS, was one who chose a different path, joining with his friend George Cockburn to form the Aeronautical Inspection Department – an activity less glamorous than flying, but vital work in a sphere where the achievement and maintenance of high technical standards are crucial. It was work, however, which was cruelly and prematurely terminated by his sudden death, due to a throat infection, at the end of 1915.

Charles Burke, still commanding 2 Squadron, in August 1914 led the first RFC component of the Expeditionary Force across the Channel to war. By November, he had been promoted to the command of a Wing and was later appointed Commandant of the CFS. He could with no dishonour have seen the remainder of the war out in the relative safety of higher command, but in 1917 he chose voluntarily to quit the RFC and return to regimental duties. On 9 April that year, he was killed in action on the Western Front while commanding a battalion of the East Lancashire Regiment.

Robert Brooke-Popham remained in command of 3 Squadron up to the very day that war broke out. At that point, just when he might have thought he would be leading them into action over France, he was plucked from that duty and found himself crossing by sea, rather than by air like Burke and the others, to take up the post of Deputy Assistant Quartermaster-General at RFC Headquarters. By the following year, he also was commanding a Wing and embarked upon a career path which continued between the wars, as he ascended to Air Rank and high command during the Second World War.

Basil Barrington-Kennett, having been appointed the RFC's adjutant, also went to France in 1914, but in the following year he too decided that his place was with his regiment, the Grenadier Guards, whose First Battalion had suffered heavy losses during the Battle of Neuve Chapelle. That April, he relinquished his post at RFC headquarters and reported to the Guards' Second Battalion at Bethune; before May was out, 'BK' had become one more name on the ever-growing list of the fallen.

Both Daniel Connor and Alan Fox (the latter having been Cammell's replacement in the Aeroplane Company) continued to fly with the RFC. The former was amongst those who flew their machines across to France in August 1914, leading one of the 5 Squadron flights. However, by early 1915, he had changed his career path to become an equipment officer. Fox, in 3 Squadron, was also appointed to command a flight, but in May 1915 was shot down and killed whilst discharging those duties.

Herbert Reynolds, after transferring from the Air Battalion to the RFC in 1912, was not among those who proceeded to France in August 1914, being then a staff officer at the War Office. After the war, he seems to have returned to general engineering duties, and in 1922 was Adjutant RE of the 48th (South Midland) Division of the Territorial Army.

Bayard Hynes also did not remain in the cockpit. Instead, he seems to have found his true *métier* amongst the engineers who gave such vital support to the flying men. He began his war with the RFC's Aircraft Park, which also established itself at Amiens, holding those spare aeroplanes which were not needed – or had been disdained – by the squadrons. Later on, when the RFC set up its own engine repair shops in France at Pont de l'Arche, near Rouen, Hynes assumed command with the rank of lieutenant colonel. It was a task which proved to be as crucial as any in maintaining the RFC's fighting efficiency, as, throughout the war, the Pont de l'Arche repair shops assisted in keeping up the flow of replacement engines to the squadrons, even for a short space in 1918 constituting their sole source of supply, as deliveries from the home factories were interrupted. After the war, he continued his work in the engineering field and in 1922 could be found back in the familiar environment of Farnborough, in charge of the Engine Experimental Department of what had now become the Royal Aircraft Establishment.

Seaton Massy, of the 29th Punjabis, having transferred to the RFC in 1912, soon directed his steps eastwards once more. In December 1913, he returned to India, where he took up the post of Commandant of the Indian Central Flying School, with the brevet rank of major. In 1915, like Broke-Smith, he found himself in Mesopotamia, having been sent there to assume command of 30 Squadron, at the time scarcely more than a flight in strength. He was just in time to join the British force besieged in Kut-al-Amara which, after holding out for several months, was forced to surrender to the Turks and endure a harsh captivity. Massy, however, was fortunate: not only was he a pilot, there were two serviceable aircraft, a Maurice Farman Longhorn and a B.E.2c, still remaining in the city. Before it fell, Massy and three colleagues flew them out and escaped to freedom.

Frederick Boothby, as a sailor and a qualified aeroplane pilot, naturally found himself in the RNAS when it broke away from the RFC. However, by then he had chosen to turn to the lighter-than-air side; in April 1912, he attended an airship course at HMS *Actaeon* and thereafter spent the remainder of his service career in that field. As for his son James, by the time that war arrived, he had left the army and had followed his father into the navy. In May 1915, as a Lieutenant Commander RNVR, he landed at Gallipoli in command of an armoured car squadron, but was killed that same day.

If some of the pioneers deserted the cockpit for different duties, there were others, already in uniform and already holding aviator's certificates, such as Andrew Board, who had been clamouring to replace them, while, as we have seen, there was no shortage of aspirant aviators in the civilian population. Between the date of the formation of the RFC and that of the declaration of war, no fewer than 628 British pilots qualified for the RAeC 'ticket'. With events allowing little more than two years for the original small company of fledglings to be converted into the first – and still all too few – squadrons of eagles, those who went on to join the new Flying Corps would all be needed.

APPENDIX I

Summary of how the names given to the units responsible for Military Aeronautics altered between the years 1878 and 1912.

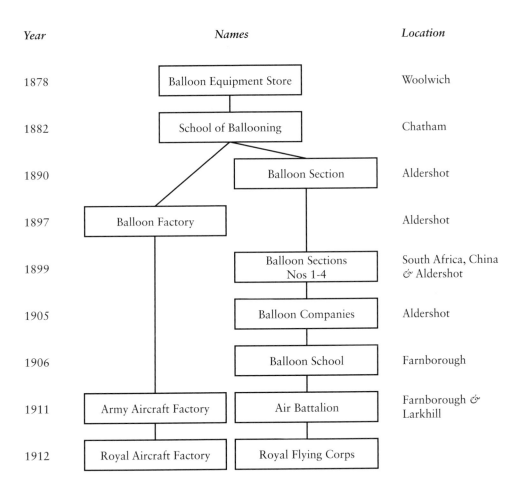

Year	Names	Location
1878	Balloon Equipment Store	Woolwich
1882	School of Ballooning	Chatham
1890	Balloon Section	Aldershot
1897	Balloon Factory	Aldershot
1899	Balloon Sections Nos 1-4	South Africa, China & Aldershot
1905	Balloon Companies	Aldershot
1906	Balloon School	Farnborough
1911	Army Aircraft Factory / Air Battalion	Farnborough & Larkhill
1912	Royal Aircraft Factory / Royal Flying Corps	

APPENDIX II

List of balloons operated by the British Army and mentioned in the text:

Name	Capacity (cu. ft)	Used in
Achilles	13,000	India
Andes	13,000	UK
Bristol	11,500	South Africa
Crusader (coal gas)	25,000	UK
Duchess of Connaught	12,000	South Africa
Elsie		South Africa
Feo	4,500	Bechuanaland
Flo	4,700	UK
Fly	5,000	Sudan
Heron	10,000	Bechuanaland
Pioneer	10,000	UK
Sapper	5,600	Sudan
Scout	7,000	Sudan
Spy	7,000	Bechuanaland
Task	10,000	South Africa
Teviot	10,000	China
Thames	10,000	South Africa
Thrasher	10,000	UK
Throstle	10,000	Malta
Thrush	10,000	South Africa
Titania	10,000	South Africa
Torpedo	10,000	South Africa
Trusty	10,000	Malta
Tugela	10,000	China
Vega	11,500	Malta
Venus	11,500	India
Veritas	11,500	Rhayader
Vestal	11,500	Malta

APPENDIX III

Aeroplanes of the Balloon School and the Air Battalion:

Serial No.	Type	Engine	Date of acquisition	Remarks
	Wright Flyer Type A	Bollée	April 1910	Bought from Rolls. Never flown.
	Blériot Type XII	60-hp ENV	Oct 1910	Gift of Colonel Laycock and Duke of Westminster.
F.1	Farman *Type Militaire*	50-hp Gnôme	Dec 1910	
F.2	Paulhan Experimental	50-hp Gnôme	Jan 1911	
F.3	Howard-Wright	60-hp ENV	June 1911	Bought from Maitland.
F.4	Bristol Boxkite	50-hp Gnôme	May 1911	
F.5	Bristol Boxkite	50-hp Gnôme	May 1911	
F.6	Bristol Boxkite	60-hp Renault	July 1911	
F.7	Bristol Boxkite	60-hp Renault	Aug 1911	
B.2	Blériot Type XXI	70-hp Gnôme		Previously Cammell's.
F.8	Bristol Boxkite	50-hp Gnôme	Aug 1911	
F.9	Bristol Boxkite	50-hp Gnôme	Aug 1911	
B.3	Breguet L1	60-hp Renault	Oct 1911	
B.4	Nieuport	60-hp Gnôme	Sept 1911	
B.5	Deperdussin	60-hp Anzani	Oct 1911	
B.6	Bristol Prier	50-hp Gnôme	Feb 1912	
B.7	B.E.1	60-hp Wolseley	Mar 1912	Ex-Voisin, gift of Duke of Westminster.

REFERENCE SOURCES

PRIMARY PUBLISHED WORKS

Amery, L. S. (ed.): *The Times History of the War in South Africa*, Volumes 1 to 7. Sampson Low (1900-1909).

Barnes, C. H.: *Bristol Aircraft since 1910*. Putnam (1964).

Brett, R. Dallas: *History of British Aviation 1908-1914*, Volumes I and II. The Aviation Book Club (1933).

Broke-Smith, Brigadier P. W. L.: *The History of Early British Military Aeronautics*. Institute of Royal Engineers (1952).

Brown, Brigadier W. Baker: *History of the Corps of Royal Engineers*, Volume IV. Institute of Royal Engineers (1952).

Bruce, Eric Stuart: *Aircraft in War*. Hodder & Stoughton (1914).

Bruce, Gordon: *Charlie Rolls – Pioneer Aviator*. Rolls-Royce Heritage Trust (1990).

Bruce, J. M.: *The Aeroplanes of the Royal Flying Corps*. Putnam (1982).

de Havilland, Sir Geoffrey, CBE: *Sky Fever*. Airlife (1979).

Driver, Hugh: *The Birth of Military Aviation, Britain 1903-1914*. The Royal Historical Society, The Boydell Press (1997).

Elliott, Brian A.: *Blériot – Herald of an Age*. Tempus (2000).

Gamble, C. F. Snowden: *The Air Weapon*, Volume I. Oxford University Press (1931).

Gibbs-Smith, Charles H.: *A History of Flying*. B. T. Batsford (1953).

Gollin, Alfred: *No Longer an Island: Britain and the Wright Brothers*. Heinemann (1984).

Gould Lee, Arthur: *The Flying Cathedral: The Story of Samuel Franklin Cody*. Methuen (1965).

Hare, Paul R.: *Aeroplanes of the Royal Aircraft Factory*. The Crowood Press (1999).

Jackson, A. J.: *Avro Aircraft since 1908*. Putnam (1965).

Joubert de la Ferté, Air Chief Marshal Sir Philip: *The Third Service*. Thames & Hudson (1955).

Joubert de la Ferté, Air Chief Marshal Sir Philip: *The Forgotten Ones*. Hutchinson (1961).

Lewis, Peter: *British Aircraft 1809-1914*. Putnam (1962).

McInnes, I. and J. V. Webb: *A Contemptible Little Flying Corps*. The London Stamp Exchange (1991).

Mead, Brigadier Peter: *The Eye in the Air*. Her Majesty's Stationery Office (1983).

Munro, R. Lyell: *Flying Shadow*. Unpublished (1991). Copy held in the Museum of Army Flying.

Nahum, Andrew: *The Rotary Aero Engine*. Her Majesty's Stationery Office (1987).

Penrose, Harald: *An Ancient Air*. Airlife (1988). Repr. by Wrens Park Publishing (2000).

Penrose, Harald: *British Aviation, The Pioneer Years 1903-1914*. Putnam (1967).

Porter, Maj Gen Whitworth: *History of the Corps of Royal Engineers*, Volume II. Institute of Royal Engineers (1889).

Raleigh, Sir Walter: *The War in the Air*, Volume 1. Hamish Hamilton (1922).

Reese, Peter: *The Flying Cowboy*. Tempus (2006).
Robson, Brian: *Fuzzy-Wuzzy – The Campaigns in the Eastern Sudan 1884-85*. Spellmount Ltd (1993).
Rolt, L. T. C.: *The Aeronauts*. Longmans (1966).
Sandes, Lt Col E. W. C.: *The Royal Engineers in Egypt and the Sudan*. Institute of Royal Engineers (1937).
Sandes, Lt Col E. W. C.: *The Indian Sappers and Miners*. Institute of Royal Engineers (1948).
Tagg, A. E.: Power for the Pioneers. Crossprint (1990).
Taylor, John W. R.: *C. F. S. Birthplace of Air Power*. Putnam (1958).
Turner, Hatton: *Astra Castra: Experiments and Adventures in the Atmosphere*. Chapman & Hall (1865).
Voisin, Gabriel: *Men, Women and 10,000 Kites* (tr. Oliver Stewart). Putnam (1963).
Walker, Percy B.: *Early Aviation at Farnborough*, Volume I, *Balloons, Kites and Airships*. Macdonald (1971).
Walker, Percy B.: *Early Aviation at Farnborough*, Volume II, *The First Aeroplanes*. Macdonald (1974).
Wallace, Graham: *Claude Grahame-White*. Putnam (1960).
Ward, Capt B. R.: *Manual of Military Ballooning*. Royal Geographical Society (1896). Repr. by Rediscovery Books (2006).
Watson, Sir Charles M.: *History of the Corps of Royal Engineers*, Volume III. Institute of Royal Engineers (1915).
Wright, Peter: *The Royal Flying Corps in Oxfordshire*. Peter F. G. Wright (1985).
Wykeham, Peter: *Santos-Dumont – A Study in Obsession*. Putnam (1962).

OTHER PUBLISHED WORKS CONSULTED

Boyle, Andrew: *Trenchard*. Collins (1962).
Brett, Maurice V. (ed.): *The Journals and Letters of Reginald Viscount Esher*. Ivor Nicholson & Watson (1934).
Carlyle, Thomas: *The French Revolution*. Chapman & Hall (1898).
Coombs, L. F. E.: *Control in the Sky*. Pen and Sword (2005).
Demaus, A. B. and J. C. Tarring: *The Humber Story*. Sutton Publishing (1989).
Dunne, J. W.: *An Experiment with Time*. A & C Black (1927).
Galloway, William: *The Battle of Tofrek*.
Gambier-Parry, Major E.: *Suakin 1885*. Kegan Paul, Trench & Co. (1885).
Harper, Harry: *My Fifty Years in Flying*. Associated Newspapers Ltd (1956).
Haydon, F. Stansbury: *Aeronautics in the Union and Confederate Armies*, Volume I. Johns Hopkins Press (1941).
James, N. D. G.: *Gunners at Larkhill*. Gresham Books (1983).
Stewart-Murray, Katherine, Duchess of Atholl: *Working Partnership*. Arthur Barker (1958).
Wallace, Graham: *Flying Witness*. Putnam (1958).

OTHER REFERENCE SOURCES

The National Archives (Public Record Office), Kew
Numerous pieces in files:
AIR1, AIR2, AIR29, ADM1, ADM116, CAB2, CAB4, CAB16, TS21, WO32, WO33, WO106, WO108.

The Royal Aeronautical Society
The Aeronautical Journal:
  'Man-Lifting War Kites' – Baden-Powell, B. F. S.: Vol. I, April 1897, p.5.
  'Flight and Flying Machines – Recent Progress' – Fullerton, J. D.: Vol. I, July 1897, pp.1-9.
  'Report on Experiments made by Major R. F. Moore (late RE), to ascertain the power and means necessary for Flight with Wings' – Moore, R. F.: Vol. I, October 1897, pp.2-17.
  'Lord Rayleigh on Flight': Vol. III, April 1900, pp.113-117.
  'The War Balloon in Africa' – Baden-Powell, B. F. S.: January 1902, pp.14-15.
  'Memorandum Concerning the Use of the Captive War Balloon during the Siege of Ladysmith': January 1902, p.15.
  'The Use of Balloons in War': Eric Stuart Bruce: July 1902, pp 43-44.
  'The Aeronautical Society's Kite Competition': Vol. VIII, January 1904, p.2.
  'Experiences with the "Power Kite"' – Cody, S. F.: Vol. XIII, January 1909, pp.15-19.
Pritchard, J. Laurence, P. B. Walker, *et al*: *The Centenary Journal of the Royal Aeronautical Society, 1866-1966*. The Royal Aeronautical Society (1966).
Chapman, Paul: 'Samuel Franklin Cody and the Development of the British Army Aeroplane No.1', lecture read before the Historical Group of the Royal Aeronautical Society on 15 October 1998.

Cross & Cockade International Journal
Wright, Peter: 'Larkhill: The Army and the Air', Vol. 31, No.4, pp.206 – 222.
Sanger, Ray: 'Clive Maitland Waterlow', Vol. 34, No.4, pp.217-236.
Dunn, Michael J.: 'The London Balloon Company', Vol. 38, No.3, pp.172-182.
Wright, Peter: 'Slow Boat to China', Vol. 39, No.3, pp.189-192.

The Aeroplane Monthly
Bruce, J. M.: A Pointless Exercise', March 1998, pp.50-55 & April 1998, pp.94-101.

Journal of the Society for Army Historical Research
Cormack, Andrew (ed.): 'No.1 Balloon Section, Royal Engineers, in the Boer War', Vol. LXVIII, pp.254-261 & Vol. LXIX, pp.33-44.

Royal Engineer Journal
'The Art of Aeronautics Applied to War, by Captain G. E. Grover RE', March 1873, pp 20-23.
'Ballooning at the Easter Volunteer Review', June 1880, p.126.
'Balloon Work on Active Service', June 1885, p.119.
'Military Ballooning', November 1897, p.223.

Professional Papers of the Royal Engineers
Watson, C M: Military Ballooning in the British Army, Vol. XXVIII (1902), pp.39-59.

National & Local Newspapers
The Times, The Morning Post, Daily Express, Sheldrake's Aldershot Military Gazette.

The Army List

ACKNOWLEDGEMENTS
(including photographic)

No small amount of the substance of this book has been derived from the massive collection of documents stored in the National Archives at Kew, that indispensable repository of the official records of the nation's recent history. Within its walls, the writer has passed so many industrious hours, has toiled through so many of its files, both bulky and slim, and has harvested therefrom so much detail, that his grateful acknowledgements to that national treasure-house of information and its staff must take first place.

Entirely appropriately, further useful information was gathered from the archives of the Museum of Army Flying at RAF Middle Wallop and I would like to extend my thanks also to Derek Armitage, as well as, latterly, to Susan Lindsey and Ken Mead, for their generous help and for the provision of the relevant photographs.

Equally appropriately, the Royal Engineers Museum and Library, at Brompton Barracks, Chatham, yielded further vital information, particularly with respect to the ballooning years. The RE Library also supplied a number of useful photographs, for which I have Charlotte Hughes to thank.

It also followed that help would be forthcoming from the Royal Air Force Museum at Hendon, particularly concerning the later years of this saga. My thanks go to that institution for this information as well as to Andrew Renwick for supplying photographs.

Additional help was obtained from Brian Waddle and Christine Woodward, Librarian and Assistant Librarian respectively of the Royal Aeronautical Society at Hamilton Place (and now the National Aerospace Library at Farnborough).

In Scotland, following the trail of John Dunne, I was kindly and helpfully received by Jane Anderson at the Blair Castle Archives, who also supplied a copy of the photograph reproduced at the top of page 114.

Very early in my research, Stuart Leslie was his usual helpful self and spared no effort in providing me with a number of photographs from his collection, for which I owe him my gratitude. (I should add that, so long has this book been in the making, this took place some time before the Bruce/Leslie collection was transferred to the Fleet Air Arm Museum at Yeovilton).

I should also like to thank Deborah Jones, at the Science Museum, and Josephine Garnier, at the Imperial War Museum, for supplying me with the photographs which are credited to each of those institutions.

If I have left two names until last, it is in order to emphasise my especial gratitude to Paul Chapman and Jean Roberts, for their hospitality as well as for their invaluable help, both in the supply of excellent photographs and for assistance with critical features of the story. It should also be mentioned that some of these latter photographs came originally from the Drachen Foundation in the USA, to which due acknowledgement is made.

All photographs not mentioned above are from the author's own collection.

INDEX

Since the ranks of many, if not all, of the military personnel featured in this history altered as the years went by, they have been omitted altogether from this index. Likewise, no titles are included, except those which had been awarded prior to that character's first appearance.

Ader, Clément Agnès, 100
Advisory Committee for Aeronautics, 153
Aerial Navigation Sub-Committee, 63, 138-48
Aero Club of the United Kingdom, see Royal Aero Club
Aeronautical Society of Great Britain, see Royal Aeronautic Society
Aeroplanes:
  Army Aircraft Factory:
  B.E.1, 183, 205, 210-13
  B.E.2, 183, 212
  F.E.1, 171-72, 180, 194, 205
  F.E.2, 205
  S.E.1, 194, 205
  Blériot:
  Type XI, 132, 146, 180
  Type XII, 149, 160-64, 172-74, 180
  Type XXI, 180, 197
  Breguet L1, 210, 213
  Bristol:
  Boxkite, 158, 167-70, 180, 197, 210
  Prier Monoplane, 210, 213
  Cody:
  Cody I (BAA No.1), 116, 124, 126-29, 134-38
  Cody II, 180
  Deperdussin, 210, 213
  Dunne:
  D.1, 111-15
  D.3, 119, 129-30
  D.4, 119, 129-32
  D.8, 237
  Henri Farman Type Militaire, 176-77, 180

Howard-Wright, 197
Nieuport, 210
Paulhan, 177-79, 180, 195
Roe, various models, 158
Sommer, 210
Valkyrie, 165, 207-208
Voisin, 119, 145
Wright, 159, 180
Agadir, 215-16
Airships:
  Baby, 70
  Barton, 67
  Beta, 72, 74, 79-80
  Clément Bayard, 76
  Delta, 72, 74, 80
  Eta, 72
  La France, 65
  Gamma, 72, 74, 80
  Lebaudy, 76-79
  de Lôme, 65
  Nulli Secundus, 67, 69-70
  Parseval, 70
  Schütte-Lanz, 70
  Zeppelin, 65, 70
Aldershot, 11, 32, 83, 87
Alexander, Patrick Young, 104, 109
American Civil War, 13
Arabi Pasha, insurrection by, 20
Army Aircraft Factory, 193-95, 205, 212-13, 221-22
Ashanti War, Second, 18
Asquith, Herbert H., 196, 217
Australia, Balloon Detachment at Commonwealth celebrations, 50

Baden-Powell, Baden Fletcher Smyth, 12,

84-85, 109, 133, 139-40
Balfour, Arthur James, 134, 196
Balloon Equipment Store, 18
Balloon Factory, 33, 57, 153-54
Balloon School, 57, 59, 83, 89, 92, 153-54, 180
Balloon Sections, 32, 38, 51
Balloon Square, Aldershot, 11, 32, 57
Balloons operated by the British Army, see Appendix II.
Bannerman, Sir Alexander, 63-64, 76-77, 80, 176, 177-78, 189, 190, 192, 204, 208, 225, 234
Barber, Horatio Claude, 165, 196
Barrington-Kennett, Basil Herbert, 190, 198, 201
Barrington-Kennett, Victor Annesley, 224
Beaumont, Frederick Edward Blackett, 15-16, 19
Bechuanaland Expedition, 1885, 21, 23
Bell, Albert, 230
Bell, Arthur Hugh, 45, 47
Black Week, 37
Blair Atholl flight trials:
  in 1907, 112-15
  in 1908, 129-32
Blair Atholl Syndicate, 142-43, 208
Blakeney, Robert Byron Drury, 11-12, 45, 47
Blériot, Louis Charles Joseph, 76, 106, 146, 149-50, 161
Board, Andrew George, 192
Bomb-dropping from balloons, 63
Boothby, Frederick Lewis Maitland, 163, 240
Boothby, James Robert, 163, 240
Boxer Rebellion, 1900, 49
Brett, Reginald Baliol, 2nd Viscount Esher, 138, 141, 175
Broke-Smith, Philip William Lilian, 55, 56, 63, 72, 77, 92, 190, 225, 234
Brooke-Popham, Henry Robert Moore, 202, 205, 230, 239
Burke, Charles James, 176, 190 198, 202, 211-12, 225, 230, 239
Buston, P. T., 51

Cambridge 'Odyssey', 201-203
Cammell, Reginald Archibald, 63, 80-81, 190, 197, 199, 203, 207-208
Capper, John Edward, 51, 54, 57, 59,

61, 67, 69-70, 72, 89, 104, 108-109, 112, 115, 124, 128-29, 132, 139-41, 152, 176
Carden, Alan Douglas, 70, 79, 131, 190, 237
Caulfeild, William Talbot McClintock, 60-61
Cayley, Sir George, 98
Central Flying School, Upavon, see under Flying fields.
Chanute, Octave, 101-102, 104, 173
Chatham, see School of Military Engineering.
Churchill, Winston Spencer, 38, 196, 218
Circuit of Europe, 216
Cockburn, George Bertram, 146, 149, 193, 239
Cody, Samuel Franklin, 69-70, 85-93, 109-11, 115-16, 123, 125-29, 134-38, 143, 154, 201, 234-237
Committee of Imperial Defence (CID), 63, 138, 217
Connor, Daniel Goodwin, 190, 202, 239
Coutelle, Jean-Marie-Joseph and La Compagnie d'Aérostiers, 12-13
Coxwell, Henry, 16, 18

Daily Mail Round Britain Contest:
  in 1911, 199-201
  in 1913, 235
Dawes, George William Patrick, 190-92
de Havilland, Geoffrey, 144, 170-71, 193-94, 205, 223
Delagrange, Léon, 119, 157
Dickson, Bertram, 150, 167-69, 219, 228
Director of Fortifications and Works (DFW), 67, 112, 128, 132, 220
Dunne, John William, 108, 111-15, 119, 129-32, 142-43, 237-38
Dunville, George, 230-31
Dupuy de Lôme, Stanislas Charles Henri Laurent, see under Airships.

Earle, R. G., 40-41
Eilmer of Malmesbury, 97
Elsdale, Henry, 19, 20, 21, 30-31, 76
Engines:
  Antoinette, 69, 105-106, 116, 181
  Anzani, 182
  Buchet, 67, 72, 112

Canton-Unné, 74
de Havilland/Iris, 74, 144
ENV, 143, 160, 182
Gnôme, 179, 183
Green, 72, 182
Humber, 183
JAP, 116, 143
NEC, 183
Renault, 182, 183
REP, 72, 119, 131-32
White & Poppe, 74
Wolseley, 183
Esnault-Pelterie, Robert Albert Charles,
    181

Farman, Henri, 119
Farnborough, *see under* Flying fields.
Ferber, Ferdinand, 105
Fleurus, Battle of, 12
Flying Meetings in Britain:
    Blackpool, 154, 156
    Bournemouth, 156
    Doncaster, 154, 156
    Lanark, 156
    Wolverhampton, 156
Flying fields:
    Blair Atholl, 112-15, 129-31
    Brooklands, 116
    Camp d'Auvours, 121
    Eastchurch, 143, 193, 222
    Etampes, 161-64
    Farnborough, 57, 61-62, 67, 77, 123-24,
        128, 134-38, 204-205
    Hardwick Farm, 201-203
    Hendon, 157, 196, 207
    Hunaudières, 121
    Issy-les-Moulineaux, 119, 145-46
    Larkhill, 55, 158, 165-74, 197, 204-205,
        222
    Lea Marshes, 143
    Mourmelon, 146, 150
    Pau, 132, 150
    Port Meadow, 198, 202
    Reims, 147
    St Cyr, 177
    Seven Barrows, 170-71
    Shellbeach, 145
    Upavon, 222
Fourteen Streams, Battle of, 45, 47
Fox, Alan Geoffrey, 190, 239
French, Sir John Denton Pinkstone, 41,
    59, 149
Fullerton, John Davidson, 103-104

Fulton, John Duncan Bertie, 166, 173,
    178-79, 190, 204, 213, 217-18, 239

Gibbs, Lancelot Dwarris Louis, 129-131,
    152, 167, 238-39
Gibraltar, balloon trials at, 55, 57
Glyn, Ralph, 219
Godard Brothers, 13
Goldbeater's skin, 20, 31, 33, 44, 66, 72
Gordon Relief Expedition, 1885, 24
Grahame-White, Claude, 149-50, 156,
    157, 163, 196
Grande Semaine d'Aviation, Reims,
    1909, 147-49
Green, Frederick Michael, 193
Green, Gustavus, *see under* Engines.
Grosvenor, Hugh Richard Arthur, 2nd
    Duke of Westminster, 160, 183, 196
Grover, George Edward, 15-16, 18, 19,
    24
Grubb, Alexander Henry Watkins, 40,
    43, 45, 47, 54
Gurr, Percy, 112, 129-30

Haldane, Richard Burdon, 138, 140, 180
Handley-Page, Frederick, 109, 158
Hargrave, Lawrence, 89
Harmsworth, Alfred Charles William,
    1st Viscount Northcliffe, 107, 123,
    134, 175
Heath, Gerard Moore, 33, 38, 40
Henderson, Sir David, 220, 222
Henson, William Samuel, 98
Holtorp, Harold E., *see* London Balloon
    Company.
Holwell, Raymond Vernon Doherty, 89
Hubbard, Thomas O'Brian, 224
Humber Ltd, 158
Hume, A. H. B., 49
Hurlingham, 51, 146
Hydrogen manufacture, 18, 21, 33, 54
Hynes, George Bayard, 190, 213, 218,
    239

India, Balloon Section in, 50
Inspector General of Fortifications
    (IGF), 66

Jones, Harry Balfour, 32, 40-41, 43-45

Kimberley, Siege of, 37, 41
King, William Albert de Courcy, 69, 70,
    83

Kitchener, Herbert Horatio, 1st Viscount
   Kitchener of Khartoum, 30, 37, 41

Ladysmith, Siege of, 37-40
Lanchester, Frederick William, 153
Langley, Samuel Pierpoint, 101-102
Lanz, Karl, *see under* Airships.
Laycock, Joseph Frederick, 160
Lee, Henry, 19
Lefroy, Hugh Percival Thomson , *see
   under* Wireless transmission and
   reception.
Levavasseur, Léon, *see under* Engines.
Lidsing, 30
Lilienthal, Otto, 100
Lloyd George, David, 138, 140, 149
Lodge, Sir Oliver, 204
London Balloon Company, 61
Longcroft, Charles Alexander Holcombe,
   226
Loraine, Robert, 146-47, 150-52,
   156-57, 169
Lowe, Thaddeus Sobieski Coulincourt,
   13

McClean, Francis Kennedy, 193, 223
McCudden, William, 228-29
Macdonald, J. R. L., 48-49
Mackenzie, Ronald Joseph Henry Louis,
   24, 26, 28, 29
Mafeking, Siege of, 37, 45, 47
Magersfontein, Battle of, 37, 41
Mahdi, The, 23
Maitland, Edward Maitland, 80, 190,
   197, 222
Malta, Balloon trials at, 55
Manly, Charles, 102
Manoeuvres, British Army:
   1880 and 1882, 19
   1904, 56
   1910, 72, 166-70
Manoeuvres, French army, 1910, 168-70
Martin-Leake, Theodore Edward, 49-50,
   60-61
Massy, Seaton Dunham, 198, 202, 240
Master-General of the Ordnance (MGO),
   112, 128, 138, 192
Maubeuge, Siege of, 12
Mawson's Antarctic Expedition, 1911,
   plan to use an aeroplane, 192-93
Maxim, Sir Hiram Stevens, 100, 111,
   139, 141
Mellor, C., 38

Meudon (*l'Ecole Nationale
   d'Aérostation*), 12-13
Michelin Trophy, 180, 182
Military Trials, 1912, 235
Money, John, 13
Moore, Ross Franklin, 109
Moore-Brabazon, John Theodore
   Cuthbert, 145
Mortimer-Singer prize, 199, 212

National Airship Fund (*The Morning
   Post*), 76, 78-79
Nicholson, Sir William Gustavus, 138-
   140, 187

O'Gorman, Mervyn Joseph Pius, 153,
   192-96, 210, 220, 228

Paine, Godfrey Marshall, 223
Palmer, Edwin, 229-230
Paardeberg, Battle of, 43
Paris, Siege of, 16
Parseval, August von, *see under*
   Airships.
Paulhan, Louis Isidore Auguste Marie,
   156
Perry, Evelyn Walter Copland, 205
Phillips, George Edward, 40
Photography from balloons, 20, 55
Pilcher, Percy Sinclair, 100
Prier, Pierre, 210

Ramsey, John, 69, 230
Ranelagh, 51
Repington, Charles à Court, *see*
   Manoeuvres, British Army.
Reynolds, Herbert Ramsey Playford,
   177, 190, 201, 202-203, 213, 239
Ridd, Frank, 212, 228
Ridge, Theodore John, 153, 205-206
Roberts, Frederick Sleigh, 1st Viscount
   Roberts of Kandahar, 37, 41, 43-47
Roe, Edwin Alliott Verdon, 109, 116,
   143-44, 176
Rolls, Hon. Charles Stewart, 133, 138-
   140, 145, 156, 159
Royal Aero Club, 63, 139, 150
Royal Aeronautical Society, 87, 98, 100,
   111
Royce, Frederick Henry, 139

Santos-Dumont, Alberto, 65-66, 105-107
School of Ballooning, 19, 32

School of Military Engineering, Chatham, 15, 176, 217
Schütte, Johann, see under Airships.
Scott's Antarctic Expedition, 1901, accompanied by balloons, 50
Seely, John Edward Bernard, 217-18, 227-28
Short brothers, 145, 157
Snowden-Smith, Richard Talbot, 190, 193
Solferino, Battle of, 13
Sopwith, Thomas Octave Murdoch, 157
Spaight, Thomas Henry Limerick, 50, 55
Steam Traction Engines, 32, 49, 53
Stewart-Murray, John George, Marquis of Tullibardine, 112, 142, 224
Stokes, W. A., 50
Stringfellow, John, 98, 100
Strugnell, William, 228-29
Suakin, 24
Sykes, Frederick Hugh, 56, 220, 222

Talbot-Crosbie, Maurice Bertie, 83, 92
Technical Sub-Committee, 220, 227-28
Templer, James Lethbridge Brooke, 12, 19, 23, 24-28, 30-33, 48, 57-59, 66, 109
Thomas, George Holt, 168
Tilney, W. A., 38
Tofrek, Battle of, 25-26
Trollope, Francis Charles, 21, 23, 33, 48

Valentine, James, 199, 201, 223, 228
Voisin, Charles, 105
Voisin, Gabriel, 105, 106, 119, 145, 147
Vortex Rings, 203-204

Ward, Bernard Rowland, 34
Warry, Bertram Arthur, 45, 47
Waterlow, Clive Maitland, 79-81, 190
Watkins, Hugh Evelyn, 190, 192-93
Watson, Charles Moore, 18
Wei-hei-wei, 49
Wells, G. F., 56, 57
Wells, Herbert George, 216
Westland, Francis Campbell, 70, 112, 130
Weinling family, 20, 33
White, Sir George Stanley, 158, 180, 210
Wilson, R. H. V., 228-229
Wireless transmission and reception:
  in balloons, 63
  in dirigibles, 72, 80
  in aeroplanes, 211
Wolseley, Garnet Joseph, 1st Viscount Wolseley of Cairo, 24, 30
Wright, Katherine, 132, 134
Wright, Orville, 102, 104, 107-108, 121, 132
Wright, Wilbur, 102, 104, 107-108, 119, 121-23, 132-34

Zeppelin, Graf Ferdinand von, see under Airships.